flesh wounds?

new ways of understanding self-injury

Kay Inckle

PCCS BOOKS
Ross-on-Wye

First published 2010
Reprinted 2012

PCCS BOOKS Ltd
2 Cropper Row
Alton Rd
Ross-on-Wye
Herefordshire
HR9 5LA
UK
Tel +44 (0)1989 763 900
www.pccs-books.co.uk

Flesh Wounds? New ways of understanding self-injury

A CIP catalogue record for this book is available from the British Library

ISBN 978 1 906254 29 2

Cover artwork by Kay Inckle and Brid O'Farrell
Cover designed in the UK by Old Dog Graphics
Typeset in the UK by The Old Dog's Missus
Printed in the UK by Imprint Digital, Exeter

CONTENTS

PREFACE

This book has certainly been a labour of love. I have worked with great care to create a collection of stories which aid dialogue and understanding about self-injury and how best to respond to it. Nonetheless, the stories – and the lives in which they are rooted – explore experiences which readers may find difficult and distressing. Therefore, I encourage readers to practise self-care regarding where and when they read this book. Relevant help and support organisations are listed at the end of each chapter, with full contact and service details in the resources appendix (at the end of the book). I have also been exceptionally mindful to avoid content which may be experienced as triggering, but even so, I cannot guarantee that some readers will not be challenged in this regard.

Please take care and please take heart as you read.

Kay Inckle
Dublin, January 2010

ACKNOWLEDGEMENTS

This book is the result of a two-year post-doctoral research project funded by The Irish Research Council for the Humanities and Social Sciences (IRCHSS), to whom I am sincerely grateful for providing me with the opportunity to carry out this work.

I was welcomed into the School of Social Work and Social Policy in Trinity College Dublin to undertake this project and I am deeply grateful to both Dr Evelyn Mahon and Professor Robbie Gilligan for their support and generosity. The community at SSWSP has been unfailingly warm, welcoming, supportive and fun, and heartfelt thanks go to all of my colleagues there.

Generosity has been the major theme of this project. People from all walks of life have generously given their time and shared resources and information with me in a genuine spirit of support, community and trust. My heartfelt thanks to Amanda; Lois Arnold; Mark Bulger; Colm; Una Donnelly; Elaine; Emma; Mary Farrelly; Joan Freeman and all at Pieta House; Rachel Friere; Joseph; Kath Kelly; Hilary Lindsay; Louise Pembroke; Clare Shaw; Terri Shaw; Jenny Smith; and Karl Tooher.

Blessings come in many guises, and I am ever thankful to be blessed with the presence of many wonderful people in my life. Love and thanks especially to Brid, Claudia, Leslie, Lucy and Lorna, Mairín, Orlaith and to my own Princess – an unfailing source of unconditional love in the way that only a cat can be! Special love and thanks to Clare.

Finally, sincere thanks also to PCCS Books for publishing this manuscript, without whom this book simply would not be.

INTRODUCTION

This is a book of stories about self-injury (sometimes called self-harm). It explores the meaning and purpose of self-injury in an individual's life; the experiences that might lead to self-injury; and which approaches and responses to self-injury are helpful and which are not. It is intended to be a resource for people who hurt themselves and for those who live and work with them.

The stories are fictional in the sense that none of the actual characters as portrayed here are real. But all of the stories – the events, people, and situations – reflect real-life experiences and are drawn from a two-year research project which I undertook in order to write this book. In the project I recorded experiences of self-injury from service users and service providers – as well as people who were both or neither. Then, paying careful attention to the key themes, issues and experiences that emerged I retold these accounts through fictionalised characters. Using fictional characters and creative writing strategies protects the anonymity of all of those involved but at the same time allows an in-depth representation of the 'real-life' inner worlds, emotions and experiences of the protagonists. Furthermore, the storytelling format makes the book and its content accessible and interesting to a much wider audience than can be reached through standard academic articles and reports. Storytelling is also an important tradition in many cultures, including Ireland, where wisdom with complex 'morals' can be shared and learned through encounters in the fictionalised world.

The 'moral' of the tales in this book point towards the need for a holistic and person-centred understanding of self-injury and one which focuses on harm reduction rather than prevention. The stories challenge the stigmatising view of self-injury as something 'mad' or 'bad' to be prevented at all costs. They highlight the importance of understanding the complexity of each individual and their relationship with self-injury alongside practices which offer acceptance and support across the breadth and depth of someone's needs. The stories are intended to enable people who work or live with people who hurt themselves to understand the experience of self-injury so that it is less frightening and alien to them in order that they may provide meaningful help and support. The stories also aim to provide a source of support and validation for people who self-injure, to recognise their strengths and build on them and to provide information and resources. The book can also be used by people who hurt themselves as an to aid communication with others in their lives. The stories can provide points of connection and dialogue between people from across the spectrum of backgrounds, perspectives and experiences and facilitate understanding and constructive communication between them all.

The book contains three factual appendices to provide more direct information to the reader. The harm-reduction appendix provides a simple outline of some of the key harm-reduction principles and practices which the stories explore. The methodological appendix explains in more detail the process of the research and writing that created this book and why this method is so suited for this work. Finally, the resources appendix lists the help and support organisations relevant to the issues covered in the book. There is also a bibliography which includes a vast range of self-injury and harm-reduction-related publications which are touched on in the stories.

In the book each story is complete in itself, but all the stories subtly interconnect with one another and some of the stories are divided into separate chapters. The book does not necessarily have to be read chronologically, but the outline below provides a brief guide to the key themes and issues of each story and those connected with it. And while it is not essential to read this outline before continuing through the book, doing so will clarify the themes and issues of the stories, and also provide additional guidance and insights for those not familiar with this approach to self-injury and the related implications.

'Faggot', is by far the longest story and in many ways helps to set the context for the stories which follow. It critically addresses psychiatric diagnoses of self-injury which focus on prevention and medication and sets them in contrast with creative art therapy and the 'slow it down' rule (a harm-reduction technique). It explores the impacts of homophobia and sexual violence and their relationship to self-injury as well as to service provision. It ends positively through exploring progressive and survivor-led possibilities for mental-health practice.

'Trust Me 1 (First Time)', is the first of a trilogy of chapters which narrate a story of self-injury from different perspectives. The first time, the story is explored from the position of a newly qualified social care practitioner, Ciaran, in his fist job in a residential unit for young people. It traces his first contact with self-injury and the circumstances through which even well-intentioned actions can have devastating implications for staff and service users who are not well-resourced in this area. Here the reader shares the protagonist's own learning journey around self-injury and best-practice responses.

'Flashback One', is a short, halting chapter which interrupts the narrative flow of the book in much the same way as actual flashbacks disrupt the flow of experience. It is the first of three chapters which use Louise Pembroke's concept of 'iatrogenic traumatic stress' – which is discussed in the notes at the end of the chapter – to explore the ways in which some medical interventions, particularly those used for patients who are defined as 'problematic', have the same impact as post traumatic stress disorder-inducing events. The first chapter addresses the experience of childhood hospitalisation and its relationship with self-injury.

'Normal', critically addresses some of the stereotypes around self-injury and explores the impacts both for those who do, and those who do not, meet standardised diagnostic criteria, and how in both instances possibilities for helpful interventions are missed. It also highlights how these stereotypes often confuse an individual's own articulation of their own experiences.

'In Between', explores the impact of user-led support groups for self-injury – something which professionals often express anxiety around. It highlights the ways in which user-led groups can provide acceptance, empowerment and support alongside information and resources for staying safe and practising harm-reduction techniques. The group is able to hold the more nuanced in-between spaces of a journey with self-injury by avoiding the need to focus on rigid binaries of crisis (pathology) and recovery (prevention). The group also demonstrates the opposite impact to the triggering or copy-cat effects that many professionals fear.

'Flashback Two', is the second of three flashback chapters and addresses the impacts of negative experiences in Accident and Emergency departments. Here service users often report being responded to with hostility – including being stitched without anaesthetic – which is intended to curtail their self-injury, but which often only leads to more damaging consequences in psychological, emotional and physical terms. This story also creates a window into the experiences and the behaviour of Anne, one of the protagonists in 'Normal'.

'Trust Me 2 (Second Chance)', is also a second instalment in a trilogy of connected chapters. This story revisits the events and characters explored in the second story but this time from the position of the young resident of the care unit who injured herself, Tricia. This chapter brings the characters forward, giving our worker an opportunity to put some of his learning into practice, albeit in circumstances which are far from ideal.

'Broken', explores the complex inner worlds of self-injury and how they become increasingly inarticulable when people search to find 'what's wrong' within diagnostic criteria. It also explores the use of a clean kit and first aid kit backed up with physiological knowledge as means of reducing harm.

'Flashback Three', is the third and final of the flashback trilogy and it explores the impact of the use of physical restraint within inpatient settings as a response to apparent disassociation. The silent inner experience of the patient reveals how the practice itself is not only triggering of a flashback experience but also of a dissociative response.

'Trust Me 3 (Third Time Lucky)', is the final chapter in the 'Trust Me' trilogy and meets Tricia, the protagonist, some time later and in radically reduced circumstances. However, an accidental near-fatal injury brings Tricia into contact with a whole new series of possibilities. These are drawn from best-practice interventions across a variety of contexts which are fitted together and explored as an ideal chain of response. The best-practice interventions here not only mirror the gaps in response to Tricia's earlier experiences, but also contrast with service provision in other stories including 'Flashback Two', 'Normal' and 'Broken'.

Moving towards the end of the collection of stories, 'Cathy and Heathcliff 1999', and the two which follow are perhaps the most challenging of the book. They demand more of the reader in terms of piecing the stories together and making meaning from them in the context of their previous reading. 'Cathy and Heathcliff 1999' critically depicts the diagnosis of borderline personality disorder, a label which is commonly applied to women with an ongoing history of self-injury (also explored in 'In Between'). In places there are glimpses as to what may lie behind the diagnosis, but these snapshots are rare. The void in the protagonist's history acts as a strategic narrative device to reflect the emptiness of the diagnosis. Through the character of 'Cathy' this chapter also portrays the sometimes tentative boundaries between issues which are diagnosed as self-injury and are therefore pathologised and those which are not, and the impacts on service-provider perceptions and responses.

'A Thousand Epilogues', provides an opportunity to revisit the characters from 'Cathy and Heathcliff 1999' ten years on. The protagonist is still struggling to emerge from the burden of her diagnosis and its implications, but is slowly beginning to find processes to make meaning from her experiences and to access support which is appropriate for her.

The thirteenth and final story, 'The House of Smiles', is perhaps the most challenging of all in both its content and method. This story operates a double fictionalisation and narrates an art performance through which a young woman explores her relationship with self-injury. It draws strongly from my research, and also touches on a number of often sensationalised debates in the media (as well as academic discourse) around borders between art and 'mutilation' and the purpose and meaning of this kind of work. It also provides closure to one of the routes opened up but ultimately left untrod by Connor, the protagonist of the opening story 'Faggot'. 'The House of

Smiles' draws the collection to a close and in doing so firmly locates self-injury outside of pathological 'mental-illness' criteria. It frames it in the broad spectrum of human experience, its myriad contexts and meanings, and diversity of responses to it.

FAGGOT

'Faggot!' Connor cannot avoid the unmistakable, snide, half-whispered threat that crackles in the air behind him. He walks on, careful not to look around or to show any sign that he has heard, or is responding to, the insult. Still, it hangs in the silence and seems to follow him, clinging to him like a mark of shame or a noxious cloud of gas that he is somehow responsible for.

Once across the other side of the barren courtyard, and safely behind the reinforced-glass doors of the corridor which leads to his office, he dares a subtle half turn in the direction of the group who assailed him. But there are so many groups of patients and their visitors huddled in their strange collectives, emitting clouds of blue-grey cigarette smoke, or walking the perimeter of the concrete-slabbed square – looking more and more like the caged animals he so often feels they are – that he cannot be sure who said it.

He pauses and catches his breath and inhales deeply, willing his heart rate to slow down and his body to return to its usual sense of solidity, not this wobbling lightness of fear that those words always inspire in him. He places his hand on the cool metal doorframe and lets his head drop forward and takes another deep breath to steady himself. He turns his attention to his feet, breathing into the certainty of them placed securely on the ground. He lets the wave of panic pass through him and gradually feels himself reassembling. Then, with careful measured resolve, he straightens himself and adopts his most professional and confident demeanour and strides along the corridor to his office.

He opens the door to his small room and at once feels at home. At his own expense, and incurring the first of many reprimands from the senior consultant he had decorated the room in sunny yellow and orange and filled it with plants and prints of art works. He has stress balls and geometric puzzles on the desk for nervous hands to play with and two small comfy chairs to the side of it. Underneath the desk is a large, well-used and paint splattered carton of art materials, its jumbled contents an enticing treasure trove of colour. He even painted the ugly metal filling cabinet and the grey bookshelves in an attempt to make the room as unclinical and as inviting as possible, and really it had worked – especially in comparison to the rest of the hospital. His office was a respite, a sanctuary for him and the patients he was assigned.

At moments like this he still finds it quite surreal that he is actually here, a newly qualified psychiatrist, in his first permanent position. It has been such a long road to get here and despite his having completed his training some years behind his peers he often feels oddly young and very out of place, the resident bad boy, in the austere and dour surroundings of St Jude's Hospital – 'The Bin', as the crumbling Victorian institution is still referred to locally – even by some of the patients.

There had been policy documents, strategic plans, meetings and endless political wrangling over the hospital for years now, which had swung like an eternally restless pendulum vacillating between outright condemnation of the existence of such an archaic institution to outrage at the prospect of its closure and the patients being turned out to fend for themselves in sparse and underfunded community care systems, which really meant homeless shelters, prison, sleeping rough, and even death for some. Connor sighed, some days, like today, he didn't know why he was there. He is so at odds with this juggernaut of psychiatry it's as if he, like his patients, could easily become caught and mercilessly trampled in the cogs of this huge soul-crushing machine. He had known at the outset he would be a lone voice in a sea of animosity, swimming against the prevailing current, often fighting just to stand still and frequently being swept mercilessly backwards by the tide of authority and tradition, but that didn't make it any easier. He had been here mere months and had already received so many reprimands he had stopped counting. Only yesterday he had been given some more of the 'friendly advice' he frequently incurred about the unconventionality of his methods.

His practice of individual and in-depth consultations with patients, and his extensive use of art therapy in his already controversial office, as opposed to the standard snatched few minutes of diagnostic review on the public ward, was earning him increasingly disparaging and hostile responses from his colleagues. He had heard his work referred to as 'peace and love with the hippy-dippy art-school boy', or worse 'a one-on-one with art school fairy'. It was amazing how much resentment his approach excited; it was not even particularly new or revolutionary, and certainly well within the repertoire of psychiatric practice as he and many of his contemporaries understood it. But not here: here, tradition and authority were the watchwords and anything else was an aberration to be punished and eradicated. He would have probably been out on his ear already if it wasn't for how well the patients were responding. As the new guy he had been given some of the 'hardest' and 'most hopeless' cases, and yet all were visibly improving through his methods, and this alone would have earned him yet more hostility if it wasn't that it made the other psychiatrists and nurses' jobs less demanding. Furthermore, the weekly group art sessions he was doing on the wards, over and above his caseload, was also reducing his colleagues' workloads and so no one was going to complain directly. They would, rather, just stick to the snide comments just out of his earshot, a wonderful model of healthy emotional communication from his peers, he often reflected!

However, this was not the first time he had had those kind of comments whispered at him by patients and that was more alarming. He had a growing sense that a couple of the consultants had deliberately gossiped with interns in the hearing of some of the more volatile patients who were not on his caseload, in full knowledge of the consequences. Most of the patients here were caught up in an endless power struggle with the staff, viewing them as a single, homogenous and hostile authority where any weakness in any of them was an advantage to be exploited. And of course, in this dinosaur institution being gay was both a weakness and an aberration.

He rested his head in his hands and wondered if he was actually crazy to be here, in this environment and culture, where even the basics of humanity often felt so alien. But deep down he knew he was here for a reason, for something he believed in so much, something that had once seemed an impossible dream.

And what an immense journey it had been to reach this small office in this biblical institution – it seemed laughable that this was the culmination of his dreams! Yet it was, and he knew he had achieved something amazing, something unheard of, and that alone gave him hope for the patients in his care. Once he had sat on the other side of the psychiatrist's desk and, seemingly lifetimes before that, he had been young and naïve, privileged and confident, but unworldly, like the rest of his peers on the medical degree. It seemed so long ago, those first two years at university, and when he looked back now he saw himself as little more than a child, but back then it seemed they had all felt so certain, filled with the confidence of infallible knowledge. Or, at least he almost had, until they had found out.

Connor had known before he started his medical degree that he would have to be careful about what was then 'his secret', but he hadn't realised quite how hostile it would really be. He had thought that with a Student Gay and Lesbian Society the University would be a safe enough place for people like him, but he had been wrong. One of his classmates had seen him leaving the local gay bar with Paul after one of the Student Lesbian and Gay meet-ups. He had been a little drunk, and giddy with flirtation: leaning too close to Paul on the way out; touching him too much as they walked toward the bus stop. The next Monday the taunting had started, whispers and nudges to begin with, comments whenever he went to the bathroom or was changing in the locker room after using the squash courts. And the more he floundered in his own embarrassment and fear, the more it escalated. He had found his second year pure hell. But he had not known how much worse it was to get by the end of that year.

There had been a small party for his year after the end of term exams, and he had gone along so as not to alienate himself even more by his absence, which would surely only lead to more comment and gossip. There were also a couple of the female students, Mary and Jean, who he got on well with and had gradually made friends of, so he was not totally isolated from his peer group. The party had been awful. A lot of the students, especially the real tough guys, had been drinking since that afternoon and there was a tension in the air that threatened to get out of hand. The staff had managed it well, however, and when they had begun to wrap things up at around 9pm it seemed like it had all been contained, and there was a sense of relief and good cheer all round as people said goodbye and wished one another a good summer break.

It was a gloomy evening; it had been drizzling all afternoon and the low cloud made it seem later and darker than it was. Connor was going home the next day as he would be working in his mother's pharmacy for the summer and he still had to finish his packing. Most of the students were heading on into town for more drinks and he was glad of a genuine excuse not to go. He didn't know how much Mary and Jean were aware of the harassment the other guys subjected him to, but he tried to hide it from them, ashamed and embarrassed of being humiliated in this way. He had hugged and kissed them goodbye in turn, and then set off across the rugby pitch at the south of the campus which formed the short cut to his bus stop. He was almost at the far exit of the grounds when he heard a horrible, familiar sound behind him, 'Faggot!' hissed with hatred through the still night air. He froze for a second and then walked on. 'FAGGOT!' Louder this time, and in a chorus of more than one voice. Fear was rising in his abdomen, he broke into a trot, he had only the pathway and the small shrubbery to clear before he was safely on the roadway. 'Get him!' He heard a cry behind him and before he could move any faster he was brought crashing to the ground by a lightning rugby tackle. He put his hands forward to break his fall, but achieved little protection. Pain, shock and panic were exploding through him and he was dizzy with fear. Still, he tried to get to his feet, but his legs were held fast and feet seemed to be crushing down on him in painful blows from all directions. A heavy boot pressed into the side of his head squashing his face into the dirt and making it hard to breath. He felt his arms and hands pulled out and weighted down. He was struggling to breathe and to piece together what was happening to him. His body and senses were fragmenting with the pain, shock and fear, as if he was splitting into different pieces and unable to draw himself together again. He could hear a voice behind him, one that he thought he recognised, but was too confused to put a name to, though it sounded like one of his regular tormentors. 'Fag', it sneered in disgust, 'This is not the place for sickos like you. You need help. Pervert. Know what they used to do to your type?' Connor swallowed hard, he was still struggling for air and desperately willing some way out of this.

'I asked you a question, FAGGOT! Answer me!' Connor swallowed again. Surely there must be someone around, he opened his mouth, 'Help!' he cried with all the energy he could muster, but all he emitted was a choked whisper, and instantly he knew it was a mistake. 'You stupid little shit!' another voice behind him yelped, 'There's no one here that wants to help perverts like you!' Angry feet kicked him hard in the stomach and chest. He curled around himself in the dirt trying to protect himself but it was too late now. A crescendo of violence descended on him, at one moment he was pulled back and punched in the face, spat on, kicked in the ribs, chest and stomach, the next he was pushed face down into the dirt again and pinned hard against the ground. 'We're going to teach you a lesson, faggot! We've got the cure for you!' A foot pressed his face further into the dirt and he felt his arms yanked up and pinned behind him, pushing him yet harder down into the ground, suffocating him in sludge and muck. Then, worse than anything he had imagined, he felt his belt being ripped out from his jeans and the waist and his shorts torn down his legs. He tried desperately to move, to cry out, to protect himself, and for a moment he thought he might almost break free he was so animated by his terror. But it was not to be, suddenly the weight of a whole body landed across him, crushing him like an autumn leaf beneath a tractor wheel. He was pinned mercilessly to the ground and to his destiny, and what lay before him was the most terrible pain he had ever experienced. It was blurry, the continual shouts, threats and insults, the driving agony as a hard kick was delivered to his testicles, leaving him retching and choking on his own pain and vomit; then feeling his flesh ripping deeper and deeper apart as one and then another and then another and then another took their turn at raping him. It seemed to go on forever. It was like dying and going to hell: an eternity of soul-crushing humiliation, of terrible, terrible pain that was destroying a part of who he was. He did not know how to escape, how this would end, it seemed eternal. He felt as if his life must surely be over now, they were killing something inside him and he could not stop them. He did not think he could survive this. He did not want to. He let go, lying in the mud and dirt at the edge of the rugby pitch, his soul crushed, his body torn and bruised, battered and bleeding, his lungs, against his own will, continually fighting through the mud and the vomit and blood for the breath that would keep him alive.

He had woken up in drizzly rain, surrounded by polished black boots. A male voice was talking loudly to him. He tried to move, but his whole body had been turned into a limp slab of pulverised meat. He could not make out the words that were being said, the tone was uncompromising, angry almost. Slowly he began to recognise and make sense of them, 'Can you tell me your name?' the voice demanded. 'Connor,' he croaked, 'Connor O'Connell'. He tried to move again, and memory flooded back to him. He panicked, where were his jeans, his shorts? He could not bear to have this humiliation witnessed. He tried to move again. 'Please, I need to get home,' he whispered. Tears welled up inside him and he swallowed them down. His body was frozen with pain and cold, he was filthy inside and out. A pair of boots stopped by his face and their owner squatted down and peered at him. 'We're the ambulance service and we're going to take you to the hospital. You look like you've had a bit of a rough night, Connor.' Connor opened his mouth again but no words came out. There was a blank space in his consciousness for a time, and then he felt himself lifted on to a stretcher placed beside him on the ground. To his relief a blanket covered him. He closed his eyes and let himself evaporate into the early morning sky.

The chaos and the violence that permeated the casualty department and his excruciating processing through it only sent him further away. He let himself disappear to a pinprick hovering just to the upper left of his forehead. He could not respond or come back into what remained of his being no matter what they did or said to him. They gave him painkillers, but he could not swallow. There were questions he could not answer, words would not form in his head or fill his mouth, frustrating and alienating those who attended him. He refused to allow them to call anyone. He just wanted them to go, to leave him, he did not want to live through this. The more they pulled and scrubbed his body, assessed and dressed his wounds the further he retreated into the distant dot of himself. But he could still hear the comments from the other side of the flimsy screen they had placed around him. 'Must have been an end of term gang bang gone wrong,' they said. 'Gays are so promiscuous, look at the state he's got himself in!' They seemed angry with him, repulsed by him, as if this was his fault and he was as bad as what had happened. He just wanted to be alone, safe, away from this so he that could shut it all out.

He hovered in the distance above himself as he was stitched by rough, uncaring hands. He was told something about the number and type of sutures used, that they would dissolve into his body as he healed, and how he should take care of them until they did so. But he was too ashamed and too far away to listen. This was not possible for him to bear; he did not want to know what had been done to him and how they had tried to piece him back together. He knew nothing could ever bring him back together after this. The doctor who had stitched him kept speaking but Connor tried to shut him out, then an inescapable edge entered his voice. 'Anyway,' he said, now sure he had Connor's attention, 'there'll be no more boyfriends for you for a while', then with a sneer he had turned sharply and walked away.

Paul had found him later on the next afternoon. He had called at Connor's house that morning to give him a lift to his train home as they had planned, and found him not there, no packing done, and none of his housemates having seen him since the previous day. He rang every one of Connor's friends that he knew before he tried the hospital and, to his horror, found he had been admitted in the early hours of the morning in circumstances that sent a creeping dread through his body. When he arrived he barely recognised Connor, his body a rainbow of bruises and grazes and he was lying utterly motionless on his belly, his eyes open but glazed over like a dead man's. The only way that he knew for sure Connor wasn't actually dead was that he closed his eyes as he approached.

Paul was the last person who Connor wanted to see him like this. Why was he here? He just wanted to discharge himself and go home and close his door and lie down and stay a long, long way from everyone. But the nurses had not let him discharge himself earlier on, and now Paul was here, and he couldn't bear it. He kept his eyes closed for a long time, and eventually when he opened them Paul was gone. He felt in the locker at the side of his bed and to his relief found his phone and his keys – his wallet was there too, not abandoned in the mud of the rugby pitch as he feared. He looked at his phone, endless missed calls from his mother, obviously waiting at the station for him. He texted her that he had to stay on a few days and that he had sent her a message the previous day, and had she not got it? Almost as soon as it was sent, she was ringing again, angry no doubt; he couldn't handle any more of anyone else's anger. He switched off his phone and lay back down again.

Somewhere out of the gloom Paul appeared again. Connor, looked at him for a long time before realising he was speaking to him. 'I can take you home if you want. They'll let you go as long as you have someone with you.' Connor nodded. Paul pulled the curtains around his bed and lifted a small pile of neatly folded clothes out of his bag. 'They said you'd need these.' Shorts, socks, jogging pants, a t-shirt and hoody, and wrapped separately a pair of new, grey runners. It was so painful to move that Connor could barely dress himself, but he sent Paul away, beyond the curtains. He would not accept his help. He could not let Paul see him now.

A marathon of pain later he was finally changed into the clothes and they left the hospital, every step Connor took felt like broken glass was being ground into the tender flesh of his body. Paul had intended to drive him straight to his parents' house, but Connor had screamed unremittingly until he had finally agreed not to. But he refused to take him back to his house and leave him alone there, and insisted on bringing him to his flat. 'Ciara's already gone for the summer,' he reassured him, 'so there's no one there.' Connor eventually agreed but more in exhaustion than willing compliance. As soon as they were in the flat Connor went to Paul's room and lay down on the bed. He felt he had just crawled halfway across the world in a field of barbed wire, and he just wanted to close his eyes again and shut all of this out.

He must have slept for it was dark when he opened his eyes again. A duvet had been pulled over him, but he was still fully dressed. He was disoriented by physical pain and a sense of something shattered inside him, something was gone and would not come back. It was a long moment before he remembered where he was and how he had got there. Then he was aware that Paul was in the room also, and that must have been what had woken him. Paul must have sensed that he had woken as he began talking softly to him, or perhaps he had been talking all along, but Connor couldn't assemble enough of himself to understand or respond to what he was saying. There was just a big wide hole between him and everything else. He felt so far away from himself now, the only thing that made him sure he existed was the physical pain in different places in his body, other than that he might have disappeared altogether. He felt Paul's weight on the bed beside him, and panic rose like thunder inside him. He curled around himself as much as the pain would allow, but Paul came closer still. He touched his shoulder. 'Don't!' Connor barked, surprised at the depth and harshness of his own voice. Paul jumped back, 'I wasn't going to ...' he began apologetically.

'I know. Just don't,' Connor ordered. He could feel Paul's woundedness instantly, even with his back to him, as Paul shrunk away, but he wasn't able to care. 'Would you prefer it if I was in the other room?' Paul asked him mournfully. Connor nodded stiffly and closed his eyes and waited for him to go away.

Much of that summer is only available to him in brief moments of clear memory, the rest is a fog, an almost dreamlike state, with a thick gauze between the place he had retreated to and the world he inhabited. He had stayed at Paul's for days, refusing any of the food or attention he repeatedly offered him, and only moving around the apartment in snatched intervals when Paul was at work.

The bruises and grazes began to fade and the stitches, as promised, dissolved into his body signalling, at last, that he could go back home for the summer as planned and pretend none of this had happened. He left one day when Paul was at work. He packed his things and caught the train home, only texting Paul when he was halfway there to say he had gone. He didn't think they had spoken to each other in days now, but that probably didn't matter anyway. He got a taxi from the station to his parents' house and went straight upstairs to his room. He had expected a sanctuary, a relief, that the last couple of weeks would just melt away when he got here and he would put it all behind him as if it had never happened. But it just felt utterly alien, as if he had walked into another reality that was nothing to do with him. Even so, he tried his best to go through the motions that his parents expected, performing as much of a semblance of normalcy as he could muster: some conversation at dinnertime, enduring the berating for his being two weeks late coming home and then not having even told them he was coming back. How his mother had been relying on him to help out in the pharmacy and he had let her down! He had better be intending to be in there tomorrow morning! His father was quiet and, thank god, had had to leave quite promptly for evening surgery, so Connor was spared the long disappointed looks he would have normally been subject to for failing to meet his expectations. His father was so anxious for him to follow him into his general medical practice, and to be all that his expectations desired. Connor had never questioned that before but suddenly, as his half-eaten dinner congealed on the plate in front of him, he knew that couldn't happen now. That Connor was dead. There was just a shell on autopilot in his place that he was using to drag his hateful body from one excruciating minute to the next, and waiting for it all to stop.

He remembered some of the days that summer when he had been in the pharmacy, snatches of mundane hours, sorting medicines and cleaning shelves. His mother had been increasingly keeping him out of sight from the customers especially on the alarmingly frequent days when he was showing up unwashed. It had become harder and harder for him to compel himself into the shower. The raw truth of his own body repelled him. To have contact with his own flesh, to own it and live in it as a human being felt impossible now, every cell and pore only emitted the shame of the violation he had become.

He had memories of his mother standing beside him in the back of the pharmacy, anxiety sending the octaves of her voice higher and higher, but he had no idea what she was saying. One day she cried and held him, and for a moment he almost came back, for a split second he woke and remembered that he used to be someone else and that he had lost a part of himself somewhere. The next thing he remembered he was back on the rugby pitch, on his knees, scouring the grass and the mud for what he had lost. It must have been raining because he was wet, or perhaps he was crying. He might have been there for a long time, but eventually he heard someone calling him. At first he wasn't sure if they said his name or 'faggot' so he got up and started to run. He cleared the low hedge in a leap, landing on the road behind it and just about falling in front of a passing car which swerved to avoid him, beeping loudly, and then rushed off into the night. He heard someone call him again, definitely by his name this time and he turned around. He saw a beautiful man, maybe a couple of years older than he, walking towards him. He realised he knew him, his name was Paul, and somewhere in another life they had gone out together. Connor was suddenly aware he was wet and covered in dirt, and he didn't even know how he had got here or why he was there. He was frightened and ashamed. He felt water coming out of his eyes and then something warm wrapped around him. He realised Paul was holding him, and it felt nice, but he could not bear it and pulled away.

More memories: of his parents, each in turn entering his room on monotonous amounts of occasions, lips endlessly flapping, emitting useless sounds. Sometimes the tones were anxious, sometimes angry, other times threatening or pleading, but just a jumble of noise that could not penetrate where Connor had retreated to. He didn't see why they were always at him, he did what was necessary most of the time: he put on his white coat every morning that he was required to do so and spent the necessary six or eight hours in the pharmacy completing the mundane tasks assigned to him by his mother; he sat at the table every evening, poking food into his mouth, chewing and swallowing, pretending to listen to his father's anecdotes and answering the odd question that was thrown at him – making an effort to pull himself together enough to meet the occasion of his address. What did it matter that he didn't go out or answer the phone? That he chose to sit in his room alone whenever possible? This was the best he could do, this was all he could do with what was left of himself, and why could they not just accept that?

Later in the summer his memories start to clear after he found a way to bring himself back. It was chance, or so it seemed, the first time. He had been sitting on his bed in the evening, the TV in his room might have been on but he wasn't watching it. He had changed into a t-shirt and jog-pants after work, or he might have been wearing them all day, or for weeks for all he knew, except it was unlikely his mother would have let him in the shop so dressed. As he sat he began to notice his arms as if for the first time, their pale skin and the forest of brown hair that grew over them. They seemed alien and distant, a weakness or a disappointment. Trying to focus his concentration, to remember why his arms felt like such a betrayal to him, he pinched a clump of hair between his thumb and forefinger and pulled it tightly into a twisle as if to twist his memory into place. Then, to his own surprise, he yanked the knot of hair out of his arm. It stung. It felt sharp and warm and bright, and there was something reassuring about the sensation. He did it again, and then again. He liked the way it felt, it seemed to draw him into himself, to make him feel more solid and real. He liked the heat and burn as he pulled out each small clump of hair and the tingling on his skin afterwards. He liked that he was doing something to his arms, there was definitely something about his arms that troubled him, but he could not remember what. And doing this seemed to propel him into feeling more awake and alive than he had felt in a long time. He could feel himself again, and he liked the sharpness of the feeling.

He started to be able to hear what his parents were saying to him more easily now, and to find answers for them which seemed to make them more relaxed. It was as if a whole tension was dissipating now and he was moving back into himself. He could focus on the TV or the radio, and had even picked up a book and begun to read again the odd time. His arms continued to fascinate him. It was like this was balancing something, something from far away, that he was calling back.

However, he had had to start wearing long-sleeved shirts all the time, even when the days grew hot. The raw bald patches of flesh were becoming quite obvious and his arms had morphed into a strange and blotchy landscape. He had found something else too. Sometimes when he pulled out the hairs tiny dots of blood would sprout from the follicles and the tingling would be especially intense. The dots fascinated him; they were like bright red imitations of the grey dot he had once retreated into, it was like looking at himself in colour. He especially loved the sensation when the dots appeared. He found he could prolong that delicious intensity if he scratched over it with his fingernails, making his skin burn all the more, and bringing him further and further out of the fog that seemed to have settled between him and himself for so long. Some days he became so engrossed that he scratched himself red raw and bleeding without realising. The first time he had shocked himself, almost like coming out of a trance to see that he had almost skinned himself. But it also delighted him, it was right somehow: it felt like himself, repulsive but real, violated, alive.

The end of the summer was arriving, chimed in by his parents' constant one-sided discussion of his return to university. It had never occurred to him that he would go back, and it seemed absurd that they were expecting him to do so. Surely they knew that that Connor was gone now. He didn't exist anymore, that was over. The tension in the house began to increase again. He could feel it constantly in the back of his head, throbbing like a vein in a bruise. It was getting harder and harder to keep things on a level now, to not become overwhelmed by managing the fragmentation of the life and the person he was supposed to be. More and more he scratched and scratched at his arms. Some days the scabs would seep and bleed almost uncontrollably and the flesh and fluid would cake under his nails, but he could not stop. It turned his stomach and frightened him, yet it still felt right, and he was always calmer and cleaner afterwards. His arms stung constantly these days and he had to be careful of the fabric of his shirts sticking to the raw and seeping flesh. But it reassured him, he knew he was alive and real, that there was something of himself there by his own making, even if that was just more shame. It made other things easier for him too, even showering was more manageable now because his attention was entirely absorbed by the stinging in his arms – tracing the water over the raw skin, taking care not to mark any of the towels he used – so that he did not have to be aware of the body he inhabited. The stinging also helped him to focus on the day-to-day chores that he could not drag his body through otherwise. It was like a guiding shard of light that kept him near enough to the present to survive it. He knew also that it was terribly wrong, that he should not be doing this to himself, but he had got lost somewhere and only this seemed to bring him back enough so that he could carry on.

And then everything fell apart again. It was a Tuesday and the dishwasher had broken. He had been trying to avoid a whole conversation during dinner about his pending return to college; about what had been the matter with him this summer; about why he had not seen any of his friends; an endless train of accusation rattling across the table in his direction. Finally, his mother got up and began to clear the plates and he thought the ordeal was over at last, but then she turned to him, 'Be a love and wash the dishes for me, will you?' He forced a nod and a smile and followed her to the kitchen, anxious that his escape to his room had been postponed, and just when he needed so much to be there. He ran hot soapy water into the bowl as his mother piled the dishes beside him. He plunged a glass deep into the water, the heat and the soap stung the raw skin of his arms through his shirt sleeves, cutting, bright and sharp. He washed the glass and took a second. His mother reappeared beside him, 'What are you doing?' she asked with incredulity. 'You're getting your sleeves are all wet!' Then, as naturally as if he was a toddler playing with clay, she lifted his hands from the water and began to roll back his sleeves. He froze. An avalanche of silence crashed between them as his mother slowly revealed his desecrated flesh. She looked at his arms, first one and then the other in shocked disbelief. Then she pushed his sleeves further back. She let out a loud cry that that brought his father rushing in, 'Oh Connor,' she wailed. 'What have you done?' His father pushed between them and yanked at Connor's arms to see what was going on. And suddenly Connor was somewhere else again, his arms were being pulled up, and he could not breathe. He felt sick. He was suffocating, there was noise and commotion around him and he was on the ground. Pain seemed to be everywhere, he could hear his mother's voice shrieking, 'Oh God, he's collapsed! Get an ambulance!' He tried to pull himself up, he did not want to be in the hospital again, but he didn't seem able to move and then the fog descended tightly around him once more.

Memories: A light is being shone into his eyes and he is being asked if he has taken anything. He hears his mother's indignant, but frightened voice, 'Drugs?! My son is not on drugs! It's his arms, look at his arms!' There is commotion all around, and he can feel his body being pulled this way and that. Being touched, having his limbs and clothes pulled, fill him with fear and confusion and sends him spinning. He begins to retch and just in time he is passed a kidney-shaped stainless steel bowl and he vomits into it. His vomit burns his throat and stomach, and momentarily pulls him back upright and into the world around him. He realises he is on a bed or a trolley in a hospital, and there are grubby white curtains pulled in a horseshoe around it. At the foot of the bed stand his father and mother, their faces contorted with a cocktail of fear, anger and disbelief. There is a doctor in a white coat beside him and a nurse in a blue uniform removing the dish from his hands and passing him tissues.

The doctor is saying something to his father about his arms and his mother is crying. Suddenly his father bellows, 'My son does not need to see a psychiatrist!' Connor watches his mother turn mournfully to him and say sadly but uncompromisingly, 'I think, Sean, he does.'

'Well not here!' his father ordered, still refusing the outrage of what was happening. 'If he's going to see someone I'll choose who that is! I'll sort it out myself!'

The atmosphere in the house is horrible now. It's obvious to everyone that Connor isn't going to go back to college and he doesn't seem to be expected to do anything anymore. He spends most of the days lying on his bed, waiting until the house is empty before he gets up, making sure he is safely back in his room when his mother and father return. A boundary has been crossed, and none of them can continue the excruciating pretence that sutured the months of the summer together. None of them know how to respond to each other anymore, and more and more Connor has to accept that he has unavoidably failed them. Shame cuts deeper and deeper into him. Every day now his mother comes into his room and checks his arms, they are healing slowly. The psychiatrist, Dr Moran, gave him pills but they just make him feel further away and lethargic, and they cloud his thoughts with a thicker fog. They have also made him put on weight and he feels flabby and gross. It must be months since he did any sport or worked out, and even though he is rarely hungry or feels like eating his body is swelling like a pus-filled boil.

There is only one thing that makes him feel better now, and that is when he takes the scissors from his desk and drags the grey metal blade into the soft thick flesh of his thigh. The pain is sharp, and when he presses hard the blood comes out quickly in a bright red line. Sometimes he has to do it a lot just to feel inside himself again, but then, when he has, he gets frightened. He looks at his thighs and doesn't recognise them anymore. The loose skin is streaked with dark red cuts and scabs and fresh pink scars. He is not even always sure how the fresh cuts got there, and yet somehow, at the same time, he knows this is how his body should be. He is very careful now about the blood and the mess and keeping any signs of what he is doing away from his mother's extra-watchful gaze. Strange, though, when she looks at his arms in her twice-daily inspection it's almost like she has to force the relief that she expresses – the 'glad he is getting better' – as if deep down they both know that this is just another façade of a lie that they are choosing to save them from the devastation of the truth.

His father seems to have difficulty looking at him at all when he speaks to him now, but he never fails to ask about his fortnightly consultations with Dr Moran, and Connor dutifully makes an effort to perform the expected replies.

After two months Connor stops taking the pills. Nothing is changing. Nothing can change, because it is in him and somewhere much deeper than tablets can reach. But still, he wonders, what would happen if he took a lot of them in one go? Perhaps that would pull him back in one big jolt? Either that, or push him further away, beyond the point of the grey dot where he hovers and into a place where he would not have to endure this anymore. He doesn't really care about the effect anyway, but he has made a definite decision to try it. Having a plan actually makes him feel better than he has in a while. His arms look normal again now and he feels almost hopeful in a ludicrous kind of way and his mother seems to feel better too. They chat a few times, and she tells him that she loves him and that she will always be there for him. He tries to appreciate her reassurances, but he cannot believe that would be true if she really knew what he was, what had happened, and especially if she saw the ever-deepening welts in his thighs. His father is pleased because it is evident that he was right to get Dr Moran to see Connor and that of course things will turn out just fine.

It is sometime around the end of November or early December when he takes the pills. His parents have gone to a belated thanksgiving dinner with their American friends and they have left Connor alone in the house. He wanders through the rooms to affirm his decision, checking one last time how alien his world had become and how desperately he needs to change something. Then he goes up to his own room. He decides to change into proper clothes. It feels like he has been in sweat pants for an eternity and suddenly he hates them. He opens his wardrobe and looks at the pile of carefully folded jeans. On top of the pile are the faded Levis he was wearing the night he was attacked. It feels somehow right that he should be wearing them now, and he steps into them, tossing the crumpled sweatpants into the bottom of the press. Funny, he can't remember the shirt he was wearing that night, but he pulls out a plain white t-shirt and grey sweater and puts them on. They smell of laundry detergent, clean and simple everyday details of life, comforting him with the inane hope of normalcy. He slips a brown belt through the first loop on the waist of his jeans. Then he notices that most of the loops are torn and the last vestige of his hope disappears as quickly as it arrived.

He moves to the locker by his bed and takes out the envelope of pills he has stashed. He is not naïve enough to think his mother's hawk-eyes do not scour the contents of the small brown jar on her twice-daily visits to his room. As he steps around his bed the hard seams of his jeans, tighter on him now, bite at the cuts and scars on his thighs, and the discomfort strengthens his resolve. He plumps up the cushions on his bed and leans against them. Then he empties the envelope of pills into his mouth and swallows them down in one gulp.

Memories: Connor is in Dr Moran's office again, but this time flanked on either side by his parents. Dr Moran, as always, is fortressed behind his huge mahogany desk, polished so that it glints with light reflected from the fluorescent strip on the ceiling above it. Connor wonders if Dr Moran is afraid that his madness might be contagious, that it might seep out of him like an uncontrollable violation of blood and pus and humiliation and irreversibly pollute him forever, and that the expanse of wood and polish form a quarantine zone to neutralise his infectiousness. Dr Moran is asking a lot of questions and Connor's father is getting angrier and angrier. 'I'll have you know there is no history of schizophrenia, or anything else for that matter, in our family, on either side!' he bellows. 'Connor was studying medicine, there is nothing wrong with his mind!' Dr Moran clears his throat and raises an eyebrow, 'Well, we can certainly rule out any possibility of a medical career for this young man from now on. Besides, we often find schizophrenia latent until late adolescence or young adulthood in men, and then it emerges in these kind of mood and behaviour patterns. Either way, Connor is obviously not well and our priority is to decide on the next course of treatment. I think we should increase his medication for a while.'

His father exploded, 'What?! Are you trying to kill him?! Look what he did with the last lot he had, and you want to give him more?!'

Dr Moran smiled condescendingly, 'If you'll let me finish, Dr O'Connell,

I was just about to highlight that a key factor in Connor's current relapse was that he wasn't being properly supervised with his medication. In which case, of course I wouldn't prescribe further medications without concrete protocols in place in that regard. If you and your wife', he added, making a cursory acknowledgement of Connor's mother in the room, and directing his accusation towards her, 'are not able to take responsibility for overseeing his dosage then we could keep him in until he stabilises. Of course if you're adamant about him not returning to that particular medication there are a few options left, but we wouldn't normally consider them at this stage of his diagnosis.'

'Go on', his father interjected hopefully.

'Well, sometimes in cases like this where there is a suspected schizophrenic diagnosis we do find ECT helpful in relieving the symptoms.'

This time it was Connor's mother's turn to shout, she leapt from her chair, 'Absolutely not! No. Never!' she shrieked. 'He's twenty years old for God's sake! There has to be something else!'

Dr Moran looked at her as if she was confirming his suspicions of a schizophrenic heritage, and then looked at Connor's father, 'Dr O'Connell?'

'I think we just need some time to think this through and consider all the options. Perhaps we could make another appointment for next week and make a final decision then?' he replied slowly.

'I wouldn't normally condone such a lengthy gap in treatment for someone who is so unwell, but if I have your absolute reassurance that Connor will be under your supervision, Dr O'Connell, and that at the first sign of any further disturbance you'll bring him straight back to me, then I'll let you take him home for now. Come back and see me again this day week. My secretary will make you an appointment on the way out.' And with that all three were summarily dismissed from his office.

Connor's father was still spluttering with indignation when they arrived home, but it felt to Connor rather like everyone had forgotten he was actually there, or that he could speak, and he had found a strange respite in not having to pretend. But they had scared him too. Despite his silence he had heard what they had said and he was alarmed. He didn't want to be put in hospital, he didn't want more of their pills or treatments, but he had no defence against them now – they had seen the way he had carved up his thighs when they had stripped him and pumped his stomach in casualty. It was obvious to all he had lost his mind; why else would he be doing this? He was afraid they might be right. His mother cried silently for most of the car journey home and her face looked red and raw, as if she had peeled a layer of her skin back, a macabre poster girl for 'skin treatments gone wrong'. Her eyes more rightly belonged to a wounded deer when she looked at Connor, as if it was him that had robbed her of her son and her happiness.

Wednesday morning: six days have passed, and they are due back with Dr Moran the next day. It seems that nothing has been decided, despite the endless arduous discussions that have taken place over the last six days and only a fraction of which have included Connor. Then, in the middle of the afternoon, and with no prior warning Connor's mother burst through his door. 'Connor, love, I have an idea that might help you!' she glowed. She sat on the bed beside him and took his hand with more tenderness than she had in a long while. 'Someone in the shop today was talking about a psychotherapist who has just set up down here, she's very good apparently, has an international reputation and has published a lot of papers. She's worked with all kinds of different people and she might be able to help you. I called and told her a bit about you and she said she could fit you in for a first appointment tonight if you would go along? Will you see her? Will you?' Her eyes searched his face, full of hope and fear and nervous excitement. Her energy was infectious, and Connor could feel hope begin to surface from far back in his mind. He squeezed her hand. 'OK', he murmured, relieved to have any plan other than to face Dr Moran as his only option in the morning. 'Yes, I'll go and see her.'

They have two sessions a week for the first three months and Connor finds very quickly that he actually likes Maureen. She is gentle, but clear and solid, and she doesn't get angry or frustrated when he cannot produce words or coherent explanations. On these days she produces paints and crayons and asks him to draw how he is feeling. At first he wonders if she is crazy or if this is some covert diagnostic test for schizophrenia or some such, but she gently guides him into that far-off place and he begins to make marks on the paper. She encourages him to be bold, and eventually he is splashing red and black in violent explosions across the page. When he stops he is often shocked by what he has produced, but also strangely satisfied, almost like the first time his arms began to bleed beneath his scratching fingers or the first bright red line of blood appeared under the pressure of the scissor blade. It feels right somehow, as if something has been told. Maureen takes everything calmly and thoughtfully, even when he tells her about his arms and legs. She does not demand to see the marks or even that he stop, but she asks him how it feels when he does it and she seems to understand that he is trying to come back. And eventually he finds he can talk to her …

Four months into therapy Connor calls a family conference. He is afraid, flanked once again by both his parents in a professional's office, though in Maureen's room they sit in a curve of soft chairs before her and there is no desk forming a dividing line of authority and culpability between them.

Maureen looks from Connor to his parents and smiles, 'I'm very pleased you came along today, Sean, Mary', she says nodding to each in turn. Connor senses his father stiffen and can imagine what is going through his mind. He is looking at Maureen and her brightly painted room thinking, 'This all seems rather unprofessional, this room is a more like a sitting room than an office, and that woman is dressed far too young for her age: died hair and some class of gypsy dress and cardigan, and knee boots! Really! Surely she should have a suit and name badge at the very least?! And fancy being addressed by my first name by someone who doesn't even have a medical degree!' But Maureen is relaxed and focused and utterly unphased by any of the animosity he emits. She is genuinely glad they are there and knows they have important work to do this session. She smiles at them both again. 'Connor has invited you here because he has something that he needs to tell you and he wanted me to be here while he did.' His father is almost beyond insult at this stage: as if he needs some painted lady in the room with him for his son to communicate with him, well, really!

Connor jumps into the pause before he has time to regret it. His heart is pounding, but he has rehearsed this over and over with Maureen so he is absolutely sure what he wants to say. 'Mum, Dad', he looks quickly at them both, and then lets his eyes come to rest on a patch on the floor between all of their feet. 'Last summer,' he swallows hard, 'last summer, just before I came home I was attacked leaving college.' He pauses. 'A group, a gang, they – they did some terrible things to me.'

'What?! Who?!' his father erupts. 'Who did it? I'm calling the Gardai![1] No one hurts my son and.'

Maureen holds up her hand. 'Please, I can hear that you are shocked and angry and upset, and I know this is difficult for you, but Connor hasn't finished yet, there is something else he has to say.'

Connor looks from Maureen to his father and then his mother, 'They did it for a reason', he falters.

'What?' his mother wails in despair. 'What reason could anyone have to hurt you?' Her eyes are wild and wounded, whirling round the room in search of an explanation. Connor takes a deep breath and focuses for a moment on his feet placed squarely on the floor, just like Maureen has been teaching him to do when he doesn't want to fly away from himself. 'They did it,' he says slowly and carefully, taking another long breath, 'they did it, because I'm gay.'

There is an intense silence in the room, seeming to rise up from the space in the centre of the floor between the collected pairs of feet, a towering impenetrable iceberg. Then his mother begins to cry, softly at first, and then

---

1. The Gardai or An Garda Síochána is Ireland's national police service, literally translates as 'guardians of the peace'.

with loud wailing sobs. His father stares at him for what feels like an eternity and then moves over to his wife and places his arms around her shoulders.

Connor takes a deep breath, he feels awful and the atmosphere in the room is terrible. Yet somehow, now, with Maureen and his parents all here, he is getting a sense that he feels dreadful, ashamed, and small, but that that might be different from him actually being all those things. Maureen looks at him and smiles and nods encouragement, she looks across at his parents who are knotted together as if under attack. Connor is sitting forward, his elbows resting on his knees and his face in his hands, and Maureen says, 'How do you feel Connor? Tell your parents how you feel now, honestly.'

'I feel terrible', he mumbles into his hands.

'Say that again Connor, and to your parents.'

He turns his body towards them, and takes a deep breath. 'I feel terrible', he repeats, and then a landslide of uncontrollable tears fall down his cheeks. In the next instant his mother is standing beside him, holding him, stroking his hair, wrapping herself around him, 'Baby', she murmurs. 'My precious baby, I'll always love you, no matter what.' She pulls back from him slightly and tilts his chin upwards, so they are looking directly into each other's eyes 'I love you,' she repeats, 'I'll always love you, no matter what.' She turns to her husband behind her. He has blanched and his hands are trembling slightly. 'We both love you, don't we?'

His father stutters, he wants to say yes, but he has just found out that his son, his only child, is homosexual, a queer, a faggot. 'I need some air', he says and leaves the room.

Maureen waits, allowing Connor and his mother to console one another uninterrupted for a couple of moments and then gently interrupts, 'Connor, Mary, I'm sorry to interrupt you but I'm just very aware that Sean is not with us. Would it be all right, Connor, if I went out and spoke to your father?' Connor nodded, suddenly aware of the depth of trust he has for Maureen and how safe he feels with her.

Maureen found Connor's father in the waiting area, pacing the room like an angry caged bear. He was a big man, which Connor had not inherited, and perhaps made larger by the air of authority he emitted. There was something rather emperor-like in the demeanour he seemed to have consciously adopted and now he was even more puffed out with discontent. He did not acknowledge that Maureen had entered the room until she touched him lightly on the arm. Close up the difference in their stature was such that Little and Large would have envied them, but Maureen was not inhibited. 'Sean,' she began softly but with her unmistakable solidity, 'I realise this is a shock to you, and a lot to take in all at once, but we have to remember that we are all here for Connor today and that he really needs your support right now. He was brutally attacked and had been deeply traumatised as a result and I know, as a medical man, you understand the implications of that. But he has been doing very well, and it would be so very beneficial for his ongoing recovery if he had your support.' She reached into the pocket of her cardigan and handed him two folded paper leaflets. 'You and Mary might find these helpful.' His immediate thought was to reject the slips of paper she proffered, but then he relented, reflecting for a moment on how much changed Connor was since he had been seeing her albeit in quiet and undramatic ways. He also had to concede she did seem to know her stuff – whatever that stuff might be. He looked at the leaflets 'The Irish Network for Parents of Gay Children' and 'Victim Support: Help for Families'. He looked at Maureen with a confusion of awe and incredulity, and then placed the sheets of paper carefully into the pocket of his blazer. Maureen smiled at him, 'So, Sean, what do you think? Does Connor have your support? Because we would really like you to join us again.'

Back in Maureen's therapy room Connor and his mother are suddenly aware of Sean's voice cascading through the quiet. 'Of course Connor has my support!' His indignant tones proclaimed, 'He's my son, he will always be my son, and he will always have whatever he needs from me!' Connor and his mother smile at one another, and as his father and Maureen re-enter the room it feels to Connor like they are all slowly coming back.

The memories become clearer and more coherent from here on, and Connor has an archive of paintings to mark the next months and years of his life. He had not only continued to paint with Maureen, but also at home, and not just to work out the darkness that he could not voice. He began to experience the world around him, that he had inhabited since his early childhood, through a new lens of colour and brush strokes which surprised and intrigued him. It added a new dimension to his perception, and it felt nurturing to flow through his material and emotional landscapes in this way. He began to work for his mother again for two days a week and enrolled on a portfolio foundation course in the local Art College. That day in Maureen's office had served as the unofficial family acknowledgement that his medical degree was now a brutally aborted dream, as unlikely of coming to fruition as his being able to fly or walk on water. Connor sometimes wondered how hard this sea change had been for his father, what inner landscape of his might be shifting and turning on it axis as a result, but anytime he broached it with him he was met with uncompromising reassurances that he wanted nothing for his son other than his well-being and happiness. Perhaps it was the revelation of his sexuality, as much as anything else, that finally ended his dream of Connor joining him in his practice, as if that was as much a part of the heterosexual family lineage as marriage and children that Connor was clearly now excluded from.

There are still many difficult days and Connor often tumbles back into that far-off place which only the red lines in his skin can bring him back from, a return which is then blighted by the shame and fear those lines signify. But even in these times painting continues to holds a focus for him, and it increasingly seems to offer him a path in place of the trajectory of his life which was so brutally voided that summer. He applies to and is accepted on the art degree course at the local college just before his twenty-second birthday.

It is strange to be starting again. He feels old, like he has already lived an entire lifetime since the day he began his medical degree. They are such polar opposite worlds in every way, the science and status of studying medicine at university, and the flux and fluidity of Art College. It seems a strange thread that has drawn his life through these disparate worlds. It is hard to reconcile sometimes, but the slowly fading scars on his legs are the inescapable reminders of the journey that led him here, and that however fragmented it may have been or become it is his life, irreversibly marked out in the body that travelled these far-flung universes.

Art College is a revelation to him. The entire campus is awash with the most fantastically indentified individuals, all clamouring for a status of uniqueness, so that his simply being a gay man, a little older than many of his peers is frankly mundane. The culture is open and dynamic, nothing is fixed and everything accepted equally. His year are a diverse cohort in age, gender and just about every other characteristic or category he had ever imagined, and he likes it here. He can relax into himself on a par with the others, not having to cover or conceal who he is.

He sees Maureen once a week, and is more and more interested in the process and the impact of the work she has done with him. He enrols as a volunteer on the student helpline and takes extramural classes in counselling skills and art therapy. The courses intensify the depth of his self-awareness and his sessions with Maureen, and he feels that he is finally beginning to grow beyond the point at which he was shattered.

He has slowly begun to reconnect with his physical self too. He has started working out again, and has, after seeing flyers at the gym taken up judo classes. The mental centring and discipline he is taught, the holding within his body that he learns to practise, and the precision of each breath and each movement brings something to life in him that was so long lost he thought it would never return. Yet this is not just the return of something lost, it is also something new and strong and more powerful than he has ever felt before growing inside him, as if the seed of his being had taken root after a long and barren winter and finally begun to flourish. He feels himself changing physically too. The borders of his body seem to have become softer, less fraught with rigidity, and expanding into the welcoming space around him. He is finally in a place, both in his inner self and in his outer world, where he can be at ease and no longer has to shelter behind artificial but fragile hard edges. His eyes and skin are bright and clear, and his hair shines in an increasingly long and loose halo around his head. His aesthetic also extends beyond the pallet and the page and he gravitates to shirts in lucid colours and designs cut to the landscape of his body, and he cultivates all of it with care, attention and depth of presence.

There is still pain, though, in unexpected jolts that threaten to fling him back down the dark road he has travelled and which form deep welts in the memories of this softening and brightening time. One night, in his second year of college, he is at a party with Brian who he has dated a few of times. Brian is the first person who he has allowed to touch him since before everything happened. He has told Brian enough that he understands that their growing intimacy must be a gradual process which he accepted with empathy and without the accusations or repercussions that Connor had feared. For Connor, now, each time they touch, each time their lips meet, or they fold their arms around one another his journey into himself expands. He had forgotten the exquisiteness of skin against skin, the fascination and awe that a human body could inspire, and he had never, ever, felt the magic of desire untainted by shame as it was for him now.

Brian and most of his friends are a little younger than Connor, despite being in their final year at college, and the party is for a twenty-first birthday and likely to be riotous. But it is still early in the night and he and Brain are in the kitchen, ostensibly getting beers from the fridge, but they had found the room empty, and the perfect opportunity for the kiss that had been hanging between them as an unfulfilled promise since they met up in town earlier that evening. Just as they are becoming engrossed in one another they are disturbed by a group of fellow partiers also on a beer-mission. Most of them are from Brian's year, and they greet them with good humoured whistles and cheers, and Brian introduces Connor to those whom he has not yet met, as well as the non-college friends who have tagged along with them. After some chit-chat, Brian and Connor drift out of the kitchen, heading into the yard at the back of the house, where coloured lights have been strewn around the perimeter wall and the space is slowly being transformed into a chill-out zone. They huddle together in a large bean bag, breathing in the cool clear night and gazing upwards at the stars. Brian lights a joint and Connor realises he left his beer on the kitchen table and goes back indoors to retrieve it. Brian's friends are still in the kitchen, so engrossed in conversation that they do not notice Connor enter. He picks up the bottle and then, as he is leaving, he suddenly realises they are talking about him. A young woman, who he has a sense of vaguely recognising, has the rest of the group captivated with her serious and dramatic tones. 'I'm telling you,' she said, 'my cousin lives two doors down from him and her folks were at the same dinner party as his parents the night he took the overdose. He'd been seeing shrinks and everything, and they said he cuts himself too!' A cacophony of voices rise from the group:

'Does Brian know?'

'I don't know, but he should!'

'God, that's really scary, we should tell him!'

'Yeah we should, after all, that's all he needs!'

'Yeah, who knows what someone like that might do – do you think he has ever done anything to anyone else?'

Connor turns. A weight of shame as heavy as the body that pinned him to the ground all those months and years ago suddenly awakes and imprisons him from within. It takes all his resolve to move his limbs, but he quietly exits the front door and closes it gently behind him. Outside, he lets the bottle drop from his hand, it clunks against the pathway but does not break. The amber liquid fizzes forlornly outwards like the spent innards of a broken promise dying on the ground.

He walks very slowly home, his phone constantly buzzing in his pocket. Brian, no doubt, but he cannot face him right now – or ever – he thinks. 'Ask your friends', he texts him, and then switches it off. Each step of his journey seems to take him further and further away from himself, from what he had come to know and trust, and to be leading him backwards into that distant void of despair that he had thought he had left once and for all.

Finally, at home, and in the safety of his room, he reaches for the box by his desk where he keeps his art materials. He knows what he is looking for: the Stanley knife that he has been using for his print work. It has a thick, dark blue plastic handle with a slot along one side for the button which protracts the blade to travel through. He presses his thumb against the button and the blade immediately responds to his summons. He is hurting so much inside. His hands are shaking. He needs this. He knows this is the only thing that will stop this feeling, the leaden far-off place that he no longer wants to inhabit. This, he knows, will bring him back, but he is also deeply afraid. There have been no new marks on his legs for a while now; the scars are fading and he has been willing their healing. He looks at his uncut flesh and feels a deep sadness for himself and what he is about to do, and he is suddenly very confused. The blade is so close to his skin, promising the relief he so desperately needs, but he also realises how intensely he does not want to do this. He exhales, it seems he has been holding his breath for a long time. He puts the knife on top of his desk. He is sweating and his chest is tight, crying out for more oxygen and relief. He takes some long deep breaths and from somewhere inside him he makes a decision to wait. He doesn't really know if he can, or for how long, but he decides to see if he can wait, just a little, maybe just one or two minutes, before he does it. He keeps breathing in a long slow rhythm and tears start to come, shaking his body in waves of tremors. He reaches for the knife. It is comforting to hold it in his hand, assured of the relief it will provide. But then he lays it back down again. He breathes. He tells himself again that he can do this whenever he wants, whenever he needs to, but that he just wants to wait for a minute or two to be sure. Over and over the cycle repeats and seconds feel like years. The blade is calling to his skin like a magnet, like freedom, like relief, but second by second, minute by minute, and eventually hour by hour he gets through the night without drawing it through his flesh.[2]

He sleeps late into the next day. He wakes confused with sleep and emotional exhaustion. He sees the knife on his desk and remembers the night before, but barely trusts the memory. Tentatively he reaches down and touches the skin of his thighs, his fingers assure him that there are no new rivers of red scoured through his skin. He slips out of bed and picks up the knife. He retracts the blade and replaces it in his art box. He feels grateful to it – its presence and possibility had carried him through the night – his wounder and saviour all in one. He lies back down on his bed, a strange mix of feelings are surging through him all at once. He closes his eyes and feels tears close behind them. He gets up and moves over to the art box again. This time he begins to paint.

By the time he reaches the third and penultimate year of his art degree the college is revamping itself into the School for Visual and Performing Arts and he has taken courses in subjects that he never knew existed, in cultural studies and in critical social theory. They have exploded the foundations of his scientific training, but also leave him oddly curious of his old discipline and the path he had so securely embarked upon in that previous lifetime.

One rainy Tuesday after his session with Maureen, he realises he has made a decision, something that will reconnect everything that he was and is, and which will allow him to practise all that he has come to understand. He feels light and alive, as radiant as the absent sunshine and taking its place in the sky. Instead of walking to college for the afternoon as his usual routine dictates, he turns in the opposite direction and catches the bus to the other side of town. From his childhood he remembers when this area was derelict,

2. More information on practising the 'slow it down' rule that Connor uses the night of the party can be found in the Harm Reduction Appendix.

quietly tumbling down upon itself in a gradual implosion of decay. But since then it has become home to many of the 'new communities' as they are known, and the streets are now vibrant with the rhythms of a multitude of tongues, and the patchwork of colourful shop fronts, eclectic street vendors, and all bathed in the aroma of roasting garlic and spices. He picks his way slowly through the South-East Asian, Chinese and West African produce, revelling in the textures, shapes and smells that surround him, committing them to memory to be reproduced later under his brush. He gathers sweet Thai basil, lemon grass, fresh coriander, cumin seeds, pack choi, garlic and dried chillies. He fills another bag with plantains, yams and threads of rice noodles, thin as strands of silk. He buys crisp vegetables and fresh cashews before catching the bus home laden down with his sweet-smelling purchases.

Connor's mother is the first to arrive home and be welcomed by the pungent aroma emanating through the hallway from the kitchen. She removes her coat and gently opens the door. For a split second she views the scene as if a stranger: a young man with soft, long hair and bright clear blue eyes is standing at the counter between the cooker and the sink with a large knife in his hand. He is chopping through a mountain of exotic-looking vegetables and tossing them into a wok which is smoking with spices on the hob. He has a turquoise paisley shirt, open at the neck and sleeves rolled up to his elbows. He is smiling and humming faintly along with a tune on the small radio which is perched on the window ledge beside him. She feels her heart contract with love. He is so beautiful, he has grown vibrant with a depth and strength that awes her. She cannot imagine, anymore, life before that terrible summer which seemed to drag on forever and to change everything – or the last time they stood in this kitchen, he with his sleeves pushed upwards to reveal his arms. She can't imagine him being anything other than he is right now: whole, beautiful, perfect, her son. Her eyes flood with tears. Connor, suddenly aware of her, puts down his knife and greets her with a kiss on the cheek. He pulls out a chair for her and opens a chardonnay he has cooled in the fridge and hands her a glass. He sits with her and they talk for a few minutes and then he returns to his chopping while she showers and changes for dinner. When his father arrives home 40 minutes later the table is set and there is an infectious glow of content in the kitchen. It is all too obvious to him that there is some special occasion and that Connor has something to share with them. At the back of his mind he worries that this is about him leaving them to go and live with his boyfriend – though he cannot be absolutely certain he is seeing anyone right now – it is a part of his son's life he is content not to keep up with. He tries to prepare himself to be happy and supportive, to combat the doubt that catches and then nags incessantly in his mind whenever he sees his son with his gay friends or any of the boys he has dated. He takes a gulp of wine, letting the chill of the alcohol subdue his restless thoughts. So, when Connor finally reveals the inspiration for this unusual Tuesday feast he practically regurgitates the wine he has swallowed in disbelief. 'Finish your medical degree?! Psychiatry?!' Are you sure?' he splutters. Connor smiles, 'Yes, I'm sure. I've never been more sure!' He swallows, it is still hard sometimes to speak about the events that have so irreversibly shaped the last few years of their lives, but he believes more than ever that is why his choice is so right. He continues, 'I think after everything that has happened, and everything that I have learnt, that I have something really important to contribute and I want to be able to do that, professionally. I want to be able to help people, I want there to be something else for people other than the likes of Dr Moran and his pills.' He looks at each of his parents in turn, and the radiance of his certainty is unmistakable. His mother's eyes are awash with tears again, and even his father's eyes seem to be glistening more than usual behind his glasses. 'Of course,' they chorus in unison, 'of course, we're so proud of you.'

Connor restarts his medical degree joining the second year at a new university the following September. He is living away from home and forgoing his weekly sessions with Maureen for the first time in years. He is acutely aware in his new surroundings that despite his age and this being his sixth year, in total, as a student that he has yet to finish any degree. But he knows he is in the right place. He is continually grateful for his parents' support and their financial commitment to him. He knows this has been a hard journey for them too, but he also knows that, just like him, they have grown and strengthened through the challenges they have faced individually and as a family.

He is keenly aware of the things which keep him strong and stable and help him to grow. He immediately joins the gym, signs up for judo, enrols as a volunteer on Niteline, joins the student gay and lesbian group and, now, the mature students' society. He also continues to read critical theory, however at odds it is with medical science, and he explores antipsychiatry, critical psychiatry and post-psychiatry through the writings of Laing, Foucault, Sacks, Szasz, Breggin, Thomas and Bracken. He gets some part-time work as a research assistant on an art therapy pilot being run by the student counselling service and achieves his first co-publication with them. He excels in his course, despite his unconventional ideas, and finishes each year at the top of his class.

The hospital placement rotations during the final years of his training are much more challenging though, and sometimes he wonders if he is indeed strong enough to endure the endless vortex of human trauma and distress the hospital contains. He understands more and more the emotional disengagement of his profession: it is a survival strategy in these macabre production-lines of devastation, but still he cannot condone or emulate it. He struggles with the coldness and the hierarchy which permeate every aspect of medicine, from the separation of mental, emotional and physical well-being, to the inequality of power and status between patients and staff, between doctors and nurses, between junior doctors, registrars and consultants. But he holds tighter to his belief that there is another way, and to the passion and the experiences that made him so sure that this was what he needed to do, and could do.

On his second psychiatric rotation his first two days are spent shadowing the senior consultant on admissions and assessments, before he is let loose to singlehandedly cover the night-shift admissions. The consultant, Mr Byrne, is an older, portly man who reminds Connor of a strange combination of his father and Dr Moran, and also, from the vantage point of the present, of the senior consultant he currently labours under in St Jude's – God O'Halloughan, as the nurses refer to him, in light of his inflated sense of his own omniscience.

He is slightly intimidated by him, and is sure that Mr Byrne encourages this as a way of maintaining his authority and status. He 'suggests' to Connor that his just-past collar-length hair is not suited to his position, nor equally is the 'casualness' of his attire under the compulsory white coat. He is obviously outraged to have to repeat the same clearly unheeded comments the second day they work together, and the atmosphere between them is arctic. That morning they are due to assess a young woman who has been referred from the casualty department of the local hospital. Apparently she has an extended inpatient history dating from her mid-teens and this is not the first time she has been here. 'A cutter', Mr Byrne comments dryly as he leafs through the brown folder on the desk in front of them, poignantly regarding Connor for a moment and then diverting his attention back to the sheets of paper. The words sting. Connor draws a long silent in-breath and makes sure nothing in his outer composure betrays the jolt of panic passing through him. For a fleeting second the thought, 'he knows', raced through his mind. But he quickly bats the thought away as the door opens and a young woman is escorted in by a nurse. She has tightly cropped hair and an Indigo Girls t-shirt and faded combat pants. Her right arm is heavily dressed with surgical wads and her left arm is an intricate map of scars in varying stages of healing. The nurse indicates for her to sit down in front of the desk and then hands her a small duffle bag and a knitted hoody which she instantly pulls on and zips tight up to her neck. She looks from one to the other of the men sat behind the desk, her eyes an initial mixture of defiance and fear, her shoulders slumped tightly in the same resigned combination. Then she gives Connor a second look and he smiles warmly at her. Aside from the deep resigned sadness that seems locked into her body she could be one of his peers from the student

LGBT society transported through time to visit his new life. He feels a longing to help this woman, who is really barely more than a girl, and far too young to be a regular inhabitant of a place like this.

Mr Byrne, meanwhile, has shuffled through the papers in her file and brought an assessment sheet to the top. He looks at her and ticks a few boxes and adds a few written comments without speaking, and then puts his pen down and interlaces his fingers on the desk in front of him. He regards her intently for a moment before he speaks. 'Well, Miss Smyth, we meet again, and not under improved circumstances I see from the casualty report.' It is a statement rather than a question but it is left to hover in the air as if demanding a response, though Connor is unsure how she could respond to such a finality. He is about to introduce himself and explain his own presence, but Mr Byrne, clearly already having interpreted the silence, added a few notes to the page and then continued with more direct questioning. 'I see you have had a change of hair too, did you do that when you did that to your arm?'

The woman across from them looked perplexed to the point of outrage by this comment, but also roused to respond. She has a soft voice which is thickened with incredulity. 'I cut my hair months ago, before you last saw me. I told you then, I did it when I came out.' She is watching them intently now, and Connor wants to interject. He wants to ask her if she has support of her family and friends, and how she feels in herself now she has made this bold declaration to the world. He opens his mouth to voice some of these thoughts, feeling a possibility of a genuine and constructive rapport and connection with her that may make him able to really help. But Mr Byrne is talking again and has written something else. Connor focuses his eyes in disbelief on the top leaf of the open file in front of them, 'unstable self-image' is etched into the page, more damming, he thinks, than any of the lines than she herself has etched into her arms.

Funny to be thinking of her now, he realises, in his sunshine-painted office in the bowels of St Jude's. He wonders where she is today and how she is. One of many, it pains him to think, that have already skirted the edge of his career, a career which was supposed to support them, not let them slip absently by into the abyss of the unknown. There are so many lost and broken souls in the world that he inhabits that it seems impossible, futile, to hope for anything than for just the tiniest few of them. Psychiatry and all its promises of miracle cures routinely abandons them to an infinite hopeless cycle of pain and dependence. He sighs. God O'Halloughan is coming to see him this morning; no doubt yet another reprimand to add to his ever-growing list. Connor smiles to himself. O'Halloughan might even bring some tobacco-wash paint with him and insist Connor use it to restore his office to something more befitting to the demeanour of the hospital as a whole.

But before that he still has a pile of admin to get through and also a session with one of the patients from the men's chronic ward. He is a young man to be so categorised, and to have been here for such a significant part of a relatively short life. He is only a little older than Connor, yet he has been an inpatient for most of his adulthood with a few periods of life in the community. Connor likes him. They have spent some time talking in regular scheduled sessions together over the last few months, and the consistent interest and attention alone seems to be having a marked impact on him. At some stage Connor wants to see if he can get him painting, but there is still some trust to be built up before then. Whenever he looks at this man Connor feels acutely aware that he could be a mirror image of himself in less advantageous circumstances, and that what kept him on the desirable side of the border between madness and sanity was no more than a combination of eclectic good fortune. For all his father's bluster and straight-lacedness, Connor knows that had it not been for him, and the money, privilege and education that his family enjoyed he too may have been trapped in the endless revolving door of psychiatry, his life held to ransom by the arbitrary cocktail of random ill luck and human pain.

He looks at his watch. Time to go and collect his patient from the ward. Connor's individual sessions are currently tolerated so long as they don't cross too many of the established boundaries. However, having patients walk unaccompanied to a psychiatrist's office for a session, as he did at the outset, was an outrage too far for the consultants. 'You're not in private practice now you know!' he had been warned. 'That's not how we do things in this hospital, and for good reason: we have the safety of all the patients and staff to consider, and we certainly can't have unaccompanied patients wandering in and out of offices at will.' Connor had reluctantly assented to a compromise where he could still work with his patients in his protocol hour-long individual sessions, but he had to collect and return them to the ward himself in order to maintain the semblance of the dividing line of power and sanity that perpetuated the mental health hierarchy. He left his office, with the door unlocked and his white coat still hanging on the back of it, and went to collect Peter from the men's ward.

From the moment he approached him Connor felt an energy about Peter that was new. Something seemed raw and close to the surface in him, as if, just as Connor once had, he had been living a long way from himself and was only now beginning to arrive back. He was thin, underweight despite the cocktail of medications which were constantly being prescribed to him, and he was dressed in faded blue cotton pyjamas. He had a green towelling robe slung around him and flip-flops in place of slippers. Those on the chronic ward were rarely allowed to wear clothes, their semi-nakedness beneath threadbare nightwear a simple and effective vehicle of subjugation.

They had only just arrived in the office and not even sat down when Peter blurted out, in a sudden rush of courage and embarrassment, 'Are you gay?' Connor looked at him but before he could reply Peter nervously continued. 'Only that's what some of the other guys are saying and I wanted to know 'cos,' he paused and took a breath, 'I wanted to know 'cos I wanted to ask you about something that happened to me once.'

Connor smiled. 'Yes, they're right, I am gay. And I'd be very happy for you to ask me about whatever it is that's bothering you.' He smiled again. 'But please sit down first!' He reached over and took one of the stress balls from his desk and tossed it playfully to him, Peter caught it in one hand and smiled broadly, and then threw it back to Connor who, even though off guard, managed to catch it in his right hand. 'OK,' he said, 'my turn for the stress – hit me with it.'

In ten minutes of fraught recollection Peter revealed a devastating history of abuse which had shattered him on every level. He shook and wept as he finished his account and Connor, deeply touched by his distress and his trust in sharing such deeply held pain with him, moved over to his side. He knelt by his chair and placed a wad of tissues in his hand, gently squeezing his arm in comfort as he did so. 'I'm so sorry that happened to you', he said, raw with emotion. 'It was wrong and you did not deserve any of it.' He gently squeezed his arm again, and then something in the room caught his attention. To his surprise he realised that the door was open and God O'Halloughan loomed in the frame sneering at the scene before him. 'I called by, Dr O'Connell, to remind you about our chat about hospital protocols, but I can see it is rather too late for that.' He sneered again, accentuating the path of his eyes from where he stood, to the empty desk, to Connor – the gay shrink – kneeling beside and apparently hand in hand with a young male patient dressed only in thin pyjamas. Connor needed no forewarning about how this would be presented, but at that moment he didn't care, he was so enraged at the intrusion and the utter disrespect it demonstrated towards him and Peter. He rose to his feet, he knew he had nothing lose now. 'I'm not sure about hospital protocol, Mr O'Halloughan, but basic good manners prescribe knocking before entering someone's room.' They stood in a silent face-off for what seemed like an age before God O'Halloughan finally broke the impasse. 'I'll see you at twelve fifteen', he commanded. 'In my office', and then turned and walked out letting the door slam closed behind him. Connor was incensed, he turned to Peter, unsure how he could recover his connection with him now, concerned for the irreparable damage done by such an intervention during his painful disclosure. He was quite taken aback, then, to see Peter gently convulsing with silent laughter. His mirth was so intense that it was a while before he could speak, but when he was finally able to compose himself he said, 'Thank you so much for that! That was the best medicine I ever had! The look on his face! That was priceless!' He laughed again, loudly and irresistibly this time, and Connor joined him. But moments later a seriousness descended on Peter and he added, 'But you're going to be in deep shit now aren't you?'

'Yes', Connor replied gravely, 'yes I am', already feeling the inevitable doom of his contract being terminated, a suspension, an inquiry or some such scourge on his career.

Connor looks at his watch, it is 12:03, and he has exactly twelve minutes before he will face the wrath and judgement of God O'Halloughan. It feels a bit like waiting for the gallows and he thinks it would be an appropriate time for a last cigarette and momentarily wishes that he smoked so that he has something fitting to do in this limbo. Instead, he clicks into his email account. There is an email from the editor of *The Journal of Post-Psychiatry* which offers a potential lift. He had recently submitted a paper on art therapy and institutional culture and eagerly opens the email hoping for news of a positive peer review. There is an acknowledgement of his paper, and some informal but encouraging feedback from the editorial team, but no final outcome of the peer review as yet. Connor reads on, his mood brightening with every sentence. The core founding team of the journal have received funding to run an inpatient project as part of their practice-based research on the impact of post-psychiatry. They are keen to include an art therapy dimension and would therefore like to invite him to join them as a full-time team member. Connor is ecstatic, he could kiss his computer he is so happy, he could even kiss God O'Halloughan at this moment!

He looks at his watch – eleven minutes past twelve – the eight minutes which have just passed have rerouted the course of his life more unmistakably and positively than he would have thought possible in such a short interval, and have equally concretely affirmed everything he has worked so intently towards, yet had so often questioned from within the walls of this graveyard of hope. He logs out of his computer and swings out of his office, his buoyant steps marching an unstoppable path along the corridor and lighting a future bright enough to rival the sunflowers which bedeck his shirt.

HELP AND RESOURCES

Full contact details can be found in Appendix Three: Resources.

UK
- FFLAG: Support for parents of people who are lesbian, gay and bisexual
- FirstSigns: Self-injury support and information for people who self-injure and those who live and work with them
- Nightline: Telephone support service run by and for students
- One in Four UK: One-to-one and helpline support for females and males who have experienced sexual abuse
- Rape Crisis England and Wales: Support for women and girls who have experienced sexual violence
- Victim Support: Confidential support for victims and witnesses of crime

Republic of Ireland
- Dublin Rape Crisis Centre: Helpline and one-to-one therapy for females and males who have experienced rape or sexual abuse
- Niteline: Telephone support service run by and for students
- One in Four: Support and therapy for females and males who have experienced sexual abuse
- Student Union of Ireland LGBTQ Support
- Victim Support: Confidential support for victims and witnesses of crime

REFERENCES AND FURTHER READING

Bracken, P & Thomas, P (2002) Time to move beyond the mind body split. *British Medical Journal, 325*, 1433–4.

Breggin, P (1991) *Toxic Psychiatry*. New York: St. Martin's Press.

Foucault, M (1989) *The Birth of the Clinic: An archaeology of medical perception*. London: Routledge.

Foucault, M (2001) *Madness and Civilisation: A history of insanity in the Age of Reason*. London: Routledge.

Laing, RD & Esterson, A (1970) *Sanity, Madness and the Family*. Middlesex: Pelican.

McNiff, S (2004) *Art Heals: How creativity cures the soul*. Boston and London: Shambala.

Miller, A (1995) *Pictures of a Childhood*. London: Virago.

Sacks, OW (1991) *A Leg to Stand On*. London: Picador.

Sedgwick, P (1982) *Psycho Politics*. London: Pluto Press.

Servan-Schreiber, D (2005) *Healing Without Freud or Prozac: Natural approaches to curing stress, anxiety and depression*. London: Rodale.

Szasz, T (2007) *The Medicalization of Everyday Life*. New York: Syracuse University Press.

Thomas, P & Bracken, P (2001) Postpsychiatry: A new direction for mental health. *British Medical Journal, 322*, 724–7.

Thomas, P & Bracken, P (2004) Critical psychiatry in practice. *Advances in Psychiatric Practice, 10*, 361–70.

TRUST ME 1
(FIRST TIME)

October 23rd, Ciaran has been working at Teen-Link for almost three months now and his probation period will be officially completed at the end of the next week. It's strange, in some ways it all still feels new and alien to him, as if he remains very much the outsider in this substitute family home of ten teenagers and a staff team of more than double that. Yet, at the same time, he also had a sense of having been there for a while, and consequently feels a little frustrated with his own lack of progress with the residents. Most of the residents have been there longer than he, and so have taken great joy indulging every possible opportunity for confusing him around rules and protocols, trying to trip him into errors that will bring brief additional privileges to themselves and simultaneously humiliate Ciaran in his mistakes. It's innocent enough, meant to be harmless, but he still finds this surface-level jousting for status so frustrating.

He had finished his degree in Youth Work and Social Care with a first-class honours and two very successful work placements and some relief work under his belt, and he had expected to hit the ground running with his first full-time permanent position. The vacancy at Teen-Link had arisen with perfect timing the summer after he had finished his degree. He had sailed through the interview and selection process; an educated, well-skilled and enthusiastic young man was a something of a rarity in this profession and he was the ideal candidate for the position. Teen-Link was unusual in that it housed both girls and boys – or young people as they made a point of calling them – and they were keen to get more male staff members on board. Ciaran had impressed the selection panel in every way; he was qualified and experienced, and he had a beautiful combination of earnest enthusiasm for the work coupled with a good sense of fun, all housed in an easy-going, funky demeanour. They even liked his appearance, he had dark hair carefully waxed into a messy indie-rock style and a smig[1] shot through with a silver piercing stud, the kind of image the kids would relate to. Overall, he was

---

1. A smig is the small triangle of beard which some men grow below their bottom lip.

exactly what they wanted and, as he already had Garda clearance[2] from his previous work placement, he had been able to start immediately.

Ciaran quickly got on well with his peers, and when the residents weren't trying to manipulate him into errors, they seemed to like him too. But, still, there was a reserve, a distance that Ciaran was keen to move beyond. He wanted to start key-working, but that wouldn't begin until after the mandatory three-month probationary period was completed. Nonetheless, he was still keen to make some impact in enabling the young people move towards full adult lives. So, in the mean time, he focused his attention on the two residents who had arrived at Teen-Link after him and who, like him, were on their own sort of probation period. Tricia had been first of the two. She was a striking-looking girl, tall and slim but curvaceous, with dark red hair and skin as pale and thin as tissue paper. She stood out amongst the other girls by the way she dressed so modestly, always in high necked tops worn long over the waist of her jeans, no cleavage or belly-rings on display from her, adding an aura of maturity to her that could have made her their senior by a number of years. Her face and arms were sprinkled with a liberal display of dark freckles, but they also somehow made her appearance more womanly than childlike. She had intense blue eyes, but she rarely looked directly at anyone with them, usually focusing to the side and near distance of whomever she was speaking to. She was quiet most of the time too, closed down in a bewildered kind of way as if she wasn't really sure how she had got to Teen-Link or exactly what she was supposed to be doing there. Even so, she seemed in her own tentative way to be responding to Ciaran's attention and to be comfortable enough with him to allow him to take tiny steps towards her. Ciaran liked her, but sometimes he couldn't help wishing that she would just fire herself up a bit, even just to get angry or defiant over nothing and show some of the energy that the other girls demonstrated in such excess.

The other new resident that Ciaran had been paying attention to was a young lad, Ronan, only just turned fifteen therefore eligible to be in the project, but actually appearing much younger. He was small and slight, certainly still much more a boy than a young man, he had mousy hair that he rarely washed and he seemed to live in the same dirty runners and tracksuit. He oscillated between becoming so small and silent that it was as if he could actually physically shrink himself to disappearing point and become invisible, to sudden bouts of uncontrollable fury and rage. Ciaran worried about that rage, at present it mostly resembled a small child's tantrum, but when Ronan physically developed Ciaran knew that same rage could well be lethal.

---

2. 'Garda clearance' refers to the police background check that many organisations working with children, young or vulnerable people require before a person can be employed.

It was seven-thirty in the evening after what had been an unusually quiet Thursday. The night workers would be on duty in half an hour for hand-over before they commenced the sleep-over shift – the most unpopular on the rota. Even so, in a perverse way, Ciaran was looking forward to getting on the full-time rota and taking on the sleep-over shifts. He knew that sleep was a bit of a misnomer, the pull-down beds in the offices and the dribbling staff shower hardly provided the facilities for a good night's rest. But there was an intimacy that grew from occupying the project at night, and the night time hours were so often where trust was built. He looked at his watch and sauntered towards the blue office – the one where the male staff sleep – imagining the time not long hence when he would finally take his turn.

Before he reached the door, however, Tricia intercepted him. He hadn't even realised she was back in the project – she had been out for the evening visiting her mum – and he worried that it must have gone badly for her back so early and also to have sneaked in without anyone seeming to notice.

'Can I talk to you?' Tricia asked him, actually looking directly at him for a moment before her eyes darted around the corridor with a sense of animated urgency. Ciaran had never seen her this charged up before, she was aglow with urgent intensity. 'Of course', he smiled reassuringly, but she had already turned and was moving ahead of him down the corridor. Ciaran instinctively followed.

He stepped into the small room, noting that its magnolia-painted breeze-block walls were bereft of the posters, magazine pictures and nicknacks which cluttered and personalised the other kid's rooms. The heavy fire door swung shut behind him leaving him alone in the small, cramped cell with Tricia. He instantly knew it was a mistake; he shouldn't be alone in one of the resident's bedrooms with the door closed, and especially not with a girl, but he felt suddenly trapped, uncertain and panicked. He had been so flattered and hopeful when Tricia had sought him out, he had seen the urgency of her need and had jumped to respond, hoping that this might be his chance to really make a difference. In heat of the moment he had not considered that she was leading him down the corridor to her room. Besides, on occasion, he was still a little disorientated by the layout of the project, especially with it having some of the bedrooms, including Tricia's, on the ground floor – the space he still associated with the offices and communal rooms. New residents were generally placed in ground floor rooms for the first six months or so of their tenure, graduating to the upstairs rooms, on either the male or female corridor, as they became more independent and proved themselves less in need of intensive surveillance and support.

For the first time since he started at Teen-Link Ciaran really did not know what he should do next. He realised the gravity of his mistake but was also afraid that if he immediately backed out of the room he would irreparably hurt Tricia's feelings, reject her trust, and undo any possibility of helping her with whatever was so obviously troubling her there and then, or, maybe even of working with her in the future. He hovered, locked with uncertainty and excruciatingly aware of the close proximity of their bodies in this tiny and highly charged space.

Tricia stepped back from him and perched on the top of the small bedside locker that filled the space between the wardrobe and the single bed facing him. She was speaking softly, urgently, but Ciaran was so caught up in his racing thoughts that he had not been able to listen to her or take in anything she had said. When he finally focused his attention on her he could not comprehend what was happening. He looked at her, and then he looked at her again. His surprise and confusion meant it was a few seconds longer before he realised what she was doing, and then a few more before he understood what he was looking at. She had unzipped her hoody so that it flopped open away from her body and then she had lifted her t-shirt up to her armpits, holding it so that her hands were shielding her breasts. She was not speaking now, she was waiting for something from him. The landscape of her body beneath the t-shirt confused him. He was used to her pale skin and the dark freckles that littered her face and her arms, so that initially he thought that her torso was almost completely covered by four or five enormous very dark red freckles, so dark that in places they even showed through what he could see of the pale fabric of her bra. But as he continued to stare in confused disbelief he realised that what he was looking at was not freckles but scabs; huge, raw scabs, that were still damp in places and that it was fresh septic fluid that he could see seeping through her underwear. An involuntary cry escaped from him, he had never seen anything quite like that before. She looked like she had been horrifically burnt. Something dreadful must have happened!

The next minutes were a blur of commotion and noise that he had no clear memory of. He was not sure if he had got out of the room and called out for help, or if his cry of shock had been heard. But, either way, suddenly there were two other people crowding into the tiny room – the project leader, Martin, who had been just about to go off duty for the night – and Paula who had just arrived, a little early, for the night shift. Ciaran was somehow at the back of the trio helplessly watching a nightmare unfold before him. Tricia was screaming at them all to get out of her room; Paula had rushed forward and was trying to calm Tricia and, at the same time, lift up her t-shirt so that she could see the extent of her injuries. Damp patches of septic fluid were beginning to visibly spread through Tricia's t-shirt around her breasts and abdomen. Tricia was trying to hold down her t-shirt and zip up her hoody and at the same time break free from Paula, but in this tiny space she was utterly confined and had nowhere to go. Martin seemed almost as uncomfortable and bewildered as Ciaran had done just moments before, but Martin had an added air of stoically maintaining his presence, as if this alone would somehow orchestrate a neat and proper outcome. But it was pure chaos, everyone seemed utterly blown apart by this explosion out of nowhere and no one seemed to have any idea what it was, or what should be done about the horrific-looking injuries on Tricia's body.

Ciaran had felt like he was watching a horror movie unfold in front of him; he had pressed play and there was no going back, no pause or stop button, and he was now compelled to see this to its inevitable apocalyptic, blood-bath of an ending. Tricia had metamorphasised before his eyes from a pretty, quiet girl with meticulously straightened dark-red hair, freckles and blue eyes into a contorted, screaming banshee, with half the flesh seared off her torso; hair and eyes wild with anger and hatred, struggling to be free of them, almost ready to propel herself out of the window on the energy of her rage. In between screaming at Palua, her venom was focused on Ciaran, 'You said I could trust you!' she spat in his direction. 'What did you do that for? You said I could trust you!' The accusation hurt him as much as if it was his own skin that was raw and weeping beneath his shirt. He wasn't even sure what he had done.

The next morning Ciaran had received an almost apologetic call from the manager of the project, Caitriona. 'I'm sorry, Ciaran', she had said, 'but last night, after the incident, Tricia said some things to the A&E doctor that we have to take very seriously and follow procedure around. No one doubts you Ciaran but it's procedure …'

'What? What things?' he stammered, 'What did she say?'

'It's not clear at the moment, but it turned out that she had done all those injuries to herself, she'd been rubbing all kinds of caustic substances, oven cleaners, bleach and the like, into herself. She has made a right mess but it should heal eventually. Anyway, she wasn't making a huge amount of sense by the time the doctor saw her. She had tried to leave twice before hand, and it was late by the time they got to her. The doctor came back to us because he was concerned about something she said. He'd asked her why she had done it and all she kept repeating was, 'He asked me to do it. I wanted to talk to Ciaran. He told me to take up my top again.'

Ciaran let out a howl of disbelief.

'Don't get too upset about it Ciaran, we know it doesn't add up, but we have to follow procedure to get to the bottom of it, and so you won't be able to come in until we have it resolved. I know this is very tough on you, especially when you're so new in, but please don't worry too much. This kind of thing is not unheard of by any means, and there is usually a simple answer in the end. It is made more difficult by the fact that you had gone into her room alone, and that is something that we will need to talk about further. Martin is going to follow-up with that and keep in contact with you over the next while. There will be an investigation and a panel that you'll have to appear before, but Martin will keep you updated with all of that. It doesn't normally take longer than three months and Martin will continue to supervise you through that period though you will, of course, have to meet off site.'

Ciaran's mind was racing, trying to keep up with the nightmarish implications of the incomprehensible occurrences of the previous night. Three months seemed like an eternity. And what Catriona had said about Tricia utterly confounded him. He had barely slept, every time he closed his eyes he saw the soft white flesh of her body, the curve of her breasts scoured raw and weeping, horrifically wounded, and now to hear that she had done that herself was incomprehensible. Nothing in any of his training or any of the books he had read had prepared him for anything like this. It was overwhelming.

'She did that to herself?' he asked, incredulous.

'Yes, self-harm is not uncommon in teenage girls but we usually see it in a phase of cutting that they go through, and it's usually much more consistently attention-seeking than Tricia. We had no idea Tricia had a history of self-harm when we took her; it wasn't on her referral. We don't generally take self-harmers, they're too difficult to work with in the kind of set-up we have here, and they tend to generate a lot of copycat incidents. Self-harmers really need a solid psychiatric placement. But, as you know, there are none of those for girls Tricia's age range. The doctor at A&E sent a referral to Child and Adolescent Mental Health Services, though it could be more than six months before she is seen and she'll be getting towards the top end of their age group by then. In the meantime, we are going to have a case review in light of her behaviour, and assess if there might be a more appropriate placement for her. Anyway, leave Tricia to us, she's not really your concern now and it's unlikely she'll be here when you come back to us. You should use this time to go over the incident report you made last night and to have a think about what you will say at the panel. Don't worry about it too much though, you're a good worker Ciaran and we think a lot of you, but lapses in judgement can have serious implications and the panel will need reassurance that you are aware of that and that it won't happen again.'

Ciaran sighed, he suddenly felt exhausted. What a mess he had made, not even passed his probation period and already suspended and under review for something he didn't understand. If only he hadn't gone into her room, if only he had heard what she had been saying, maybe then he could make some sense of it. He felt useless, stupid, forlorn, and as soon as he was off the phone from Catriona he went back to bed. He stayed in bed all day, not able to sleep but not able to get up and face the world either. How could he tell anyone what had happened, that he was suspended from his job, under investigation?

But he could not hide forever either; he was supposed to be cooking for Gina tonight, and he had already heard Dave arrive home from work. He could hide away in his room from Dave for a while and Dave would just assume he was out and that he had the flat to himself, but when Gina arrived his cover would be blown. 'Better get ready to face the music', he thought, and dragged himself out of bed and into the shower.

Gina reacted surprisingly badly when he meticulously recounted the events of the previous night and it took a while before she came round again. 'What?!' she had screeched. 'You were in a girl's bedroom and she was undressing in front of you?!'

'It wasn't like that', he sighed. 'She was all burnt up or something, I think she wanted me to help her. I don't know what happened.' He wasn't sure whether Gina was most outraged by his breach in protocol or by a certain sneaking jealousy that he was starting to notice bubble up now and then, for instance, when he paid attention to his female friends. He saw her try and contain it, but it would slip out in barbed comments or tight-lipped glances that escaped her before she got the better of herself. He could never make sense of it; she was gorgeous, she had a great body, she was smart and popular, and they had been together for nearly a year now since they met at the college film-soc ball. She had been a year below him studying social psychology and hoping to go on and do a Masters in clinical psychology. He had not been with anyone else since then, or given her any reason to be insecure so why, he often wondered, was she being so jealous and untrusting? They had never talked about it directly; she would always manage to divert the focus away and redeem herself by some means or other. And this time it was the self-inflicted wounds that turned her from jealous indignation to genuine interest.

'She had burnt herself?'

'Yeah, something like that, with chemicals or something. I don't really know to be honest. I've never seen anything like it before, it was really awful.'

'I should ask Mary about that. She's doing her thesis on self-harm and is always going on about how people don't really understand it; they think it's just about people trying to kill themselves, or using blades and overdoses and how there's so much more to it. She probably knows loads about that kind of thing.'

And true to form, and perhaps as continuing amends for the barb of jealousy that she had only just reined in, Gina did talk to Mary and Mary enthusiastically supplied Ciaran with a whole reading list of books and a draft of her thesis. With little else to do in his suspension period he devoured the books, he read *The Language of Injury* by Gloria Babiker and Lois Arnold; *A Bright Red Scream* by Marlee Strong; *Beyond Fear and Control* by Helen Spandler and Sam Warner; *Self-Harm: Perspectives from Personal Experience* by Louise Pembroke. He read accounts from 'Cultural Psychiatry' (Favazza, 1996) to feminism (Smyth, Cox & Saradjian, 1998) and psychotherapy (Sutton, 1999; Turp, 2003). He read reports and research about self-injury by Helen Spandler, by the Bristol Crisis Service for Women, and from the National Inquiry in the UK, and he read Irish research that had been written up as a book of short stories. He trawled through a network of online sites, and found a number who advocated something called harm reduction, (harm-ed.co.uk; kreativeinterventions.com). So that in the three months between his first encounter with self-injury and his review panel he had undertaken a personal crash-course which had transformed his previous innocence to an informed advocacy position on best practice.

He thought of Tricia often during that time and how he had let her down; how unprepared he had been for what she revealed to him, and how all his training and education had left him so unskilled to deal with happened. He worried about the consequences of his actions, especially that he had quite literally not heard what she had said to him, knowing now that his full and present attention could have led to a profoundly different outcome. He had been told that Tricia had withdrawn the allegation she had made against him and that, in fact, her withdrawal was making further placement for her even more difficult. Foster families and residential centres alike were reluctant to take a self-harmer who was known to make false allegations. They were looking for an all-female unit for her, but the most likely reality was that because she was sixteen she would be left in limbo, using up emergency beds in an array of short-term facilities, to all intents and purposes out on her own in the world. It still didn't make sense to Ciaran. There was a piece of the puzzle missing, and it looked like no one was going to be around to help Tricia put it back together.

The date of the review panel arrived, and Ciaran made the journey across the river to the south side of the city where the Teen-Link headquarters were located. He picked out a suit for the occasion, charcoal grey with a purple pinstripe running through it, he matched it with a purple collarless shirt and shiny black square-toed shoes. He felt uncomfortably overdressed but, despite the allegation being withdrawn, his job was still on the line and he knew he had to make an effort. He walked self-consciously into the recently regenerated industrial park where the Teen-Link headquarters were located. The refurbished buildings squatted, almost embarrassed by their corporate makeovers in the unchanging grey of their surroundings. Teen-Link occupied a two-storey building that had been refitted so that the entire front of the ground floor was now made up of large glass panels. Inside, three tall potted plants added some greenery and there were two dark blue couches and a large coffee table to the left of the entrance. In front of him was a large dark-wood curved reception desk, from behind which a young woman with blond hair eyed him enthusiastically. He certainly wasn't in the mood for flirting, and she quickly responded to his reserve and became cool and prompt as he explained who he was and why he was there. He was ten minutes early and she directed him over to the seating area, pointing out the water-cooler on the way. His mouth was dry but he didn't feel he could swallow anything, nor could he make himself comfortable on the hard, low sofas. He stood up again and stared out of the window, waiting fatalistically for the minutes to pass before his destiny would befall him. Eventually, the phone on the reception desk buzzed, and after a few quick words exchanged into the receiver, the receptionist ushered him towards the board room where his review panel awaited him.

He took a deep breath and entered the room. There was a circular table made of pale wood with a horseshoe of bodies arranged around one side of it. Martin and Caitriona he recognised instantly and both smiled warmly at him. Maggie Breen, the head of personnel who had been on his interview panel was also there, along with two men he did not recognise. The first man was introduced as Director of Services for the whole of the Teen-Link organisation and the other man had been seconded from a sister organisation as an independent panel member.

Ciaran found himself increasingly nervous despite their efforts to put him at ease with their friendly introductions. And as the review progressed he felt more and more humiliated by the whole procedure: all of them sitting quietly around the table with wads of printed paper in front of them, while each report of the incident, including his own, was read out. He felt so exposed by the bare detailed facts of what had happened, and all the more so that he had no concrete explanation by which to understand it. It was overtly apparent he had fallen a long way short of protocol. He should not have been in her room. Why did he have no idea what she had said? Why had he remained there while she was removing her clothes? He felt ashamed, uncomfortable in his own skin, and it was difficult to keep from physically squirming before them.

Finally, he was offered a chance to speak for himself. Maggie invited him to respond to what he had heard before they came to their final decision. He owned his mistakes and apologised profusely. And then his months of reading and his unending attempts to piece it all together came tumbling out in a nerve-induced rush. 'The allegation Tricia made against me, I think it might be connected to something else. I've been reading a lot about self-injury in the last months and it's very often connected to having experienced different kinds of abuse or difficulties at home. She had just come back from visiting her mother that night, and some of those marks were fresh, as if she had just done them. I think she was trying to tell me something.'

The curve of faces before took on an array of expressions from uncomfortable surprise to outright displeasure, but that did not deter him. 'I know I made huge errors and that I am responsible for most of what took place, but I don't think the way we reacted helped at all …'

Before he could continue the Director of Services cut in, 'We have clear policy guidelines around responding to any self-inflicted violence, which have been carefully developed and with the safety of all residents and staff in mind. All acts of deliberate self-harm are categorised as Level-Two incidents and require immediate reporting to the on-call manager and the attention of emergency services, including psychiatric evaluation. We cannot take any risks with this kind of behaviour, we do not want to be dealing with a suicide or with interpersonal violence in any of our projects.'

'But that's my point', Ciaran interjected, smarting at the pejorative terminology and ill-informed understanding of self-injury being bandied so recklessly around before him, all too aware of how hurtful it was to the people to whom it was applied, and how drastically it failed to capture their experiences. 'People who self-injure, especially in the way Tricia did, are absolutely not attempting to kill themselves, and they are certainly not a risk to other people. It's a way of coping and it can be a way of trying to communicate something really difficult as well, something so difficult they might not even be able to speak about it.' Ciaran scanned the faces in front of him, hoping that they were willing to embrace this revelation and share his new way understanding of self-injury. However, the visages before him were becoming increasingly hostile, and only Martin directly met his gaze and, with an almost imperceptible shake of his head and widening of his eyes, signalled to him to quit, now! But Ciaran couldn't stop. 'She was trying to tell me something and I let her down.' At this stage, exasperated, Catriona interrupted, 'We have a lot of experience of working with troubled young women and their problems at Teen-Link, and the point of the review today, Ciaran, is to reassure ourselves of your suitability to continue working with us, not to challenge policies and procedures that have been established on the basis of years of experience and expertise. You were involved in a Level-Two incident and a serious allegation was made against you. And even though that was withdrawn, we need reassurance from you that you are not going to let yourself be manipulated into compromising situations by volatile and vulnerable young women. We are here to assess your practice and your understanding of your role and the correct policies and procedures, not to make elaborate critiques of our policies.' The Director of Services folded his arms and threw a brief satisfied glance in Catriona's direction. 'She's good', he thought to himself, 'very good: clear, to the point, and no messing, an impressive air of authority about her, not bad looking either.' He smiled inwardly at his own appreciation. 'We could do with a few more like her in this organisation', he mused, before returning his attention to the young man in front of them, thinking. 'Now him they could probably get on pretty well without.' He didn't like his type – a metrosexual or whatever the term was these days for guys who spent far too much time in front of the mirror – but still, like everyone else he was due his second chance, but hopefully he would just use it to hang himself completely next time.

Ciaran, meanwhile, had opened his mouth to respond, Tricia still visible in his mind's eye, in one moment slowly and calmly pulling up her t-shirt to reveal the ravaged skin beneath it, perhaps having already confided the darkness of her pain to him, and in the next moment wildly clinging to the fabric of her clothes as she was cornered by Paula, her room suddenly a sea of panicked authority figures closing in on her. It was all so wrong. He was about to form his next sentence, to try once again to articulate the truth that they all seemed so remote from, but in the corner of his eye he saw Martin frowning and visibly shaking his head. He stopped. Suddenly realising he could not win this battle, not here anyway. He sighed. 'I'm sorry,' he said, 'I'm sorry for all of it.'

To everyone's relief the next step in the proceedings was for Ciaran to step outside while the panel reviewed the meeting and made their final decision. Ciaran slunk back into the reception area and hovered by the water-cooler for a moment. The receptionist was nowhere in sight, making his heart sink further, he would have appreciated some small-talk or even some flirting right now, anything to distract him from how quickly his career was unravelling before him. Twice now in just over three months he had made unbelievable blunders that could well cost him not only this job but his whole career. He stepped outside as, despite the windows, the reception area suddenly seemed incredibly claustrophobic, as if the whole organisation was bearing down on him in judgement. He felt wrong and stupid. He took a deep breath of the cool air. 'Then again,' he thought to himself, 'is everything I said just now really such a blunder? After all,' he reasoned, 'wouldn't I stand over everything I just said?' And, more than that, he suddenly knew without doubt that he could not but advocate that truth for anyone who had hurt themselves. Wouldn't he do that for Tricia and for all the other people whose stories, whose unheard voices, he had read about over the last months? 'Of course I would', he thought to himself – it was not even a choice, he could not undo what he had learned. Deep down he knew that he was right about this but sometimes, as he had recently begun to discover, being right was a very lonely island to inhabit. He sighed and turned back towards the building that he had been drifting with his thoughts away from. The receptionist had returned to her post, but she barely glanced at him as he re-entered the building and busied herself in a stack of files in front of her. Ciaran hoped that none of them were his.

After what seemed like a decade they called him back in. They decided that he could return to Teen-Link on an extended probationary period which would be reviewed after another three months. Any further incidents or concerns around his practice, he was sternly informed by the Director of Services, would be viewed very seriously indeed. He was asked if he understood and he nodded and assented. There was paperwork to be completed and signed before they were finished, and a general air of discomfort pervaded the room throughout the remainder of the proceedings. Ciaran knew he had made himself very unpopular and that the enthusiasm with which he was greeted in his early days was probably irretrievably lost. Still, in a last effort, Ciaran mustered all the optimism he could find and thanked them. As he did so he tried his best to re-embody the motivated demeanour he occupied during his initial interview and his first weeks at Teen-Link in order to reassure them, and himself, of his continued suitability for the position – but all the while hoping that they were more convinced than he.

HELP AND RESOURCES

Full contact details can be found in Appendix Three: Resources.

UK
- The Basement Project: Information and resources about self-injury for people who hurt themselves and those who live and work with them
- The Bristol Crisis Service for Women (BCSW): Telephone, text and email support for women and girls who self-injure and also wide range of self-injury resources and publications (www.selfinjurysupport.org.uk)
- FirstSigns: Self-injury support and information for people who self-injure and those who live and work with them
- 42nd Street: Free and confidential support for young people experiencing stress and mental health problems in the Manchester area
- harm-ed: Self-injury training and resources

Republic of Ireland
- Kreative Interventions has available free downloads of *The Hurt Yourself Less Workbook* and *Cutting the Risk: Self-harm, self-care and risk reduction*
- Pieta House: Free one-to-one therapy for people who hurt themselves

Northern Ireland
- Zest: Free one-to-one therapy for people who hurt themselves

REFERENCES AND FURTHER READING

Babiker, G & Arnold, L (1997) *The Language of Injury.* Leicester: BPS Publications.

Favazza, AR (1996) *Bodies Under Siege: Self-mutilation and body modification in culture and psychiatry* (2nd ed). Baltimore, MD: Johns Hopkins University Press.

Pembroke, LR (1996) *Self-Harm: Perspectives from personal experience* (2nd ed). London: Survivors Speak Out. Forthcoming as a free download from www.kreativeinterventions.com

Smith, G, Cox, D & Saradjian, J (1998) *Women and Self-Harm.* London: Women's Press.

Spandler, H (1996) *Who's Hurting Who? Young people, self-harm, and suicide.* Manchester: 42nd Street.

Spandler, H & Warner, S (eds) (2007) *Beyond Fear and Control: Working with young people who self-harm.* Ross-on-Wye: PCCS Books.

Strong, M (2000) *A Bright Red Scream: Self-mutilation and the language of pain.* London: Virago.

Sutton, J (1999) *Healing the Hurt Within: Understand and relieve the suffering behind self-destructive behaviour.* Plymouth: Pathways.

Turp, M (2003) *Hidden Self-Harm: Narratives from psychotherapy.* London: Jessica Kingsley.

REPORTS: UK

Truth Hurts: Report of the National Inquiry into Self-Harm among Young People. London: Mental Health Foundation (2006).

Women and Self-Injury: A Survey of 76 Women. Bristol Crisis Service for Women. Bristol: The Mental Health Foundation (1996).

RESOURCES

Arnold, L & Magill, A (1998) *Self-Harm: A resource pack.* Abergavenny: The Basement Project (see Appendix Three: Resources)

Cutting the Risk: Self-harm, self-care and risk-reduction. Originally published by the National Self-Harm Network and now available as a free download from www.kreativeinterventions.com and www.harm-ed.co.uk

The Hurt Yourself Less Workbook. Originally published by the National Self-Harm Network and now available as free downloads from www.kreativeinterventions.com and www.harm-ed.co.uk

LifeSIGNS (now FirstSigns) (2004) *The LifeSIGNS Self-Injury Awareness Booklet: Information for people who self-injure/self-harm, their friends, family, teachers and healthcare professionals.* FirstSigns Self-Injury Guidance and Network Support (see Appendix Three: Resources)

FLASHBACK ONE

There are two deep parallel gashes in my upper chest which the pharmacist has sprayed with an antiseptic concoction that has turned my skin a jaundiced yellow. It could have been worse though, she had initially picked up a spray can of Wasp-Ease and aimed it at my wounds before she realised and then, thankfully, corrected her mistake. But she had laughed about it – a lot. The pain and damage her error would have done to me seemed to amuse her. I laughed too.

I had been cycling down a steep hill when a car driver had swung his door wide open into my path and felled me instantly, the hard metal of the door cutting deep into my flesh and cracking against the bones in my breast. 'You were going very fast', he said two me two days later when he called at the place where I was staying to see how I was. There seemed an expectation that it was partly, if not completely, my fault.

There had been such a commotion. I was lying in the road and people were pulling my limbs from all directions, trying to lift me up and move me out of the path of oncoming vehicles. Dazed as I was, I was still acutely aware that the elastic in my trousers had snapped and I was desperately clutching at them so as not to be exposed and humiliated. But I was at the mercy of the copious hands and the staring throng who seemed to have appeared out of nowhere to witness my downfall.

Two Gardai[1] arrived. It seemed, just as my ill-luck would have it, that they had been passing as the incident occurred and were now obliged to get involved. They kept trying to insist on calling an ambulance and I persistently refused: I knew that I could not let them take me to hospital. I was terrified of what they would do to me. Also, because of my age, I was afraid they would contact my parents. The gards eventually relented and brought me and the buckled bicycle back to the small flat I was sharing with a friend for the summer. I sat and waited for her return.

When she did return I had already resorted to vodka to ease the impact

---

1. The Gardai or An Garda Síochána, often referred to as the gards, are Ireland's national police service. An Garda Síochána literally translates as 'guardians of the peace'.

of the accident. She instantly removed it from me and, from a few cursory questions, decided that I had no broken bones or serious injuries despite the pain I was experiencing and that I was increasingly losing the use of my hands. She took me to the chemist to obtain the aforementioned remedy for my flesh wounds.

In the days and weeks that followed my cracked bones caused me immense pain, and I was only gradually able to use my hands without an immobilising agony searing through my chest. But it was the gashes which fascinated me: deep welts in my flesh which filled with dried blood and eventually scabbed over in thick lines. First, concave curving inwardly into my skin and then convex, a dark ridge standing against the pale tissue that wrinkled tightly around it. There were traces of yellow at the edges of the scabs and then, later, the same yellow appeared in between the cracks along the length of the thick red-brown trails.

I constantly pick at the scabs, selecting small areas for the intricate attention of digging it away. It nauseates me, yet it is also utterly compelling. I want to dig out sections of the thick brown lines of scab and reveal the skin beneath. Partly I think that the skin below the scab may have healed, and that by forcibly removing it I am simply speeding up a return to a normal appearance, to an unblemished and untainted self. It feels as if my body takes so long to heal because of how bad I am.

Initially, I feel angry and disappointed when only fresh blood and some traces of pus spring out to fill the fleshy dents exposed by the excavated scab. Angry, disappointed, and also that I have nothing to lose now – it is not healed; I am still a mess – I grit my teeth and quickly yank away the remainder of the scab. It comes away in a repulsive tare of pain and relief. I feel sick and a little shocked as I rip out the thick line and I quickly dispose of it in the bin. But I also have a strange satisfaction of having somehow punished myself, and a deep sense that that is somehow part of the healing process.

Most of the time, I merely pick at the edges of the scab, telling myself I am just testing small areas to see if the flesh beneath is finally back to normal, and on many occasions I manage to make myself leave it alone after only reopening a small area. But when I am very angry or frustrated or disappointed with myself I cannot help but tear out the whole scab again, and re-live the horrible, nauseating satisfaction it instils in me. And, despite doing so in moments of pure self-loathing, I really do believe that this will somehow make me right again; that once I am stripped to the bare flesh and bones of my pain and my shame, then healing can begin and I will be normal again.

Eventually, a long time after the end of that summer, the gashes do finally seal over for good. They form two thick keliod scars which run in parallel lines across my upper chest and which will remain for the rest of my life.

***

I am lying naked on top of a hospital bed, surrounded by nurses and a flimsy makeshift screen which, at any time and without warning, anyone may walk around and indeed, they often do. I have to beg for even that pathetic shield to be in place before they expose my body to the next group of medics, patients, visitors or whoever happens to be passing by. It seems that the adults enjoy the vulnerability of the scanty protection that is offered me and are amused by how distraught I become about my privacy. After all I have only just turned nine years old. Still, I am considered 'advanced' for my age, with puberty and the accompanying physical changes already well underway. I am horrified not only by the shocking changes that are sprouting without warning from my aberrant body, but also by the attention these changes attract. I always thought these parts of my body were private and not to be looked at, touched and commented upon. The way they touch me, and the things they do and say feel all wrong. I don't like it. I hate it. But they are adults, doctors and nurses, and I am only here because there is something wrong with me. Everyone already knows that I am bad, so it must be me that is wrong. There is no choice anyway. It seems that all of my body, me, is fouled by everything that is happening and there is nothing I can do to make any of it better or right again.

Nothing is private and everything is wrong. The nurses are cross when I need to use the bed pan; they are angry when I cannot. They resent having to wash me, but are disgusted when I am dirty. Never has my body and its once private regions been so subject to the whimsical and incomprehensible moods of adults and the violating behaviours which accompany them. The shame and humiliation thickens inside me and becomes as much a part of me as my rancid bones.

Years later I find in my medical records that I am not only described as 'physically advanced' for my age but also as 'very compliant'. I wonder if this is a code that they used to communicate between themselves that there will be no consequences for anything they choose to do to me. As soon as I am sent copies of my medical records the originals are destroyed. No complaints against medical staff or institutions can be pursued without the original records being in existence.

I am told again and again that I am in the hospital for my own good. There is something terribly wrong with me and they are going to make me better. I am told that I am lucky, that other people suffer much worse than me, and that I must not make a fuss.

Before my first operation the consultant comes over to my bed and asks me which side he is operating on. I am nine years old and no one has ever asked me for information or permission for what they do to my body. I am very nervous about getting it right and the consequences of getting it wrong. I don't trust anything I know about myself, how can I? He draws crosses on my right side with a dark, inky-blue marker and then stands at the bottom of the bed, surrounded by other men in white coats. He laughs and says, 'I have no idea what I am going to do!'

I am supposed to be in hospital to be 'made better', but my body has been cut and my bones sawed and pinned together in strange formations. When I awake from the surgery, sick and disoriented with anaesthetic I am devastated by what they have done to me. I am completely immobilised and one side of my body is now totally misshapen and has a huge gash running down it which is an inch-and-a-half thick in places and is twenty-two stitches long. The pain inside, in my bones, is much worse than it was before I was brought here to be made better.

Over the days and weeks which follow I get sicker and sicker. I can no longer eat without vomiting and I have turned a jaundiced shade of yellow. The gash erupts with blood and pus that leaks down my crinkly and now feelingless skin. Many of my nerves have been cut, and sensation will never return to the flesh of my thigh but, ironically, the intense pain in my newly restructured bones will be lifelong. In turn, a number of the stitches turn septic and have to be yanked out of the rotting flesh. They are pulled out quickly, one by one, and yellow and red quickly oozes into the spaces they leave, and then soon becomes raw with infection.

The nurses get angry with me for vomiting so often; for the mess that seems to seep uncontrollably from me; for my somehow being the author of all this badness. I vomit and a nurse angrily tells me, 'Don't think we don't know what your game is!' I vomit, my parents tell me they will not come and see me again if I do not finish the meal that I have just been sick from; I vomit the vile tasting pills they force me to swallow and am told I will never get well if I am not a 'good girl' and keep them down.

After four weeks they finally seem to realise that I am not doing this on purpose and that I am actually quite ill. I am given a blood transfusion and intravenous feeding to try and bolster my strength against the bone infection that is now rampant in my body and which has diminished me to within inches of my life.

But their final answer is more surgery. And that is how I have come to be lying on the bed, naked and surrounded by nurses. There are still about sixteen stitches remaining in the gash. Some areas of it have stuck together, while other places flop hopelessly open like a forlorn mouth polluted with toxic sorrows. I am so ruined now that I am almost beyond fear – but not quite. One of the nurses brandishes something that looks like a larger version of the crochet hooks my mother keeps in her sewing basket. I desperately, and utterly illogically, want to try and preserve whatever of the tiny molecules of my shattered self might be left, and I say something out loud. One of the nurses frowns angrily and tells me not to be so cheeky. The other nurse inserts the hook into the base of the gash in my body and rips it forcibly upwards along the length of the wound.

From my thigh to my waist I have a long, misshapen and keloid scar. It is an inch or more wide in places, and dotted around with blobs of raised pink flesh where the stitches were roughly removed. It will remain for the rest of my life.

GENERAL NOTE

Louise Pembroke (personal communication) uses the term 'iatrogenic traumatic distress' (ITD) to describe the emotional and psychological damage which results from medical interventions and treatment.

> 'Iatrogenic traumatic distress' or 'iatrogenic post-traumatic distress' means healthcare provider- or therapy-induced trauma. [It is] physically or psychologically damaging/abusive treatment which then results in vivid and disabling flashbacks after the event/s. The flashbacks are similar to those experienced by CSA [childhood sexual abuse], hostage, torture, witness to a traumatic event, survivors. Indeed, ITD could be viewed as a result of medical torture in the case of being deliberately sutured without an anaesthetic. The repeated exposure to persistently negative/abusive responses can result in adjustment behaviours as seen in sexual abuse/violent assault survivors such as dissociation and passivity in an attempt to survive the circumstances without incurring further damage.

Louise Pembroke discusses ITD specifically in terms of responses by medical professionals to self-injury. In the three flashback chapters I broaden the use of the term to incorporate ITD that may be experienced in other areas of medical intervention. In this way the term dovetails with the increasing recognition of the traumatic impacts of medicalisation on young children and the propensity of young people and adults who experienced chronic illness or disability in childhood to self-injure during their life (Babiker & Arnold, 1997). Moreover, those with physical and intellectual disabilities are much more subject to medical intervention and 'handling' throughout their lives which is often experienced as highly violating, traumatic and abusive. Likewise, those of us with disabilities experience heightened vulnerability to incidence of direct abuse within a whole range of 'care' or 'treatment' relationships (McCarthy, 1996; Shakespeare et. al., 1996).

Furthermore, as Louise Pembroke notes, in settings where self-injury is treated via prevention and restraint policies these are also commonly experienced as deeply traumatic violations which have profound and long-term impacts on the mental, emotional and psychological well-being of survivors (see also: Breggin, 1991; Clarke & Whittaker, 1998; Shaw & Shaw, 2007; Shaw and Hogg, 2004). Enforced restraint and treatment practices also have human rights implications which are increasingly being brought to public attention through survivor movements (see Shingler, 2007, *Only Smarties Have the Answer*).

ITD may result from a range of medical interventions and both direct and indirect forms of violation. These may stem from old-fashioned notions of 'tough love' or 'for your own good' attitudes to treatment adopted by some practitioners, especially towards children or patients who are viewed as 'problematic' (Miller, 1990), as well as overt physical, emotional and sexual abuse. Recognition and redress is notoriously difficult at the best of times as is evident in the length of time and amount of damage caused by notorious medical practitioners such as Harold Shipman (UK) and Michael Neary (Ireland) before they were arrested. This is even more so when the patient/victim/survivor is already labelled as mentally ill, intellectually or physically disabled or attributed with other diminishing circumstances (Breggin, 1991; McCarthy, 1996; Ussher, 1991).

Finally, because self-injury is overly associated with cutting and overdosing – largely as a result of statistics gained from emergency and primary care settings in which other forms of self-injury may not be recognised, or may only very rarely require medical intervention – many incidents of self-injury, including ITD-related incidents, pass unnoticed. For example, recent research among university students in the USA (Gollust et al., 2008) showed wound interference to be the most common form of self-injury followed by head-banging. Both of these may easily be ITD responses, as in the story above, and yet are rarely accounted for in this way. Similarly, people with learning disabilities are often reported as having pathological tendencies to head-banging, as symptomatic of their disability rather than as an emotional or ITD response. Current research is, however, redressing this imbalance (see Jones, Davies & Jenkis, 2004; Bristol Crisis Service for Women: www.self.injurysupport.org.uk).

The three 'Flashback' chapters address the implications and after-effects of a range of medical interventions/treatments and their relationship with self-injury. They also highlight the ways in which the survival or mirroring responses of the recipients may then become the subject of further punitive diagnosis and intervention and result in an endless downward spiral of damage and diagnosis.

HELP AND RESOURCES

Full contact details can be found in Appendix Three: Resources.

UK
* The British Association of Counselling and Psychotherapy: Professional body for counsellors and therapists
* The Patients' Association: Support and campaigning organisation focusing on the concerns and rights of patients

Republic of Ireland
* DisABILITY.ie: Information and support for people with disabilities by people with disabilities
* Irish Association for Counselling and Psychotherapy: Voluntary regulatory body of accredited counsellors and therapists in Ireland
* Irish Patients' Association: Support and campaigning organisation focusing on the concerns and rights of patients

REFERENCES AND FURTHER READING

Babiker, G & Arnold, L (1997) *The Language of Injury.* Leicester: BPS Publications.

Breggin, P (1991) *Toxic Psychiatry.* New York: St. Martin's Press.

Bristol Crisis Service for Women (2009) *Hidden Pain: Self-injury and people with learning disabilities.* Bristol: BCSW.

Clarke, L & Whittaker, M (1998) Self-mutilation: Culture, contexts and nursing. *Journal of Clinical Nursing 7*, 129–37.

Gollust, SE, Eisenberg, D & Golberstein, E (2008) Prevalence and correlates of self-injury among university students. *Journal of American College Health, 56*(5), 491–8.

Jones, V, Davies, R & Jenkins, R (2004) Self-harm by people with learning disabilities: Something to be expected or investigated? *Disability and Society 19*(5), 487–500.

Liebling, H et al. (1997) Why do women harm themselves? Surviving special hospitals. *Feminism and Psychology 7*, 427–37.

McCarthy, M (1996) Sexual experiences and sexual abuse of women with learning disabilities. In M Hester, L Kelly & J Radford (eds) *Women, Violence and Male Power* (pp. 119–29). Milton Keynes: Open University Press.

Miller, A (1990) *For Your Own Good: The roots of violence in childrearing.* London: Virago.

Shakespeare, T et al. (1996) *The Sexual Politics of Disability: Untold desires.* London and New York: Cassell Press.

Shaw, C & Hogg, C (2004) Shouting at the spaceman: A conversation about self-harm.

In D Duffy and T Ryan (eds) *New Approaches to Preventing Suicide: A manual for practitioners* (pp. 167–77). London: Jessica Kingsley.
Shaw, C & Shaw, T (2007) A dialogue of hope and survival. In H Spandler & S Warner (eds) *Beyond Fear and Control: Working with young people who self-harm* (pp. 25–36). Ross-on-Wye: PCCS Books.
Ussher, J (1991) *Women's Madness: Misogyny or mental illness?* London: Harvester Wheatsheaf.

REPORTS (IRELAND)

Department of Health (2006) *A Vision for Change: Report of the Expert Group on Mental Health Policy.* Dublin: Stationary Office.
The European Patients' Charter for Ireland available online from the Irish Patients' Association: www.irishpatients.ie
Mental Health Commission (2007) *Knowledge Review: Code of practice on admission, transfer and discharge to and from an approved centre.* Dublin: Mental Health Commission.
Mental Health Commission (2008) *Quality Framework: Mental health services in Ireland.* Dublin: Mental Health Commission.
The Royal College of Surgeons (2007) *Children in Hospital: Rights and responsibilities of children and parents.* Dublin: Royal College of Surgeons.

DVDs

Only Smarties Have the Answer (2007) Aiden Shingler. Available from Mind Publications, Granta House, 15–19 Broadway, London, E15 4BQ England. Email: publications@mind.org.
Visible Memories (1997) Croydon Mental Health Service Users. Available from The Basement Project and Mind (see Appendix Three: Resources).

NORMAL

Sarah, the triage nurse, let herself out of the reception area and the door closed and locked itself behind her. Audrey eased herself into the uncomfortable chair and looked again at her watch. She was hopeful, almost as if she really believed that the five minutes that it took to go to the toilet and make a cup of tea would have miraculously transformed into hours and the night shift receptionist would be arriving in as the clock simultaneously turned to midnight.

Audrey's mug was very full and the strong sweet tea slopped slightly over the edges as she placed it on the counter in front of her. She didn't like the late shift – though it was a million times better than the overnight stint – she preferred the earlys, eight until four, and then at least she had a couple of hours to herself before her dad got back from the day centre. She could head on into town: go for coffee and cake or get her nails done; treat herself the way she so rarely got to do these days. She didn't really mind looking after her dad, after all, the kids were grown now and she and Tony separated years ago, so it made little sense for her to be living in their old house all on her own when she could just as well go back to her dad's and save him having to sell his house and go into a nursing home. It was probably crazy trying to hold onto both houses; she had had trouble renting hers out and there was still a bit left of the mortgage, but she wanted to try. She wanted to make sure the kids were properly provided for, especially after she and Tony had split up and everything that must have put them through. She felt guilty, she had tried to make it work, but in the end he had left anyway, moved in with someone else and started all over again.

The maintenance didn't last long after his new girlfriend got pregnant so Audrey had gone on a FÁS[1] scheme and trained as a receptionist. It had been years and years before that when she had left school with her not very impressive Junior Cert[2] results and had gone straight to work in the local

1. FÁS, or Foras Áiseanna Saothair, is the Irish National Training and Employment Authority, i.e. the job centre/dole office.
2. The Junior Cert, or the Junior Certificate (Teastas Sóisearach), is the first level secondary school qualification in Ireland, the equivalent of GCSEs (or O levels) in the UK.

biscuit factory. That was where she had met Tony. He was the supervisor, a few years older than her and already engaged to one of the other girls. But it had been love at first sight and he had eventually broken off with her and taken up with Audrey – well, actually, it was the other way round, he had got together with Audrey and then he had left his fiancée. They used to laugh together that they fell in love over fig rolls. When did they fall *out* of love? she wondered, probably after Anthony was born, their third child and first son. It had been a difficult labour and had ended in a Caesarean and hysterectomy, so no chance of any more after that. Audrey had been heartbroken, she had always wanted more kids. Six: that would have been her perfect family, her own little tribe to love. But she had just had 'to get on with it', that was what women did then. Some of her friends who had more kids than they could handle had even told her she was lucky, not to be having to worry about missed periods and counting the days of every cycle to see if she was 'caught' again. They didn't seem to understand that she really did want lots more kids. The hysterectomy also tolled the final death knell of their sex life. It was like Tony just totally lost interest in her; didn't see her anymore. She used to wonder if Tony didn't think of her as proper woman now that her womb was gone and all her private parts had been torn apart and then sewn back into place again. She reckoned he was already seeing someone else by then anyway, but he got through a fair few more before he finally settled on Josie and moved in with her. Anthony was thirteen then.

The day Tony had left Audrey had looked in the mirror and barely recognised herself. She had put on so much weight, and she looked so old. She was suddenly a dumpy middle-aged woman; she looked like someone's grandma already. Actually, she looked very much like her own grandma but she would have been much younger than the point in her grandma's life that she resembled. She had slumped on the bed, utterly dismayed by herself. She opened a packet of biscuits, hating herself for eating them when she was so overweight and ugly looking already, but at the same time no longer caring, feeling that since it was too late now anyway she might just as well eat. At least it gave her a bit of comfort, and after all what else was there?

When she started the FÁS course she had gone along to Weight Watchers with a couple of the other girls there. It always made her laugh that plump middle-aged women could still think of themselves as girls. Girls were young and slender, with long legs, tight stomachs and pert breasts not yet sagged and stretched by an army of hungry babies. She had done well at Weight Watchers to begin with and had lost three stone pretty quickly, but then she had put most of it back on again. It was like anytime she started to feel good about herself she would eat, and then the more her eating disgusted her, the more she would do it, until she was back up to her old weight again. Having to face the weigh-ins was the worst of it, the public humiliation at gaining, not losing, pounds each week, which only made her want to go and eat more. In fact sometimes on Saturdays she would go and have a cream tea straight after the meeting to console herself. One time, after reading an article in about bulimia in *Women's Way* she tried using laxatives to stop herself putting on weight, but she only felt more disgusted by her loose bowels and the smell and the mess than she did by her fat so she quickly gave them up. She told herself she didn't care. What did it matter what she looked like or what she weighed anyway? At her age there was really no one to be bothered for.

When her dad had started to need help that had been her excuse to stop going to Weight Watchers altogether, though she would still sporadically put herself on diets, making up complicated charts to figure out the number of points in each food item, and how many biscuits she could eat if she substituted those points for her dinner or the glass of Guinness she liked the odd evening. She would drastically reduce it all down and start to look really well for a while, but whatever she lost she would put back on again, like she just wasn't really ready to live without the layers of flesh and cellulite that cushioned her from the world.

The late shifts were really bad for it. She got herself through the infinite hours with endless cups of sugar-loaded tea and at least two packets of chocolate and caramel biscuits. She hoped the nurses didn't notice, she felt ashamed in front of them; they all seemed so young and beautiful and thin, especially the Philippine girls with their smooth dark skin, jet black hair and almond eyes. Audrey felt like a different species: saggy, puffy and pale. It seemed impossible that she had been young and beautiful once, that Tony had left his fiancée for her, that she had once been more than this flaccid shell of wrinkles, fat and stretch marks.

She sighed and picked up her tea, it was only eight o'clock and she had already eaten more than halfway through the second packet of biscuits. Still, she could always get a Mars Bar out the machine later if needs be.

Nora peered out from behind the screen in the treatment area towards the waiting room. It was fairly quiet tonight, though Tuesdays were never the busiest anyway unless there was something going on it town – or the lead up to Christmas, of course, when the whole country went on a bender and it seemed like the majority of them ended up here in A&E. Well, that was how she had thought of it when she began her internship, but the stories from her peers who were placed in some of the other city hospitals made her realise that things could certainly be a lot worse; at least the facilities here were fairly new and they had good security. Some of the A&Es just became a macabre circus at the weekends, a nightmarish combination of a detox, a wet house, a homeless shelter, a Gerry Springer show, with car wrecks and fires and God knows what else thrown in for good measure. It didn't even seem hygienic to have everyone all mixed up together like that, with people vomiting and bleeding and fighting all in such close proximity and traipsing in the dirt from outside. It seemed even less reasonable to expect any real level of treatment in those circumstances, but somehow that was how they carried on. And then there were the really bad days when even here in Saint Martin's it was just like a butcher's conveyor belt, an abattoir of pulped bodies that it felt impossible to manage. Nora would go home physically and emotionally wrecked from it, certain that she could not survive another shift, and yet she always did. And as the weeks went by she found herself developing a barrier of resolve against it all. But not completely, it could still get through to her sometimes, and she would find herself not able to sleep or to shake off the imprint of a face or a voice and the pain that had wedged behind her eyes. Eventually, when she was totally exhausted she'd take a sleeping pill just so she could get some rest, but she was wary; she had heard all those stories about doctors who got too attached to the contents of their medicine cabinet and she didn't want to turn out like that, she wanted a career. It was all still so new, she told herself, she would get used to it eventually just like everyone else had done, and she would be able to do the work and move on without getting all emotional over it. She glanced round the waiting area again. Two of the faces there looked familiar, perhaps they had been here before, or perhaps they had just been waiting for so long that it seemed like she knew them already.

Tim shifted in his chair, it was hard to get comfortable on these hard metal rows of seats bolted to the floor. He couldn't even move a chair to put his foot up. His ankle was really starting to hurt now, and he could feel it swelling, puffing out by the minute, feeling like it would soon be so big and so painful that it would take up the whole room. It seemed pretty quiet in here tonight though, and he couldn't understand why it was taking this long. He was sure the last time he was in, when he had broken his hand, that it hadn't taken this long. He almost wished he wasn't here, but he could feel that his ankle was really badly fractured, possibly even broken, and he knew that it needed attention. Besides, Paula was with him, and she had insisted. It almost felt like an unspoken deal that if he got it properly seen to then she wouldn't say any more about it, she would just play the game, like it had been an accident and they wouldn't have to have the conversation that he had no idea how they could possibly have anyway. What could he say?

He was actually surprised she was still here with him. He would have expected her to just up and leave after what she had seen, not to hang around to bring him to the hospital and be all cool about it, although cold might be a better description. It was hard to tell though really, they'd only been going out six weeks so he didn't really know her all that well, and now she felt like a stranger sitting quietly beside him in the drab and mundane chaos of night-time A&E. If it wasn't for the pain he would have felt embarrassed, but his ankle was hurting so much now he couldn't really feel any emotions at all. It was like he was just calmly commentating on his own life from a safe distance. Paula looked at him, 'I'm going to go and see how much longer they're going to keep you waiting – that really needs to get x-rayed and plastered up soon.' She stood up, he was about to protest about not making a fuss, but then he thought better of it. Since she now knew his secret, or a part of it anyway, he thought it perhaps best to let her have her way and then maybe she would say no more about it. Maybe she just wanted it over with so they could forget about it and carry on as normal like before. He hoped so.

Paula walked over to the reception counter where a thick Perspex screen with a circle shape of drilled round holes separated the dowdy middle-aged receptionist from the rest of the room. The woman looked up and smiled and Paula leaned towards the holes as she didn't want Tim to hear her. 'I'm with Tim Delaney', she explained, though Audrey already knew that. She had seen the two of them come in together, which might have been what started her thinking about her and Tony and the old days. They were a nice looking couple this girl and Tim Delaney, just as she and Tony must once have been. Audrey nodded. 'That's right', she said. 'Suspected broken ankle.' 'Yes', Paula replied and then turning around and checking behind her to reassure herself that Tim was firmly out of earshot she continued, 'I just need the doctors to know something about it.' She swallowed and paused, and Audrey nodded again in encouragement. Taking a deep breath Paula leaned yet closer to the Perspex grill and whispered, 'It wasn't an accident. He did it himself: on purpose. I saw him.' Audrey continued to look at the girl who let out a long slow out breath. 'Will you write it down so the doctors know', it was more of a direction than a question. 'They should know that he did it himself', she affirmed, suddenly assured that she had done the right thing by letting them know. Audrey nodded again and pulled over the stack of files which were waiting for the doctors to collect, one-by-one, as they called each patient into the treatment area. Paula seemed satisfied. 'Thanks', she said and turned and walked back across the waiting room and sat herself down again beside 'Tim Delaney suspected broken ankle'.

About an hour later Tim and Paula were sat in a curtained cubicle in the consulting area with two huge x-rays of Tim's foot and ankle blown up on the screen before them. 'I'm afraid you've a nasty fracture there', the doctor said pointing with her pen at a line in the image on the screen. 'You're lucky it wasn't a complete break though, that would have put you out of action for three months or more. With this you could be back running around again in two, possibly a little less.' She smiled at Tim, 'You were running?' Paula looked up at her, had she not read the notes? Or was this a trick to try and get him to tell the truth? She looked at Tim. He cleared his throat, 'Yeah', he said in a casual tone, too casual. Even from their brief relationship Paula could hear the forcedness of it. 'I was training and I went over on it going down some steps.' He didn't look at Paula. There were a few seconds of silence and then the doctor spoke again. 'Not the first time by the looks of things?' It was a question but she didn't leave enough space for an answer. 'By the looks of this x-ray you've had a good few mishaps', she said, waving her pen in the direction of all kinds of apparently telltale signs on the images. The statement hung in the air. Paula swallowed hard and looked at Tim, not quite wanting to believe what she was hearing. He'd had a black eye and bruised ribs when they met, he said from his kick-boxing class. She'd also seen the pictures of him and his friends on Facebook, where his hand was all strapped up. Now it seemed his feet had been broken before. Paula swallowed again, the information slowly travelling down from her brain in a sickening blow to her stomach. He'd done it all himself: all of it. He'd been smashing his own body up, just like she saw him do to his ankle earlier. She looked at the doctor, why didn't she say something? Do something? Tim shrugged in a non-committal way, briefly glancing at the doctor and then looking off into the middle distance. An almost perfect performance of an uncommunicative young man well used to the rough and tumble of masculinity. 'Well, we'd better get you plastered up, and you'd better learn to take things a bit easier and not to play quite so rough!' the doctor smiled. Paula opened her mouth to say something. She wasn't sure what but she had to say something, she couldn't let this charade continue. But just as she was about to speak a commotion broke out in the corridor and the doctor's bleeper started sounding. 'Oh, emergency', she said, 'I'll have to go. There'll be a nurse along to plaster you up in a bit.' With that she was gone and Tim and Paula were alone in the cubicle with the unmistakable images of his shattered bones on the screen before them and the unspeakable truth hanging in the air in between.

Four a.m. and the A&E department was really quiet now. There was a homeless woman sleeping on one of the benches. She would come in sometimes wanting to be admitted to see the psych team in the morning, but she would always be gone by the time they arrived. She was just accepted now as one of the regulars that nothing could really be done for. The only other person left in the waiting room was the woman with the self-inflicted injury. She had been left until last, even though she seemed to have quite a serious cut in her arm. Nora had wanted to call her in a number of times but the consultant had reminded her not to. 'She's a compulsive cutter, that one.

Always in and out of here, if you make a fuss over her she'll only be back sooner, doing it again. It's best to leave her until last, that way she might think twice about doing it next time. Besides, there are people here who are really sick and need our attention first. Really, it's better that way.' Nora had been a little surprised by his reaction. Instinctively she had assumed that if someone was doing that to themselves a lot then they might be at risk and should perhaps be prioritised, but the consultant didn't seem to think it was serious at all. 'You'll get used to the cutters after a while', he said. 'Every emergency department has their own regulars.' 'Repeat attenders', he had called them – it sounded so close to 'repeat offenders' that Nora briefly wondered if maybe he had got the two confused.

Nora finally called Anne Reed 'compulsive cutter' through to the treatment area. She looked awful. She was thin, very thin, and ageless in a weird kind of way. Yet at the same time she also looked a lot older in that moment than the thirty-five years her file revealed. Nora felt uncomfortable, she had always thought of cutting as something that teenagers did, not women in their thirties. Her file revealed that she had even needed stitching in her groin one time. Nora shuddered, what was wrong with her? Why would she keep doing stuff like that to herself? She felt nervous having to deal with her, unsure how to handle someone who had cut herself, and kept cutting herself. She almost felt frightened, as if something about this woman's misery might be contagious. At the same time she couldn't help feeling sad for her too, after all what must her life be like to be on this endless cycle, cutting up her body and spending hours and hours on hard metal chairs in A&E waiting to be sewn back together again, just to return in the same state days or weeks later.

Nora had smiled at her, but the woman's eyes remained downcast and she didn't notice. She didn't really seem to see Nora at all; she just meekly followed Nora's instructions as she guided her into the cubicle. 'Right, sit yourself down there and I'll get the nurse to prep that and then I'll stitch it for you.' Nora left the cubicle long enough for the nurse to clean up the wound and administer a local anaesthetic. It gave her a breather to gather herself and to try and think of something to say to this woman. She had never felt so uncomfortable dealing with a patient in her life.

She returned to Anne who remained impassive in the chair. 'That looks nasty', Nora couldn't help saying as she looked at the wound. 'It's going to need about fifteen stitches.' She was about to add that it would leave a scar, but then she saw that the whole of Anne's arm was a criss-cross texture of scars, some of them very rough looking indeed. It confounded Nora to know that she had done all that to herself. Why would she want to make that kind of mess of herself? It just wasn't normal! Perhaps she was quite seriously mentally ill? She thought about admitting her for a psych assessment, but then she remembered what the consultant had said. She was 'uncooperative', a 'repeat attender'. Nora decided it would be best if she just stitched her up and sent her home as quickly as possible.

As she worked on the sutures she could sense Anne tensing up in her body even though her facial expressions barely changed. But she was definitely reacting, like she was grimacing inwardly. 'Surely you can't feel that?' she asked, incredulous that someone who could cut large chunks out of herself could be reacting to the barely perceptible tug of sutures that would be apparent through the anaesthetic. Anne looked at her as if she was a murderer but said nothing. Nora was feeling more and more uncomfortable and just wanted to get this woman stitched up and away from her and fast. She didn't understand her at all, and she had nothing to understand her by, no diagnosis, no special training, just a growing sense that there was a certain kind of person that did this and who were the permanent shadows of every emergency department.

After what felt like an eternity Anne was all stitched up and gone, and Nora had chance to grab a quick cup of tea in the staff room. Sarah was there. 'That was your first time with Anne?' she asked, as if sensing how disarrayed Nora was by the whole experience. 'Don't worry, you'll get used to her eventually. She's been coming here for years, usually with cuts, occasionally an overdose.' Nora swallowed her tea and thought for a moment. 'The weirdest thing was the way she reacted to the stitches, like it was hurting her. How could she possibly feel anything with an anaesthetic compared to what she had done to herself?!' she asked, genuinely incredulous and seeking an answer. Sarah looked matter-of-factly at Nora, 'Oh, she would have felt it all right. We don't use anaesthetic on self-harmers; it only encourages them.'

'What?!' Nora spluttered out her tea in disbelief. She had just put fifteen stitches in a woman who had not been anaesthetised?! She felt sick.

'Yeah, the thing is with self-harmers if you're nice to them they just do it more, to get the attention and the sympathy or whatever, so the best thing is just to keep a distance and to make sure they don't get any special treatment. Then they might not do it again so quickly.'

Nora was disgusted. She sat down. She was not sure who she felt more appalled by: a woman who repeatedly hacked up her arms; a nurse who failed to administer an anaesthetic and thereby surreptitiously making Nora complicit in causing pain to a patient in order to enact some barbaric kind of behaviour modification programme; or herself, the doctor who could sit in front of another human being and stitch her without even realising that it was hurting her, and never once stopping to check if she was OK or that procedures had been followed. She had stitched her fast as well to get it over with. It must have been excruciating, and that woman had never said a word throughout it all. Nora felt the familiar pain starting behind her eyes but she had a couple more hours before she was off duty.

By the time she got home Nora was exhausted. She lay down thankfully on her bed to welcome much needed sleep, but her brain would not switch off. Her mind kept replaying the events of the shift. She couldn't erase the image of the way that woman had looked at her while she was stitching her from her mind. She felt terrible. Sick. Sick at herself; sick at Sarah; sick at what she was supposed to have done and had totally failed to do. And then she felt angry. Why was that woman behaving like that anyway? Why did she not say something? Why had she put Nora in that position and then looked at her that way, as if she was the one at fault? As if she was the cause of it, as if she was the guilty one? Nora was suddenly livid, she would not be manipulated into feeling guilty for something that was not her fault! Immediately she understood all the consultant's warnings about cutters: the way they manipulated and played games with you; and not even just for attention, it was passive-aggressive behaviour, just so they could stay the victim, cutting themselves up and looking for sympathy and attention and all the while making you the monster in it all! Now she knew why they left them 'til last! There were people who really needed help and who appreciated it, like that guy with the fractured ankle, nice fella, if not very communicative, but a nice normal guy and his girlfriend just getting on with their lives. God, if only everyone that came in was as easy to deal with as that: straightforward, no messing, no games.

It was ten a.m. and she still hadn't slept; her head was pounding now with tiredness and anger and the image of that woman looking at her as she drew the sutures through her skin. She got up and went to the medicine cabinet in the bathroom and took out the bottle of sleeping pills. It rattled ominously, her supply was dwindling much faster than she had intended. She washed a tablet down with handfuls of water from the cold tap and padded back to her bedroom. She lay on her bed and waited for sleep to overtake her and to remove the image of Anne Reed and her messed up arm from her mind.

In the taxi on the way home Audrey ran through the events of that night in her mind. That young couple especially stayed with her, and she mulled over what she had done or, more precisely, what she had not done. When the girl had spoken to her she had obediently pulled out Tim Delaney's file and opened it. She had been surprised to see he had been there a number of times before with breaks and fractures to his feet and hands, and once with concussion. Then she had remembered him. He'd had a black eye the last time he was there and he'd broken his hand a few months before. She had looked at the file again. 'Sports injuries' were listed by a lot of his previous admissions. Audrey had looked back up at the young man and the stoic-looking girl beside him. In the far corner Anne Reed 'compulsive cutter' was sat clutching a blood soaked dressing to her arm. She'd been there hours. She looked terrible and Audrey guessed that as usual she'd probably be there a few hours more before they finally took her through and patched her up. And she had been right; Anne Reed had still been in her corner when Audrey had gone off shift.

She felt bad for them, all of them, and in a weird kind of way she felt like she knew what it was like. She had never done anything really bad like 'compulsive cutting' or 'suspected broken ankle' but she had hit herself sometimes. Times when the failure of her body, the failure of her femaleness, and the emptiness of her existence seemed too much to take; times when she felt like her life had disappeared with her womb and all the babies she could never have, and all that there was between her legs was a lie of womanhood that she had to swallow wretched hormones to maintain. When it all got too much she would just drive her fists into her thighs and groin and stomach, making her body hurt and turn a motley shade of grey-blue bruises. Somehow it reminded her of how she felt just after Anthony was born and before the last few drops of love evaporated from her life for ever. It was like she was beating the grief out of her body for a few moments, punishing her failure, giving her humiliation of a body what it deserved. She always felt ashamed afterwards, and each time she promised herself never to do it again. And quite often she would be nice to herself for a while. But then it would all bubble up and she'd be all bruised and sore for a few days again. She always felt especially bad and confused about it when she saw Anne Reed and heard the way the doctors and nurses talked to her. The worst had been the time Anne had done something to her private parts, that had really scared her. But then she reminded herself that it wasn't the same thing at all really. She was normal and it only ever happened sometimes when things just seemed too much to bear and even then never so bad as that. It wasn't like she cut herself or broke anything, at worst it was just a few bruises that were gone again in a matter of days. And, most of all, no one ever knew.

She reflected on the night. She had made a decision that was totally out of character and that surprised her and yet also felt oddly right at the same time. She had looked down at Tim Delaney's file after the girl had spoken to her and thought about what she could add to the notes that she had filled in when he had arrived. Then she had looked again at Anne Reed 'compulsive cutter' sitting alone and destitute in her empty corner and that had made her decision. She had folded up the file and put it back on the pile. Some things are definitely best left unsaid she thought to herself, and she watched the night-time cityscape slipping past the window of the taxi.

HELP AND RESOURCES

Full contact details can be found in Appendix Three: Resources.

UK
- The Bristol Crisis Service for Women (BCSW): Telephone, text and email support for women and girls who self-injure and also wide range of self-injury resources and publications
- OA (Overeaters Anonymous): 12-step recovery group for people with all forms of eating distress
- The Patients' Association: Support and campaigning organisation focusing on the concerns and rights of patients

Republic of Ireland
- BodyWhys: The Eating Disorder Association of Ireland: One-to-one, oneline, telephone, email and group support for people with all forms of eating distress
- Irish Patients' Association: Support and campaigning organisation focusing on the concerns and rights of patients
- OA (Overeaters Anonymous): 12-step recovery group for people with all forms of eating distress
- Pieta House: Free one-to-one therapy for people who hurt themselves

IN BETWEEN

RADIO GAGA

'Good afternoon, you're very welcome to the show', the smooth male voice crooned confidently from the radio and instantly a hush fell in the cramped sitting room and twelve bodies became alert and attentive. Some of the women smiled nervously at one another while others squeezed hands in support. It was a big day for them all, but even more so for Tammi who had become their spokesperson, their collective voice, for the afternoon. Katie had gone with her to the studio, but had texted them to say they hadn't let her any further than the guests' lounge – for the show Tammi was on her own.

The presenter quickly explained that the issue for the afternoon's *Hot Topic* slot had arisen from the self-harm phone-in the previous week, and that his two special guests had contributed different sides to that discussion. He said he was very pleased to welcome Dr Christine Butler, resident psychiatrist at St Jude's hospital, and Tammi, he faltered momentarily about to give her second name and then, remembering not to, corrected himself and announced Tammi, from the Self-Injury Support Network.

The silence in the crowded sitting room was palpable, a pause that was over in a heartbeat but which had a feeling of eternal stillness. In the studio Tammi felt it too, her heart had been racing all afternoon, but suddenly it slowed to its usual rhythm; it would all be over in fifteen minutes. Katie sat in the guest lounge rolling her way through a two ounce packet of tobacco, anything to keep her hands and at least a part of her mind occupied. She would rather have been able to go in with Tammi, she felt useless out there, but at least she would be there for Tammi afterwards when she came out. And Tammi would be great. She was easily the most articulate of the group, and although she spent so much time persecuting herself for being stupid, she was really smart and her ability to think on her feet was amazing. None of them, apart from Tammi, had any doubts that it should be Tammi to go on air and talk about the group.

'So Tammi, first of all, tell us a bit about the Self-Injury Support Network, who you are and what you do.' This was the only part of the debate that Tammi had been able to predict and prepare for; she had memorised the key points that she and the others had agreed were most important. She felt surprisingly calm and collected. 'First of all thanks for having me on the show as a representative of the group', she said and then launched into the mental list she had been carrying around in her head for the last few days, rehearsing it over and over again to herself to be sure that she didn't forget anything or mess up on the day. 'The Self-Injury Support Network is a self-help group run by and for people who self-injure. We have fifteen members at the moment and we meet twice a week, with usually around eight to ten of us at any one meeting. The ethos of the group is to be a supportive, non-hierarchical, non-judgemental and safe space for all of us. That means that we're all equal and we all decide together what is on the agenda and what we're going to do. We have a set of ground rules that we read through before we start each session and everyone takes a turn at facilitating the group. We share and support each other through all kinds of issues and experiences, not just about self-injury, and one of the things that has been really important in the group is the experience of being heard and listened to. We offer support and friendship to one another, which is really powerful 'cos no matter who we are or what we are going through we still have a lot to offer. The group is also important in making sure none of us feel alone with self-injury. Many of us for a long time thought we were the only one who did it, so the support and friendship and helping one another are really important. We also talk about good things that are going on too, things that have really helped us ...'

Tammi was almost finished with her semi-rehearsed speech, but the doctor interrupted her before she had completely done. 'That's all very well', she said, 'and I have nothing against patients forming groups themselves or having advocacy groups for them, but it's very important to remember that we're dealing with self-injury and there can be specific dangers here. We know from studies in hospitals and young offenders centres that self-injury has an element of contagen at the best of times, with patients triggering each other or sometimes even getting in competition with one another with their injuries. So to form a group specifically around self-injury, without professional intervention, could prove very counterproductive. There are often compulsive and addictive elements to self-injury and I would have concerns about an unregulated group constructing self-injury as so acceptable that it simply becomes forum for learning new methods of self-injury.'

Tammi, fired-up, jumped in. 'And do you not think that the high rates of self-injury in psychiatric hospitals and prisons and young offenders units might have something to do with the environment and the way that people are treated there? And also if you know that people's self-injury increases when they're in hospital then why admit people in the first place? Why do you lump people together who are only going to make each other feel worse in an environment that would drive the most normal person crazy after a few weeks?'

The atmosphere was almost palpable through the airwaves, they had been on air less than five minutes and already battle lines were being drawn. Tammi swallowed she hadn't meant to be quite so argumentative.

'I was making a serious point', Dr Butler retorted icily.

'So was I', Tammi replied, glad of a chance to de-escalate the interaction. 'All of the people in our group who have been in hospital describe it as highly triggering, unpleasant and even unsafe. Can you imagine what it's like to be in distress and to be taken into an environment where you have all your possessions and clothes removed and are surrounded by other highly distressed people, with no privacy or autonomy 24/7? In those conditions self-injury often becomes a way to survive the hospital.'

'Hospital is a last resort, granted. As professionals we certainly don't want to see the people in our care ending up as inpatients for long periods of time. But, sadly, people can and do become so unwell that they are a risk to themselves – and much more so a risk to themselves than a risk to others – so for their own protection they need to be in a place where they can be kept safe and stabilised.'

'It's true that sometimes people get overwhelmed by the things that are happening and they can't cope and need a safe place to go, but hospital is not, on the whole, a safe place. We know how emotionally difficult it is for people with physical illnesses to go into hospital for treatment so it's going to be much worse for people who are already in distress and where that distress is the reason for them being hospitalised in the first place. It just doesn't make sense to cram crowds of distressed and anxious people into one place and expect them to feel better![1] You only have to look at what happens with celebrities who get into addiction or have a breakdown of some sort to get my point. They get taken to some private exclusive resort where they have peace and privacy and luxury. They are treated with understanding and are pampered with lots of personal, individual attention and have access to all kinds of therapies and treatments from massage and psychotherapy to art. Their autonomy and identity are recognised and respected, and we have the absolute opposite in the public mental-health system where people are in large-scale underfunded public facilities with no privacy or dignity, and often in mixed sex wards, and in a structure that is not dissimilar to penal facilities.

1. This and some of the preceding points which Tammi makes are drawn from Clare Shaw's dialogue with Christine Hogg (2004) in 'Shouting at the Spaceman', for full reference see p. 89.

We get routinised treatments mostly based on medication and then people are labelled as not responding to treatment when we aren't getting any better. Who would get better in that kind of environment? Tell me honestly, Dr Butler, if someone that you loved, a member of your family, was injuring themselves, would you want them to go into St Jude's?'

'Things have changed a lot in psychiatric practice over the last decade, it's not like *One Flew Over the Cuckoo's Nest* anymore!' It was obvious from her tone of voice that Dr Butler was smiling as she spoke, but there was still an unmistakable and uncomfortable edge of ice in the air.

'But still', Tammi interjected not wanting to let this point go without the attention it merited, 'when you're in hospital, by virtue of being there, there is something wrong with you, you are sick, and everything that you do or say or feel becomes a part of that label. In our self-injury support group we can be really honest about how we feel and what we have done without anyone putting a label on it or changing how they see us. That's such a relief and so important, I can't even begin to put into words how important that is. Except that, I know for me personally, it's like when I speak in the group the things I say make sense to the others, and actually help them, but so much of the time in my head I think I'm useless and stupid and not right, and that's how I have felt when I have been treated by doctors too, like it's just me and there is something really wrong with me. From being in the group I know that I'm not alone. I'm not the only person that feels this way or that does these things, and I'm also more than those things too. We all are. And we really get to see and share one another's strengths and individuality and creativity and that is a great source of courage and hope to us all.' Tammi smiled to herself, thinking of the time when they had improvised their own idea for a psychiatric hospital cabaret called Family Misfortunes.

'We're having a huge response from listeners already, and texts are pouring in', the host chimed in. Tammi realised that she had completely forgotten his name, and when she tried to remember it she came up with a blank. She was obviously still very nervous then, even if her body felt more physically calm than before. Then she remembered, he was Mike, Mike something or another. What was his second name? Mike Raphone she wanted to call him and smiled to herself again. Then she caught herself and returned her full attention to the texts he was reading so that she could give her very best response. 'Here is one that I think people would like to hear your comments on. It's from Maggie in Tullamore, she says, "My daughter self-harmed for years. She was diagnosed with Borderline Personality Disorder and was in and out of hospital for a long time but she wasn't getting any better. And then, Easter two years ago, she hung herself." Dr Butler would you like to respond to that first?'

'Yes, well first of all I'd like to give my sincerest condolences to Maggie and her family, such tragedies are really horrendous to live through, and are sadly still more common than we would like among people with chronic conditions like Borderline Personality Disorder, which is a complex, and unfortunately incurable illness. But there have been massive leaps forward recently in the treatment and management of BPD so that people can go on and live relatively normal lives.'

'I'd just like to say something there.'

'Yes, go on Tammi.'

'In our group we see that label as really part of the problem in not understanding people and their needs and issues. Giving someone a BPD diagnosis is like a death sentence around their neck. Can you imagine what it feels like to be told there is something incurably wrong with you, and that it's not even really an illness, it's your personality, it's *you* that's not right. That's a terrible burden to lay on someone, especially someone who is probably already feeling pretty crap about themselves anyway.'

'Diagnosis and treatment of BPD is complex and there have been significant developments in working with BPD over the last number of years which include recognising a number of the points that you raise, so that with the right help people can go on and contribute to their families and society.'

'You mean DBT, don't you?'

'Yes, DBT would be one of them.'

'OK ladies, just before you lose us completely perhaps one of you would explain to the listeners what DBT is ... Doctor?'

'DBT is Dialectical Behaviour Therapy which was developed especially for the treatment of Borderline Personality Disorder.'

'Or, depending on your point of view,' Tammi couldn't help interrupting, 'it's diabolical behavioural therapy, or doing bollocks therapy.'[2] Tammi giggled despite herself and earned a frosty look from Dr Butler.

'As I was saying,' the doctor continued, deciding to just ignore Tammi's interjection, 'it's a complex treatment model which combines some of the most progressive practices and not just from psychiatry but from a range of other disciplines as well, so it's quite holistic, and it has proved very effective in counteracting self-injury.'

'But that's because if you hurt yourself you get thrown off the programme!' Tammi ejaculated. 'So of course the people who complete it are the ones who can stop! And even then, how do you know that they haven't just turned to something else, or are doing it differently, or in secret?'

'Is that true doctor, do people get taken off the treatment if they self-injure?'

---

2. 'Diabolical behavioural therapy' and 'doing bollocks therapy' are Louise Pembroke's terms.

'It's a little bit more complicated than that, but certain aspects of the programme are suspended if someone self-injures during it, yes. But only as part of a carefully worked out care plan which each person signs up to, in full knowledge of its contents, before they commence the programme. There are clear protocols for this approach within the treatment. The aim of the programme is to help people develop functional emotional regulation, self-control, and coping strategies that don't include self-injury. They have access to twenty-four hour support throughout the treatment, and both individual and group therapy in addition to a broad range of treatments and interventions. So there really is no need for someone to injure themselves during the programme and it would be counterproductive to allow that to happen. At the end of the day mutilating one's body is not a healthy or normal behaviour under any circumstances, and it's important to remember that we are dealing with a very specific group of people here with a very specific illness.'

'But that's not true! Nearly half of the members of the Self-Injury group have been diagnosed with BPD and they're no different from the rest of us or anyone else. And none of them have found DBT to be useful, in fact they have found our group much more helpful for providing support and developing coping mechanisms. Besides, using DBT to get people to repress difficult emotions like anger or sadness is what makes people crazy in the first place. People need to be angry about the things that have happened to them in order to deal with them and take care of themselves and move on. Anger turned inwards hurts yourself physically and emotionally. Anger channelled properly can empower people to make changes and to take action. We need recognition and support, not methods to repress our feelings and experiences.'

'That's a very simplistic interpretation of a very complex treatment which draws on the latest developments in psychiatric, behavioural and neuroscience research. And it works. I have to say I am quite shocked by your attitude towards something that has provided huge relief and benefit to countless people and their families who have been suffering terribly.'

'OK, we're still getting a huge response from listeners and I'll just read out a couple of texts that have come in. There is one here from Sandy in Galway and she says "I used to cut myself and I was always told I was attention-seeking and that I could just stop if I wanted to and that wasn't true. There was no support or understanding when I was doing it and I would have loved to have had a group that I could go to, that would have made a real difference to me. I think Tammi is great." And then there's another one here from JP in Dublin and he says, 'Anyone who cuts themselves up must be seriously mentally ill and needs to be put in hospital not just for their own good but to protect other people as well.'

Before Mike can even invite comments on either of the texts Tammi jumps in. 'Actually most of the dangers to society like violent crime, rape, murder and assault are committed by heterosexual men under the age of forty-five, not by people who self-injure. Is JP suggesting that we should equally lock up all men for the protection of society? People who have been diagnosed with mental illness have become scapegoats in society. You only have to look at movies or the media to see that any serial killer, mass murderer or rapist is depicted as having a mental illness.[3] You don't see people with terminal cancer being depicted as serial killers, so why is it OK to stigmatise people who are in emotional and mental pain as being bad and dangerous?'

'I have to agree with Tammi there', Dr Butler interjected. 'Medical science is demonstrating more and more that our minds and our mental health can be understood in just the same way as our bodies and physical health, and that the moral panics connected with mental illness are entirely unfounded and only add another burden to sufferers and their families. Advances in psychiatry will help to challenge the stigma of mental illness and the fears and stereotypes that exist in the public domain.'

Tammi wanted to say something about psychiatry adding to stigma and marginalisation but before she could interject Mike was speaking. 'We're coming to the end of time for the *Hot Topic* for today, and since we finally have found something that the two of you agree on I think that's a good place to leave it for now. We have time to read out a couple more texts but before we do that I have to take an ad break.'

THE SAME BUT DIFFERENT

Sheila, who was facilitating the group for that month, had barely finished reading through the opening notes and ground rules for the session when Bernie jumped in. It was unlike Bernie to be first to speak. She was one of the group's founding members and was generally quite reserved and reflective, contributing only after she had put some thought into it.

When she had first joined the group she was only recently out of a long stint in hospital and had been struggling to get back on her feet. Her self-confidence had been shattered and her apparent 'inability' to stop injuring herself and her diagnosis had left her feeling hopelessly despairing. But, with

3. Where people with a mental health diagnosis have committed serious violent crimes, such as a number of the recent school shootings in the US, there is evidence to suggest that their violent eruptions may have resulted from a reaction to the medication they had been prescribed. See Peter Breggin's website for up-to-date information and debate on this issue (www.breggin.com).

the support of the group, she had pursued her dream of going to college and had applied for, and been accepted on to, a degree programme in Youth Work and Social Care. She was now in her third year of that course and at twenty-seven years of age could easily have passed for a model. She exuded an air and appearance that couldn't have been more at odds with the descriptions of her in the wads of paper that made up her medical history. She was tall and slim, with glossy black hair cut asymmetrically around her classically featured face. She tended to dress-down, in pants and flat shoes in unremarkable colours, occasionally adding a smear of lipstick or a gloss of nail varnish to brighten herself. However, even as she attempted to merge into the background there was something rather striking about her, perhaps the flawless neatness that she always maintained, along with her naturally striking good looks. But today her composure was ruffled by this uncharacteristic urgency.

'I have a big problem', she stated, leaning forwards with her elbows resting on her knees and looking intently around the room at the circle of faces surrounding her. 'You know I've been doing this tutoring scheme that's run through the college?' She looked around again for confirmation or negation but then continued the explanation anyway. 'Basically it's for kids who have ended up over here as "unaccompanied minors", they've come from war zones and God knows what, and a lot of them have been trafficked in the sex industry. Anyway, they get to Ireland and one way or another they are picked up by the authorities and they end up in these holding centre places while their claims for asylum are being processed. They do let them go to school though, and that's where the tutoring comes in. They get students to go in and help the kids with their homework or their English, or whatever, for a couple of hours a week. And that's what I've been doing for the last few weeks. I go in and – God, it's barbaric really, I can't quite get my head around it still. There are all these kids from all over the world in this place that looks like a prison to me. And who knows what they have been through, and they don't even have support staff, just security guards to run the place and if they're lucky they might see a social worker every three weeks or so! I don't know how they survive, I really don't. What they must have been through and then to end up there? I don't know, it's beyond words.'

Bernie paused and shook her head. She rubbed her face in her hands. She felt a physical pain in her chest whenever she thought about the kids in that place or whenever she went there, it was all so wrong. But one thing the group had taught her was that she could make a difference, and that was what she was determined to do, to make a real difference to people's lives. She took a deep breath and continued. 'So, as I say, I've been going in every week for the last while and helping this girl, Sartje.[4] Now, when we signed up for this scheme we had to do this whole orientation thing about how we can't talk about anything other than the homework or general chitchat stuff. We're not supposed to talk about ourselves or allow any kind of disclosure from the kids, it's all really tightly boundaried. We do one-to-one tuition with them in a room by ourselves, or sometimes with maybe one or two other pairs of people, but the door is always open and the scheme supervisor sort of wanders in and out. It actually looks a bit like how you see prison visits on TV where you sit across a table from the other person, with the inmate wearing a coloured tabard so you know they are the prisoner. But you don't need the tabard 'cos everyone knows it's the people with white skin that get to go home after the two hours are up. Anyway, I have been working with this girl Sartje, she's just sixteen and is from somewhere in Africa. She told me her tribe and the place but the names are in her own language and I don't know enough to figure out where she means, but anyway, it's a place where there has been a lot of intertribal conflict. I'm there to help her with her English, which is great 'cos it means that we have an excuse to talk a lot, which is actually what we have been doing mostly.'

She took a deep breath. 'God, this is tough. Anyway Sartje has been telling me about how she ended up there.' Bernie swallowed, becoming increasingly upset. 'She thinks it's about two years since she has been away from home now. She originally thought she was being taken to the city to work as a domestic and go to school: that's what the men from the agency told her parents, and that she would be safe and get a good education and be able to send some money back to them. But she was just used for sex, to start with still in Africa somewhere and then in different places. She doesn't know where, but from what she said at least two other European countries before she ended up here. They got rid of her 'cos they said she was too old now.'

There was a visceral silence in the room. Each woman holding the space for that pain and that experience to emerge and take the shape it needed to.

'And she's pregnant.'

The silence intensified. Two of the women had tears noiselessly making their way down their cheeks. Others sat with their eyes closed or in downcast acknowledgement of this young woman's pain; their own pain and struggles to this point in their lives bearing witness to it.

'They won't let her out to have an abortion. She's too young to travel anyway, so she has to have the baby. I checked it out in college and it's true. I found this article that was talking about how even adult women asylum

4. I have used the name Sartje here in memorial of Sartje Baartman, or Sarah Bartman as she was known, who was trafficked across Europe as the 'Hottentot Venus' during the nineteenth century 'scientific revolution' (see Garland Thomson, 1997, 5–80).

seekers can't leave for an abortion regardless if they got pregnant by rape or trafficking or whatever. Apparently a few have taken the boat over to England, but they end up in prison when they get back and likely to be deported for breaching the terms of their application.'

One of the women was crying openly now, in loud sobs. 'What's wrong with everybody?' she asked no one in particular, 'Why is this allowed to happen?' The women on either side of her comfort her for a while and eventually Bernie continued.

'The thing is', she said, 'she's hurting herself too. I kind of wondered to begin with but now I'm sure. I want to be able to talk to her about it, but I don't even know what words she will understand. It's also really difficult 'cos if they find out about me it's likely I'll be kicked off the tutoring programme. And then if they investigate more deeply they'll easily find out about my history and that I lied, well, that I "neglected to disclose my diagnosis" on my college application form. I don't expect they'd be very happy about a self-harming personality disorder case out there working with the youth of Ireland!' Bernie said it with an ironic edge which masked the anxiety she carried inside: a daily companion to the ever-real threat of being discovered. And, despite having internalised some really compelling positions around mental health politics that she could theoretically use to back up the filled, or rather unfilled, boxes on the application form, they somehow don't make her feel any less vulnerable to the authorities and their power over her or the implications and consequences of her diagnosis.

Her thoughts returned to Sartje and her predicament. 'I know she needs something like we have here, or even just some information, anything at all, just so she knows she's not alone and she's OK. I mean, oh God, it's just too awful: she even has a terrible time at school. She says the other kids are always calling her nigger and stuff, and that they keep asking her about what she puts on her skin and saying that she must have to use shit for moisturiser to keep it that shade of brown and the teachers don't do anything about it. The worst thing is she actually likes school, 'cos at least it gets her out of that prison she lives in. But she said as soon as they find out she's pregnant they'll stop her going there too. That makes me even more worried about what would happen if they knew she was hurting herself. That's what I wanted you guys to help with. What can I do to help her without blowing it for either of us?'

There was a pause and then Bernie spoke again. 'There must be something we can do! I mean I've never really thought of it before but what about people who can't come to the group? How can we help them? And what about things like racism? And what can we do about that or to make ourselves more open to people from different cultures, especially those who may not have a great command of English?'

'Maybe there needs to be separate groups. Do you remember all that stuff we sent off to England for a while ago?' Sheila mused. 'I think a lot of that was looking at needing to have specialised services?'

'But we're a peer support group, not a service, shouldn't we include everyone?' Bernie asked, not quite seeing the relevance.

'Men too?' Aine suggested with a tone of surprise and taking up another thread completely.

'God, that's a point – there has only ever been women in the group, even though we didn't necessarily set out to be that way.' Sheila jumped in, 'And now we're in Solstice House could we have men in? And how would we feel if a man wanted to join anyway?' she asked the group.

'Do you mean a gay or a straight man?' Katie chimed, "Cos I think that would make a difference. Like for me, it would be great if there was someone else who was gay in the group 'cos there are a lot of things that happen that straight people just don't get. Like there was so much homophobia from the doctors and nurses and stuff anytime I was in hospital – one of the psychiatrists was always making comments about me shaving my hair like it was another form of self-harm or a sign of my madness or something!'

'Really?!' Bernie leaned forward again, suddenly interested in this new direction. 'And what would you prefer then, separate services for lesbians and gay men, or being part of a women's group?'

'God, I don't know if I had to choose', Katie paused for a moment. 'Actually, both! I'd like to have a women's group and also a lesbian and gay group and maybe a lesbian women's group as well!' she laughs. 'Are there any limits to what I can chose?!' The others laugh too.

'No limits at all', Tammi chipped in. 'But don't forget I'm bi, not straight.'

'Sorry, I didn't mean to be excluding you', Katie responded. It was only since she had met Tammi in the group that she had to constantly remind herself to be more sensitive about bisexual women and to admit that they too experienced some of the prejudices gays and lesbians faced except that they often faced them from gays and lesbians as well! The swirl of thoughts finally took shape in her mind, 'Yeah, that's why I think it's good to have mixed groups as well, 'cos we get to learn from each other and people we wouldn't meet otherwise and to find shared ground, and that's really important and helpful, but I do think that separate groups are important too sometimes.'

'So our group should be open to anyone, but we should also be able to have special groups for different experiences?' Bernie asked. There was general nodding and assent around the room. 'But what about Sartje? This doesn't make any difference to her because she wouldn't be allowed out to come here! And I really want to be able to do something!'

'Wait a minute', Sheila said getting up from her seat. 'I'll have a look in that box of stuff and see if there is anything useful there.' She went over to the cupboard that had been allocated to the group and pulled out a large semi-transparent plastic storage container and brought it back to the circle. She placed it on the floor in front of her chair and knelt beside it and began to unload its contents. The other women moved forward and joined her, unpacking their treasure trove. It was full of books and pamphlets, on self-injury, on self-help groups, leaflets for family and friends, leaflets for workers, there was a DVD and also some oil pastels, crayons and coloured paper from some art work sessions they had in the early days. There were even two Halloween masks and a set of devil's horns that no one could remember how they had got in there, but passed around to try on all the same. Soon all the contents were spread out on the floor and they began to assess what they had.

'Do you think any of these would be of help to her?' Sheila turned to Bernie, 'We could photocopy some of them for her?' Bernie leafed through the pamphlets. There was one for Black and minority ethic women in England, but it didn't really seem to be relevant to Sartje's situation – she wondered if there could possibly be anything that had been designed to meet the needs of someone in such dire and irredeemable circumstances! She continued leafing through the pamphlets and the other women started to select and hand her booklets that they thought would be useful. She thumbed through them and decided on *What's the Harm? The Self-Harm Help Book, Hurting Inside, The Rainbow Journal, Self-Help for Self-Injury* and *The Pain Inside*. She could read through them and pass them on to Sartje bit by bit as they got comfortable about it and she got a sense of what would be a help to her. It was something. She looked at them and smiled, 'Yeah, I think this is a great idea. I could photocopy them and make them look just like stuff to read for her homework in case anyone is looking, and then tell her that they're just for her and they're from a group I'm in, and that way she'll know it's OK.'

'Thanks', she said, looking round the room and acknowledging everyone. 'I knew I could rely on you guys – you never let me down!' She smiled again at each woman in the room and her eyes glazed over. 'Everyone should have a group like this', she said, 'everyone'.

NEWBIE

It's Maura's first time to facilitate the group tonight and she's feeling extra nervous on account of there being a new person there, and also a larger than usual number of regulars to contend with. She has the sheet in front of her with the format for the meeting that they all agreed on when the group began – and which they have collectively felt the need to revise only once or twice since then. She folds the corner of the laminated page, the resistance of the plastic absorbing her nervous energy for a few moments while the group settles down. Once they are quiet she reads through the format and the ground rules and then, as is their protocol, she announces that they have a new member, a newbie, and invites the woman to introduce herself. The woman shifts in her chair, and looks around the room, looking edgy and animated.

'I don't even know if I should be here, to be honest', she says quickly and looks around again and then at the floor. 'I feel a bit of a fraud.' Her head dips lower. 'I have been working in psychiatric nursing for nearly fifteen years and I have seen people come and go who do all kinds of things to themselves and I've never really understood it at all – well a bit, obviously – but not really like this', she says and looks up again as if there is something tangible in the room she is addressing herself to.

Maura is suddenly very uncomfortable, she had no idea this woman was a psych nurse. She thought she was here to be a part of the group, not to come looking for answers for her patients. She fidgets, wondering if she should say something. She hates this kind of responsibility. She looks around the room trying to ascertain if the other women are equally uncomfortable about this nurse being here – who has not even told them her name – and if they are expecting her, Maura, to do something about it. I'm not ready for this, she thinks to herself, her nerves and discomfort colliding inside her and making her wish she had never volunteered herself to facilitate. I'm really not able to handle this, she tells herself again.

The woman is still talking, she is sitting with her hands under her thighs and her shoulders hunched up towards her ears. Her hair has bunched up on top of her shoulders making a strange mousey brown shape. She has painted her lips in bright scarlet to match the scarf she has tossed around her neck, but both clash with the orange and brown pattern of her top. She looks thrown together somehow, as if she has tried too hard to create an external appearance that looks casual but respectable and now her discomfort has completely sabotaged that pretence. Maura doesn't like her already, she feels angry at her for coming along under false pretences and leaving her, Maura, responsible for sorting it out. She tries to tune in to what the woman is saying and at the same time think about how she is going to have to deal with asking her to leave the group. This is a safe space, a self-injury support group, she thinks resentfully, not a classroom for medical practitioners.

'It's, it's ...' The woman is looking quite distressed and keeps anxiously looking around the room, almost as if she is actually expecting to be ejected at any moment. 'It's just that all these memories have started to come back to me. Well not even memories really, it's kind of like I always knew about it, remembered it, but I never understood what it was. I'm still not sure really. I don't know if it counts or not. I mean I look at people who come into hospital and I can see very clearly that they have serious issues going on and that they are injuring themselves because of that, but me? I don't know; I don't know if it counts, or if it's the same. God, I just don't seem to know anything anymore!'

Her face crumples and tears slip from her eyes. She bats them away with the back of her hand and tries to compose herself. 'Sorry', she chokes in a voice strongly intoned with shame. Bernie picks up the box of tissues and moves over and squats beside her for a second. 'Here', she says offering the tissues, 'It's OK to cry here, no need to keep it all in if you don't want to.' The woman forces a smile of thanks through her rumpled, tear-streaked face.

Maura is watching closely. OK, she thinks to herself, Bernie has been here since the beginning and she seems OK with her being here. Maybe it's all right and I don't need to do anything after all. She feels her body start to loosen as the anxious responsibility that was holding fast inside her gradually abates.

Bernie is back in her seat, the woman is looking at the floor and quietly twisting a wad of tissues in her fingers. She doesn't look like she is going to say anything else. The silence holds for a few minutes more and then Rosin speaks. 'I had been hurting myself in different ways from a very young child, pretty much as young as I can remember, and so for a long time it just seemed normal to me, not even normal, it just wasn't really anything. I mean I never thought of it as self-injury, it was like that was something different from what I did. And even when I started hurting myself in quite significant ways, I mean ways that would be quite obvious to other people, I never saw any connection between it all. That took a long time. It was like the words and what I felt and what I did, and what I felt about what I did, just didn't add up to self-injury. It's like that was someone else's word for something that didn't fit me and my experiences. I still find it hard sometimes to really accept it too; that those words are about me and my experiences, 'cos to me it's all just me and part of my life and who I am. And those labels just don't seem to fit right or to bring me closer to my experiences or to explain them properly.' She pauses and then Tammi speaks. 'That's exactly how it was for me about the abuse: the words just not fitting the experience, and then also being told that my bisexuality was a way of acting out because of it. As if I was confused, and as if being bisexual was about being promiscuous and taking risks, which I did do for a while, but that wasn't about my sexuality, that's separate. But there don't seem to be ways to say that without getting put into one pigeonhole or another that doesn't fit, and that actually only makes it worse.'

The woman is looking up again now, wide-eyed, and staring from one to the other of the women who have just spoken, with a mixture of relief and incredulity crossing her face. 'But I'm a nurse!' she ejaculates. 'I've had training and read books and done courses and treated people and talked to their families, and all the while I had no idea it might be about me! I feel so stupid! You can't imagine how stupid I feel! And scared, terrified. It's like if I look at this, if I see what it is, then it feels like everything is just going to fall apart all around me and there will be no way back. I'll never be normal or OK again! Oh God, I feel such a mess! I can't believe this is happening!' She begins to cry again but this time sobbing violently. Sheila, who is sitting to one side of her, turns to her and says softly, 'Would you like a hug?' The woman shakes her head. 'No, no, please don't, sorry.' 'That's OK', Sheila responds as softly as before. 'Is there anything that you would like?' The woman shakes her head and then after a moment changes her mind. 'Some water maybe?' Sheila crosses the room and takes a pink plastic beaker from the shelf above the sink, she runs cold water into it and brings it back to the woman. She swallows it down as if the volume of it will submerge her tears, and pretty soon it does. 'I'm sorry', she says, actually sounding like a nurse for the first time that evening. 'I've just come to your group and blurted all this out and made a real show of myself, and I don't even know any of you.' She looks around the room expectantly as if handing back the burden of disclosure to the other women in the group. Bernie waits for a few seconds and then, as it becomes apparent no one else is going to speak she opens her mouth, 'But that's why we're here, to create a safe space for anyone who hurts themselves to come along to and share what's going on for them.'

'You're so nice', the woman says. 'I'm so glad you're here, thank you.' She looks at the floor again as if to indicate she really isn't going to take up any more of the group time with her own talking.

Patti who has been listening intently makes a decision to speak. She's still quite new to the group herself and sometimes feels a bit unsure about the boundary between sharing her own experience and apparently attempting to 'fix' someone else – which is a big no-no here. She takes a deep breath, 'I used to hit myself a lot and I never thought that was the same as what other people did 'cos I didn't have cuts and scars and I didn't have wounds that anyone could see or that needed stitching up. It was like there was no real problem 'cos no one knew and it didn't need any attention, so it didn't matter, and it wasn't real or the same as other stuff. It was only after I had been in therapy for a while that I started to realise that it's not about the injury, or it's not the physical damage that matters or measures how "real" or how "serious" it is. It's actually how I feel that is the important thing. What is inside is just as important, more important, than what's going on or visible on the outside. But people only respond to what they can see, so if they don't see it, or if it doesn't look like much to them then it's not real or important. And that's what I really believed too for a long time. But now I'm really starting to get a sense that what happens inside me is important and worthy of attention regardless of what it looks like on the outside. I always used to think if I looked OK and acted OK – if I could pass for normal – then that was it. But I was in so much pain inside, and I hated myself for feeling that way too, and it was just getting worse and worse. But now I'm starting to accept that how I feel is the most important thing, and to understand and respond to that as it is and as I am, rather than trying to measure myself by external marks or lack of them.'

The woman has been watching Patti intently all the time she is speaking. 'But you're so articulate, most people are not like you', she says. 'And besides what you're talking about is different isn't it? It's not all the same thing surely?'

Patti smiles. She wants to answer the question directly, to tell her that no, she isn't any different, she has bulimia and dyslexia and a whole list of other deprecating diagnoses which equally don't match up her outsides and insides. But she hesitates not sure if lines are being crossed and if she should respond to the question.

Maura is becoming increasingly frustrated with the woman – how can she not know? she thinks crossly to herself. She feels very hostile towards her, all the more so for remembering all the times when nurses had spoken so sharply to her, accusing her of 'attention-seeking' or 'not really meaning it' when they thought her wounds were superficial, and now here was one of them taking up all the time and attention in their safe space, the space that was there for them to get away from people like that, and not even able to own what she was doing. Now that was mad. Everyone was being so nice to her too! Maura looks at the woman intently, she can picture her in her uniform, all superior and self-righteous dishing out meds and punishments and then having the nerve to come here and make out she's still somehow different or better than the rest of them.

Bernie is speaking again, answering the question that seemed directed to Patti in a more generalised way. 'That's the whole point, we're all different! None of us are the sum total of any of those labels, or the things we do, or the things that have happened to us. None of the words or the categories or the diagnosis and treatments fit who we really are. We're all completely different and what we do means different things to each of us, as well as different things to us individually over time. That's why we have this group, to accept all of our differences as well as to share our similarities and needs and experiences. That's why we don't try and fix each other or compare or measure ourselves, because we can only each know our own truth and our own process. We each have to find our own way and the best way to do that is by accepting and listening to one another in a safe and supportive space.'

'But what can I do now?!' the woman asks, reverting to her distressed self from her nurse demeanour. 'I can't go back to work now can I? What if anyone found out, what if they knew I came here? It wouldn't be right anyway – what can I say to people, or do for people now I know it's about me too? I'm just a liar and a fraud – hardly qualified to nurse people through it themselves!'

Bernie smiles at her. She's being much more directive tonight than she would normally be, but she's listening carefully to her gut instinct and it feels right. She's just trying to help their new member get a sense of how they work. It must be very hard for her coming here from such a radically different environment where everything is clear cut and regimented and everyone knows who is what and why. 'When things have settled down for you a bit you might discover that you actually couldn't be more qualified to work with people and to offer them really meaningful support.' She smiles again, the woman wipes at her eyes with the dishevelled tissues and looks at the floor, trying hard not to break into uncontrollable sobbing again. She knows they said it's all right to cry, but she doesn't like it, she never cries in public and she's afraid that if she starts again she won't be able to stop and pull herself together. And she's on the early shift tomorrow.

Maura looks at her watch; they only have about ten minutes left. She hasn't really facilitated anything, she feels like the whole session has really crossed lines that would normally be carefully adhered to and they still don't even have a name for this woman who everyone seems so desperate to help. For the second time that night Maura finds herself uncomfortable and resentful of the woman who seems to be making it so challenging for her, taking up all the space and making it so that Maura doesn't feel like she can handle the role. Perhaps she should just say that she's not able to do the facilitator role and pass it on to someone else. She looks around the room again, taking in all the faces, some of whom she knows so very well, others less so and the one not at all. For a moment she simply sees a room of women: women of different ages, shapes and sizes, of wildly varying appearance from the hippy to the business woman; from the almost sexless to the porn-star look-alike and she realises in her heart for the very first time that there really is no them and us, no oppositional battle lines, just a constant shifting hue of human experience and pain embodied in a rainbow of human variation. And suddenly she understands why it is so important that this woman, the nurse, the newbie, is there just like the rest of them. She checks her watch again and smiles to herself, perhaps facilitating is actually not such a bad thing. It might have a thing or two to teach her beyond simple authority and orderliness.

HELP AND RESOURCES

Full contact details can be found in Appendix Three: Resources.

UK
NB: In the UK abortion is legal and information and access to all options are available through mainstream health services. However, some general medical practitioners may as 'a matter of conscience' not refer onwards if this conflicts with their religious beliefs. In these circumstances women and girls do have the right to seek the services of other practitioners.

- The Basement Project: Information and resources about self-injury for people who hurt themselves and those who live and work with them
- The Bristol Crisis Service for Women (BCSW): Telephone, text and email support for women and girls who self-injure and also wide range of self-injury resources and publications
- One in Four UK: One-to-one and helpline support for females and males who have experienced sexual abuse
- Rape Crisis England and Wales: Support for women and girls who have experienced sexual violence
- Victim Support: Confidential support for victims and witnesses of crime

Republic of Ireland
- Crisis Pregnancy Agency: Irish government agency that sponsors information and links to resources for women and girls with unplanned pregnancies
- Dublin Rape Crisis Centre: Helpline and one-to-one therapy for females and males who have experienced rape or sexual abuse
- Irish Family Planning Association: Information, support and campaigning around all aspects of sexual and reproductive well-being
- NASC: The Irish Immigrant Support Centre: Support on all issues facing immigrants and asylum seekers
- One in Four: Support and therapy for females and males who have experienced sexual abuse
- Positive Options: Funded by the Crisis Pregnancy Agency (see above); provides free information about services relating to unplanned pregnancies
- Victim Support: Confidential support for victims and witnesses of crime

REFERENCES AND FURTHER READING

Arnold, L & Magill, A (1998) *What's the Harm?* Abergavenny: The Basement Project.
Arnold, L & Magill, A (1998) *The Self-Harm Help Book*. Abergavenny: The Basement.
Arnold, L & Magill, A (1998) *Hurting Inside*. Abergavenny: The Basement Project.
Bristol Crisis Service for Women (2004) *The Pain Inside*. Bristol: BCSW.
Bristol Crisis Service for Women (2006) *Self-Help for Self-Injury*. Bristol: BCSW.
Bristol Crisis Service for Women (2006) *Self-Injury and Self-Help Groups*. Bristol: BCSW.

Bristol Crisis Service for Women (2006) *Women from Black and Minority Ethnic Groups and Self-Injury.* Bristol: BCSW.

Bristol Crisis Service for Women (2007) *The Rainbow Journal.* Bristol: BCSW.

Garland Thomson, R (1997) *Extraordinary Bodies: Figuring physical disability in American culture and literature.* New York: Columbia University Press.

Newham Asian Women's Project. (1998) *Growing Up Young, Asian and Female in Britain: A report on self-harm and suicide.* London: Newham Asian Women's Project and Newham Innercity MultiFund.

Shaw, C & Hogg, C (2004) Shouting at the spaceman: A conversation about self-harm. In D Duffy & T Ryan (eds) *New Approaches to Preventing Suicide: A manual for practitioners* (pp. 167–77). London: Jessica Kingsley.

Smith, G, Cox, D & Saradjian, J (1998) *Women and Self-Harm.* London: Women's Press.

FLASHBACK TWO

'Every emergency department has its own regulars.' 'Repeat attenders', he had called them.

There was quite a lot of blood on her legs already, but it didn't seem enough. She still wasn't right yet. She had pushed the screwdriver into the flesh of her thighs: the soft parts of her body that betrayed her, vulnerable. She needed hardness, like bone, why was her whole body not hard like bone? She pushed the screwdriver into her thigh again. She didn't really feel it anymore but she could see the torn flesh and the blood. It looked bad. It looked like something she didn't have words for, something far off inside her that she needed to get out on the surface where she could see it. If it was outside of her and she could see it she would feel OK again: safe, back in control. It was a mess but she couldn't stop now, not when she might just be really close to it feeling OK again. Her fist tightened around the bulb-shaped red plastic handle. She could feel all the energy in her body suddenly rushing into her shoulder and down her arm to her clenched fist. She knew she was going to do it now and, this would be it. She aimed at her groin.

***

Blood is spurting. Oh God, oh God, it's coming out like jets of a water pistol, but all red. This is bad. This is too much. This is really bad. Shit. What have I done? Oh God, I need help. Oh God, oh God, help me. I didn't mean this, I don't want to die, please, I need help.

AMBULANCE
  I'll have to tell them.
  Anne Reed.
  I did it.

'That looks nasty.'

HOSPITAL

'You've made right bloody mess haven't you?! What did you do that for?!'

What was that? Oh, she wasn't talking to me anymore. But I still heard. I still know. She's angry. I'm a time-waster, there are people who really need help.

I think they have taken my skirt and underwear.

The ceiling above me is spinning.

I don't know if people can see me or not.

This is worse than anything.

Please God help me, get me out of here.

I didn't mean for this to happen. Now they know again.

I have this thing pressed against me. It feels like a matted clump of blood and tissue and hair.

Oh God, what have I done? I don't want to be here, please God help me, I'm terrified, I don't think I can stand this.

Then I remember Precious.

Precious, she was once a mangled clump of blood and fur and lice dumped half starved at the bins out the back of the flats: her back leg broken in three places, barely clinging on to life. When I first saw her I drew back, disgusted, I thought she was a dead rat or something. But then she made this tiny mewing sound and it was like my heart just cracked open and this unending wave of love came pouring out. I had been so afraid to handle her, terrified of hurting her, or causing her worse damage, but I had to get her out of there. I brought down a cushion from the flat and very carefully placed her on that and then put that into a box. I took her to the Blue Cross and they referred me on to a veterinary hospital. They were so lovely there and took such good care of her. The vet very tenderly patched her up; he touched her so gently and talked her very softly all the time he was treating her. He showed me how to feed her with a pipette and I sat up for nights on end with her, willing her to stay alive, feeding her and cleaning her until she got well again. She recovered amazingly. She was soon jumping around the place like any other little kitten, with her pointy little tail poked high up in the air and her big eyes and ears alert to everything.

She totally adopted me. She loves me so much it scares me sometimes, but she is so small and sweet it's just the most gorgeous thing anyone could ask for. She follows me round the flat all day just so happy to be with me, and then at night time she sleeps curled at my feet. But the thing I love the most is the mornings and the way she seems to know the exact minute I wake up, so that as soon as I open my eyes she's there on the pillow beside me purring loudly, just so happy that I'm awake, the sides of her plump little belly going in and out with the rhythm of her purring. I love to rest my face into her soft fur and inhale her sweetness. It is the most beautiful start to each day, to have a little creature so happy to see me and so excited for the hours ahead. Precious is more precious than life itself.

The vet told me I should have her spayed. I really didn't want to, it seemed so cruel to subject the poor little thing to a horrible operation and especially just after she had got well. But he insisted it was the kindest thing to do in the long run and he was always so nice and gentle. He said that it was probably more upsetting to me than to her. I agreed eventually but I still felt terrible, especially when I came to collect her and I saw her side all shaven with ugly black stitches in her bald skin. She had to wear a hideous white plastic cone round her head to stop her biting at them. It was hard for me to look at: I knew exactly how she felt with those monstrous things in her skin and the desperate need to pull them out.

'Sit yourself down there and I'll get the nurse to prep that and then I'll stitch it for you.'

The consultant will be in to stitch you in a minute.

Oh God, please don't let him be angry.

I want to cover myself.

I want to disappear.

Please God, I feel so tired and weak I just want to go home. I want to be with Precious.

Please God, make it OK.

Male voices.

I have one here for you Seamus, you can do the stitching. Good chance to get some practice. She's a repeat self-harmer so we certainly won't be getting sued if you don't leave a very pretty scar!

Chuckling sounds.

***

The curtain opens and two men appear, one in a white coat, young: younger than Anne by quite a long way and another much older man in a suit who must be the consultant. He looks at Anne and moves over beside her, 'Now young lady this is Dr Mitchell and he's going to stitch you up again, if we can just have a look at the mess that you've made there.' He lifts the drenched wad of dressing from her groin and pokes at the sides of the wound. The pain is suddenly immense, unbearable, as if every millimetre of her skin has returned from a far-off land and now contains a thousand million nerve endings each of which is being seared apart. The consultant looks at Dr Mitchell. 'That should go back together fairly easily', he says, and then pokes at some of the other wounds in her thigh. 'Mm, these might be a bit more tricky, there are some layers of tissue damage there, but don't worry too much about getting all the layers fused, we just need to get her sewn up so her insides don't fall out, as no doubt she'll be back again, mm?' He half chuckles again, addressing himself only to Mitchell, as if Anne isn't there or as if she is not human enough to merit his notice. She might just be a wad of pulverised meat, one big raw nerve ending, devoid of soul or dignity, for them to cut and stitch.

'Surely you can't feel that?!'

Mitchell injected an anaesthetic into her side and then immediately began to prepare to stitch her, the consultant watching all the while. Mitchell pressed the wound together and then began to pull the sutures through her skin. Anne gasped, she didn't think she could take much more. 'I can still feel it', she whispered. 'Can you wait a minute?' Mitchell looked up surprised, and was about to draw back. 'Carry on', the consultant ordered. Then he looked at Anne and said in a harsh measured tone, 'I'll not have the likes of you questioning my doctors, young lady. Dr Mitchell knows exactly what he is doing, and if you don't like it, well then, you might think twice before coming in here and taking up valuable time and resources that other people need.'

The cubicle fills with shame and hate as noxious and excruciating as the pain that is ripping through her body. She cannot think anymore. She cannot protect herself. There is only pain and hurt. Everything has been sucked out of her and she is nothing but a raw shell of agony silently imploding on itself. There is no core, no solidity anymore inside or out. She leaves herself a long way behind, watching the spectacle below unfold from a safe distance.

It seems to take forever for Mitchell to get through all of the cuts that need stitching. Even if he isn't bothering to work with all the layers of tissue that need repairing he still seems to require an inordinate amount of time. So, just as he had started before the anaesthetic had taken effect, he finishes after it is wearing off.

From her vantage point Anne knows better than to say anything, and her body lies still, powerless and humiliated while he hurts her. She waits, simply willing time forward.

***

Home?

Home, yes, I can feel Precious.

Little head nudging against me.

The smell of her fur.

Her rough tongue on my face.

I'm home, I'm safe.

Thank God.

Thank you, God.

Precious.

Have to get up and feed her.

Might just take a minute.

Hard to walk still.

Never again, God help me, I'll never go back there again.

I'd die first.

I would.

I'd die.

Oh god, but then what about Precious.

Precious, Precious, more precious than life itself. I could never abandon Precious.

Precious, I'll always make sure you're all right, I promise. I love you. I'll look after you. Come on, let's go and see if I can get you something to eat in the kitchen.

HELP AND RESOURCES

Full contact details can be found in Appendix Three: Resources.

UK
- The Basement Project: Information and resources about self-injury for people who hurt themselves and those who live and work with them
- The Bristol Crisis Service for Women (BCSW): Telephone, text and email support for women and girls who self-injure and also wide range of self-injury resources and publications
- The Patients' Association: Support and campaigning organisation focusing on the concerns and rights of patients
- The PDSA: Animal welfare for people on low incomes

Republic of Ireland
- Irish Patients' Association: Support and campaigning organisation focusing on the concerns and rights of patients
- The Irish Blue Cross: Animal welfare for people on low incomes

- Kreative Interventions: Where you can download *The Hurt Yourself Less Workbook* and *Cutting the Risk: Self-harm, Self-care and risk reduction*
- Pieta House: Free one-to-one therapy for people who hurt themselves

Northern Ireland
Zest: Free one-to-one therapy for people who hurt themselves

REFERENCES AND FURTHER READING

Arnold, L & Magill, A (1998) *What's the Harm?* Abergavenny: The Basement Project.
Bristol Crisis Service for Women (2006) *Self-Help for Self-Injury*. Bristol: BCSW.
Bristol Crisis Service for Women (2007) *The Rainbow Journal*. Bristol: BCSW.

RESOURCES

Cutting the Risk: Self-harm, self-care and risk reduction. Originally published by the National Self-Harm Network and now available as a free download from www.kreativeinterventions.com and www.harm-ed.co.uk

The Hurt Yourself Less Workbook. Originally published by the National Self-Harm Network and now available as a free download from www.kreativeinterventions.com and www.harm-ed.co.uk

TRUST ME 2
(SECOND CHANCE)

A few weeks after the review panel Ciaran was taking the long route into work. He was on the afternoon shift and he liked to amble through town on his way to Teen-Link, perhaps stopping to buy a CD, or to browse at books or magazines on the way, indulging the freedom that his irregular hours afforded him. On this particular Tuesday he was a long way from work, just at the point where Thomas Street merges into the Corn Market and where Gina had sent him on a pilgrimage to a designer paint shop. They had been talking about moving in together lately and Gina was already mentally decorating the apartment that they hadn't even found yet. Her enthusiasm was infectious though, and Ciaran would laugh and tell her she was wasted in psychology, that she should be an interior designer instead, and then he could live off her fame and fortune – to the point where he had begun to sound half-serious even to himself. He had been less and less sure about his work since the review panel. Gina reassured him over and over that it had just knocked his confidence and in a few more weeks he would be flying again. He kept hoping she would be proved right. One of the things they had always shared was their deep commitment to their work, their sense of doing something really meaningful and supporting people who were less fortunate than they.

He looked at his watch, it was still early yet, and he ambled across the street to the coffee shop that now occupied the old bank building. As he crossed the road he noticed a figure alighting from a bus which had stopped just down the road to his right. He started. It was Tricia. He felt an overwhelming urge to speak to her. After everything that had happened and everything he had learned since then it felt like a second chance, an opportunity to redeem himself and to make some reparation. He was just about to dash towards her, when he realised she had already begun walking in his direction and had spotted him too. She hesitated and he waved at her. He could almost feel her weighing up whether to pretend that she had not seen him and turn around and walk the other way. He waved again and began to move towards her smiling. Finally she made a decision and continued on her path towards him, but looking uncomfortable and uncertain. 'Tricia!' Ciaran beamed, so glad of this opportunity to talk to her and find out how things had worked out for her – it being far too taboo to enquire at work at this early stage of his return. 'It's *so* good to see you!' He gushed enthusiastically, 'How *are* you?' Tricia looked bemused, taken aback by the genuineness of his warmth towards her. It was not the kind of reaction she would have expected, after all there had been an investigation and he had been suspended. 'Do you have time for a coffee?' He asked indicating the coffee shop just behind them. Tricia nodded, uncomfortable and uncertain, but it was a cold day and it wasn't exactly as if she was Miss Popular with things to do and places to go.

Ciaran let her pick a seat while he got her a tea and a large cappuccino for himself. She chose a place on a long wooden bench that ran across the back wall of the cafe. There were small shiny wooden tables placed at neat intervals in front of the bench each with a matching dark wooden chair tucked underneath. Spreading forwards through the centre of the café, larger tables surrounded by four or more chairs led towards the front window where a large sofa accompanied by an equally large squat table sat empty. There were not many people inside the café, but still Tricia was too self-conscious to sit on the sofa, afraid of drawing attention to herself, despite how much she would have appreciated the light and comfort it offered. Instead she settled into the safety of the quiet inconspicuous space in the back corner.

When Ciaran turned to carry the mugs over to where she sat he suddenly noticed how frail she had become. Her skin looked almost grey and she had dark rings around her eyes, her once-perfect hair was now clumped and ill-kempt in an untidy knot at the back of her neck. He sat down in front of her wizened frame. 'So how are you?' he asked again.

Tricia glanced briefly at him and then looked down at her tea, but she said nothing.

'Where are you staying now?' Ciaran tried again.

'The Mission House', she replied very quietly.

Ciaran swallowed. The Mission House was really a last resort hostel: an ancient poorhouse building which had been converted into an emergency women's hostel. It was technically only for adults but a lot of teenage girls ended up there if they had nowhere else to go. Although after a couple of nights most of them would prefer to take their chances on the streets than to continue to stay there. It was mostly populated by older women, forlorn yet volatile creatures, the dregs of institutions, prisons, psychiatric hospitals, and the last of the Magdaline Laundries. Women who had been institutionalised and brutalised from a young age, poor and uneducated, usually with un-tended mental and emotional difficulties and often with equally neglected intellectual or behavioural disabilities. Their basic unmet needs alone would have been trauma enough to destabilise anyone but added to the years of abuse and brutalisation they had experienced, periods of life on the street, and the unending pain and continuous losses that their marginalisation heaped upon them, being housed in the dirty, leaking, unsanitary environment of the Mission House was the final breaking point for most. What reason or means were there left to curb the most devastating of their defences?

Ciaran swallowed again, he didn't know what to say. He felt fear and sadness curdling like sour milk in his chest. What was he doing? What did he think he could do for her now? What could be done for anyone who was so young and in such a desperate place? He felt confused and useless, all his good intentions aborted into a messy and hopeless defeat. Then a thought popped into his head. It made him nervous. Yet he couldn't let it go, even though it was so far beyond the bounds of all the practice guidelines that were now reigning him in more rigorously than ever. Nonetheless something inside him told him to follow his instinct. 'Are you looking after yourself?' he asked, smiling gently and allowing his hand to flutter loosely in the direction of his chest and abdomen so his meaning was clear. Tricia looked at him in surprise and then, to his surprise, she laughed. It was a strangled laugh, a voice for an emotional reaction that had no other vehicle, even though laughter was the least representative possible expression of what she felt. She looked around the sparsely populated cafe as if to find an answer there, but it simply echoed back the void of words that would enable her to explain any of it, even to herself. Ciaran, suddenly animated, jumped up from the chair in front of her. 'Wait there a minute!' he urged her, and then hurried out of the cafe.

Tricia stared at the scene before her and felt a weight pulling down on her. He had barely touched his coffee, it was still steaming in the round white cup with most of the froth intact. She sighed and rested her head in her hands, her elbows on the table, facing into the murky surface of her tea, berating herself for having messed up again. She couldn't move or look up or face those around her who would have just witnessed her being so quickly abandoned. She wished she wasn't there. She felt trapped in an armour of humiliation that clung to her skin, making her every thought or movement a clumsy hyper-visible statement of her own ugliness and failing as a person. She could not imagine how she would ever have the strength to move from her seat through the café and out of the door. She wished she could just disappear.

Some people at a table midway through the throng of chairs got up and left. And Tricia realised that if she only very slowly sipped her tea, by the time it was finished everyone who had been in the cafe when she and Ciaran arrived together would have gone and then she could leave without being exposed. She took a tentative sip of her tea and looked again at the coffee cup in front of her. The froth was sagging on the surface and the brown power on top was becoming darker and more wet looking. She'd never had one of those coffees before. She only ever had coffee out a glass jar, crispy granules that melted into a dark liquid the instant you put hot water on it. Danny always used to put the milk in first but then the coffee never properly dissolved. She had always thought that was pretty stupid. She wondered what the coffee in the bowl-shaped cup in front of her tasted like. She was always too afraid to ask for anything other than tea in case she showed herself up. At least with tea she knew what she was getting.

She took another slow sip of her tea, and then another, needing to be doing something and longing to gulp it down, but at the same time not wanting to rush to the bottom of the mug and to have to face leaving the café. It was hard work, just staying here, slowly outwaiting her humiliation.

Then, she realised that someone was coming over to her table. She panicked, wondering if she was going to be asked to leave – they probably could tell she was homeless and didn't want her in there. She looked up, ready to bolt before things got nasty. But, to her surprise, she saw Ciaran pulling out the chair and sitting down in front of her again. He smiled, more tentatively than usual, and took a slug of his now steamless coffee. He looked almost nervous and Tricia's heart tightened. He passed a paper bag with a chemist's logo across the table to her. As he did so he touched her arm very gently. 'It's really important that you take care of yourself', he said softly. 'This might help till things get a bit better.'

Cautiously she took the bag in her hands and drew it close to her. She opened the top and peered inside. She had no idea what to expect, but she would never in a million years have guessed the contents of the bag. It contained anti-bacterial soap, non-stick dressings, and a whole array of creams and lotions for various kinds of burns, scalds and skin infections. There were leaflets on wound care and how to deal with caustic burns. There were dressing tapes and some latex gloves. Tears welled up behind her eyes. She did not look up at Ciaran but she could feel him watching her intently. 'I know it is very difficult for you right now', he said softly. 'But you really need to take care of yourself – if you can. Will you try?'

Her eyes were stinging with tears and she was afraid that if she opened her mouth to reply it would bring an avalanche of tears with it. She swallowed hard, so hard that her throat hurt. She nodded without looking up.

Ciaran took another large swig of his coffee, hoping more than anything that he was doing the right thing. He was in utterly uncharted territory now and was desperately clinging to the belief that all the books he read over the previous months had taught him well enough that he could trust his instincts in this once again potentially compromising situation. He swallowed more coffee and caught the face of his wrist watch. He was going to have to leave pretty soon to get across the other side of town and make it in to work on time. He felt bad to leave her so suddenly, with so little said, but his job really was hanging in a precarious balance. And he could hardly use having been in Tricia's company to excuse his lateness! 'Tricia, I'm really sorry but I'm actually going to have to head in to work in a minute', he said. 'I'm on the evening shift and it's going to take me a while to get across town.'

Tricia, finally drew away from the far-off dimension she had retreated to, roused back into the present by Ciaran's mention of work – the once shared territory of Teen-Link. She looked up with a sense of urgency. 'What happened?' She stared at him intently for a while, and then looked away. 'They said there had to be an investigation. They said I said something to the doctor about you. But I never did. I wasn't talking about you. I tried to tell them, like I tried to tell you, but they didn't listen. I wasn't trying to get you in to trouble, honestly.'

'I know that Tricia, and it's OK you don't have to worry about it.'

'But tell me what happened.'

'I couldn't go in while they did the investigation and then I had to go before a panel. They have extended my probation period.'

'So you still have your job?'

'More or less, it will be reviewed again in three months.'

'God, I'm sorry, I didn't mean to get you in shit with your job, I, I just...' She trailed off, defeated by the uselessness of words once again, defeated by her own uselessness and her constant inability to know how to handle anything. She felt tears behind her eyes again; she had almost screwed up someone else's life as well.

Ciaran saw her tears and touched her hand and tried to look into her face, but she kept her eyes firmly cast down. 'It's OK, really, please believe me. It was all a muddle and it was my fault just as much as yours. And really you haven't messed up my job, I've learnt a lot and I think because of all this I now know how to do it better – or I hope so anyway!' He smiled at her again but she was still not looking at him or allowing him to lighten the mood. He took a final glug of his coffee and checked his pockets in his usual routine for keys, phone and wallet and then continued, 'But I really do have to go now, or I *will* be in shit with work.' She glanced up and this time forced a smile roughly in his direction. 'It was really good to see you though, Tricia.' He hesitated, he would have liked to meet up with her again, to see how she was getting on, to try and support her or help her somehow, but he knew that he had to be extra careful around boundaries now, any more perceived improprieties on his part and he would be out of his job and his career for good. But he still did not fully understand what happened that evening and knew he was not going to get any answers from Tricia, or at least certainly not now. He wondered if he ever would really know what it all meant. He was left with a residue of confusion that made him more cautious and less confident than he would like to be. Even so, he decided to take one last risk. He knew he was only guessing by then, but also that this might be his last chance ever to do something helpful for Tricia, and to redeem himself for the mess that had taken place between them and caused her to be out of the project. Gina had told him a thousand times that it was inevitable that Tricia would have been found out self-harming at some stage and then moved on anyway, but that didn't placate him. He *could* have done better, he *should* have done better, and perhaps this was another chance. He looked around for something to write on. The only thing to hand was a napkin, still folded neatly on his side of the table where he had placed it when he brought over the drinks. He took a pen from his back pocket and began to write on it, 'These are all places you can go to if you need someone to talk to', he said and then discretely folded the napkin in half and slid it across the table to her. 'They're all free and completely confidential', he added. 'And I know they would be very happy to hear from you.' He looked at her again, and wondered if he had gone too far – he was pretty much out of his depth now. He sighed to himself, he so wanted to get it right, but for now he had better leave it be, he could do no more and he didn't know what harm he might cause with anymore of his well-intentioned fumbles. Nonetheless, as he stood to leave, he almost forgot himself and instinctively lent over to give her a brotherly hug. He quickly corrected himself with a clumsy shrug, hoping that she either didn't notice, or didn't take offence.

Tricia did notice. She saw that spontaneous gesture of warmth, as if for a moment he mistook her for a family member or a friend' for someone who was important to him, and that meant more to her than anything else that had passed, that someone liked her, that *he* liked her even after everything that she had done. She watched sadly as Ciaran walked out of the café and onto the busy pavement outside, feeling both very small but also more alive inside than she had for a long time, like a spark of light awakening in the deadening numbness of depression that had become her constant companion.

Ciaran's cup sat empty in front of her. There were traces of foam clinging in off-white ridges on the inside of the cup, clearly delineating each interval where he paused between gulps: a conversation marked in sludge lines in porcelain. Her mug was still about one-third full and she took another sip. The tea was only lukewarm now, but she was no longer so uncomfortable there. She fingered the paper package, holding it close to her body and felt her skin sting in response. It was hard to keep clean in The Mission House, and there was nowhere to wash her clothes aside from running them under the tap in the toilet and they were becoming increasingly hardened and discoloured with the runny liquid that continually seeped from her scabs. She kept her cardigan and coat tightly buttoned. She could not bring herself to shop for more clothes, even when she had the few Euro that would certainly buy a top in Penny's. The thought of the bright lights and all the people bustling through the coloured clothes were too much for her. She felt so wayward and alien most of the time, a reeking blot of stigma made out of rotten flesh and blood, unmistakably obvious for what she was, and repellent to all those around her. A piece of her life had been torn away and all she had to show for it were the rancid wounds seeping over her heart. She held the bag tightly. It seemed to promise some kind of hope – at least she might be able to keep a bit cleaner now; it might not get so bad, things might even start to get better. She actually felt all right around Ciaran, she always had for some reason – perhaps because he reminded her a bit of Jimmy, her eldest brother who had moved to England years ago. She would have almost trusted Ciaran except that trust always seemed to make such a mess.

'Trust me, you know you can trust me.' Danny's soft words echoed in her mind. How many times had she heard him say that? His voice intoned with what she recognised as a far-off, veiled threat, which was always somehow more obvious and more menacing when he was quiet than when he was shouting.

The first time he had said it she had really believed him. She had come home from school, her face tear-streaked, and had found Danny alone in the house. He had been staying over a lot in the last few weeks and she had already guessed that her mam wanted him to move in. He had a corpo flat in Ringsend, but he was not about to give up the tenancy on that or it would be gone for good. So he just called over there the odd night of the week to pick up some of his things or when he had to sign on and spent the rest of his time at their place. Tricia's mam was doing extra shifts at the pub now, working long hours, sometimes from midday to the early hours of the morning. They paid her most of it in cash, officially employing her for only nineteen hours a week so that she didn't lose her single parent benefit and so they didn't have to get into taxes and stuff. It was a great setup for all of them, except for Tricia, who rarely saw her mam at all these days.

Tricia had been surprised to see Danny at home in the afternoon. The house was usually empty if she came straight home from school, mam at work and Danny hanging around with the guys he did a few nixers[1] with here and there. He had noticed her face – her eyes red and puffy with tears – the minute she had walked in and he had come over to her all concerned and

---

1. 'Nixers' is a colloquialism which describes casual, illegal work done on top of receiving state benefits.

fatherly trying to find out what had happened and who had upset her. To begin with it had been almost impossible for her to tell him what they had been saying she felt so ashamed, but he had eventually coaxed the details out of her. He had been gentle but persuasive, and he kept telling her that she could trust him, so that she finally blurted it out. She told him how the girls in her class, and some of those who had left this year – not even trying for their exams and many of them already pregnant – had started following her and taunting her. Calling out to her, in front of their boyfriends, passersby, anyone, asking were her pubes as red as the hair on her head and did her tits have freckles too.

Even before this she had already felt betrayed by her body. And it seemed more than ever now that everything that happened to her was because of the way it was. She hated it. She hated to look at herself, especially in comparison to her peers. She seemed so large and sweaty and swollen and sprouting forests where others had none. She felt like a different species. 'A red and white speckled gee-bag,'[2] they called her, and inside she had agreed. They said they were going to get their fellas to pin her down and have a look to see if she was red and spotty down there too, and then they could try her out to see if she fucked like other girls, to see if it was different when you were red. She had felt a vortex of fear spinning around her, but she tried not to let them see how afraid or upset she was; they only seemed to enjoy her tears and take them as encouragement to increase their persecution. She had no idea where and when they would stop, but she was terrified she was going to find out.

After she told him Danny had smiled; he had a strange smile, it didn't really suit him somehow, as if his face was only ever meant to be deadpan or scowling. He had put his arms around her and hugged her, 'Don't you worry about those stupid little girls and boys', he said. 'I won't let them do anything to hurt you, I promise.' He had pulled back from her slightly and gently chucked his hand under her chin so that she was looking up into his eyes. 'And don't be listening to any of that rubbish either, you're a beautiful girl and any real man would appreciate that, and so will they when they are a bit older and a bit less stupid.' He smiled again. He was still holding her, she could feel the length of his body against hers and she felt a little uncomfortable, it didn't seem quite right him holding her like that and saying those things. Then, almost as if he read her thoughts a slight frown crossed his brow, 'You know I'll always look after you and that you can trust me don't you? I'd do anything for your ma's daughter.' He smiled and released her, 'Her ma's

---

2. 'Gee' is an Irish slang/swear word which is the equivalent of cunt. It possibly originates from the Sheela-na-Gig carvings which depict hag-goddesses holding open their vaginas and which originally symbolised entry into a sacred domain.

daughter', he had said. 'You can trust me.' It was all right then. She must just be weird to think anything else, or maybe she was still feeling bad from before. 'Go and get washed and changed', he said. 'You're mam's in work so we'll go for a burger.'

It was not long after that, maybe only days, that he had made the very same promise to her again. She had been getting changed after school, her mam at work again, and he had come into her room. She had been shocked, him standing there in the doorway, watching her with that weird smile on his face. She had stuttered to ask him to leave and tried to cover herself with the t-shirt she was about to pull on. 'It's all right', he had said, so calmly that it must be true. 'I just wanted to see how you were getting on at school – if you'd any more trouble?' Tricia was totally confused, she was half undressed in her room and Danny was standing there like it was totally normal, perhaps it was normal. 'No, no', she stammered. 'It's been alright.'

'Good', he said and moved towards her. He squeezed her shoulder gently, 'I told you you'd be all right with me, you can always trust me. You know that don't you?' It was more like a quiet demand than a question.

Tricia nodded, utterly confused, a maelstrom of feelings surging inside her and Danny all calm like everything was perfectly normal. Danny turned and left the room and she flopped down on her bed. She felt a bit sick, but she didn't know why. He was looking out for her that was all, and she hadn't had anymore trouble at school, so why did she feel so weird? There must be really something terribly wrong with her that all those kids could see and Danny just hadn't noticed yet.

A few days later Danny came into her room again and closed the door behind him. Tricia was already in her jeans and had a t-shirt in her hands which she pulled quickly over her head. 'Don't be like that', Danny had said. 'You have nothing to hide from me, not Danny. You know you're such a pretty girl those lads don't know what they're talking about.' And then he had walked out of the room and closed the door behind him like he had never been there.

The next time it was different though. He had caught her while she was still unbuttoning her school shirt. 'Come here to me', he had said, and she had hesitated. 'Come here to me', he repeated with an edge descending into his voice that she dare not disobey. 'I'm not going to hurt you', he cajoled. 'I just want to give my special girl a hug.' He held out his arms, and feeling weak with confusion and hating herself for being so weak Tricia stepped towards him. He met her with a tight embrace and held her body close to him. 'No more trouble at school then?' he asked, and then, without waiting for a reply, he continued, 'That's good. I told you you could trust me to sort it out. And I know that I can trust you too, cos your ma is not so well at the moment. She wouldn't say it to you herself, but she's been drinking a lot again. So, you know, if anything upset her it might just do her in totally. You know what I mean?' Tricia's heart was thumping, she was afraid he would feel how hard it was pounding as he continued to hold her against him. What he was saying and what she thought he meant could be totally different, or totally the same, she didn't know what to think, or what anything meant anymore, it all just felt messed up and horrible. But maybe it was just her. Maybe she was messed up and horrible. She must be stupid or weird or sick or something. She wished her mam was there like in the old days before Jimmy and Tony had gone, like when she was a kid, just after their da had left, and it was just the four of them and everything was finally allright. But she knew that was a stupid idea, that was years ago, she was nearly sixteen now, what was she thinking? She nodded against Danny's shoulder, desperately trying to figure out what she should do or say for this to just be over. 'Now give Danny a bit of a hug like you mean it!' He said, chuckling. And, despite herself, she squeezed her arms around him. For one horrible moment she thought she could feel him getting hard in his jeans. She felt sick, but then all of a sudden he was gone and she was alone in her room in her school skirt and half unbuttoned shirt as if nothing had happened.

The next time he had been visibly tense. All the muscles in his body seemed close to the surface of his skin and he closed the door hard behind him making her jump. 'Sorry,' he said, 'I didn't mean to scare you.' He stepped quietly towards her, seeming more like he had scared himself. 'You're a good girl', he said. And even though he spoke softly there was a hard edge to his voice, a bit like that tone her da always had just before things got nasty and when her mam never did seem to learn that this was the time to quit talking back, or crying, or whatever she was doing, and just shut up. Tricia was rigid. 'Don't be frightened', Danny said, seeming suddenly less tense and more in control. 'I'm not going to hurt you, you know you can trust me', and then he took hold of her t-shirt and pulled it off her body. With his hand on her shoulders he gently pushed her down so that she was sitting on the bed and he was standing before her. Tricia felt dizzy. It was no longer as if this was happening to her, it was like watching someone else, mute and numb, from somewhere else. 'Put your arms around me', he ordered and she obeyed. 'See, that feels nice doesn't it?' He pressed his groin into her chest. She could feel him through the thin fabric of his tracksuit bottoms. Tricia felt sick. She didn't know what was going to happen next. He pressed himself against her. 'Hmm, you feel good', he groaned. He squeezed her against him and then let her go. He stood back from her and chucked her chin again so that their eyes met, he had that same strange smile on his face, 'See that didn't hurt now did it?' Tricia obliquely shook her head. 'I'm never going to do anything to hurt you, I promise you that. And you know you can trust me don't you?' Tricia nodded. Her head and her stomach were spinning. She had no idea what had just happened. She felt terrible. It made her sick. But at the same time he was right, he hadn't hurt her, he hadn't really done anything had he?

From then on Danny visited her room most of the nights that her mam was at work. No matter what Tricia did to try to avoid it, it still happened. It happened if she spent the evening hanging about on the street pretending she was with friends, going cold and hungry late into the night; it happened even if she was already in bed in her pyjamas with the covers pulled up tight around her when Danny got home. In fact, if she was already in bed then it made it worse. He would lie on top her, grinding his penis against her chest, flesh against flesh, until he spattered her with his cum.

When the house was finally quiet she would get up and wash herself, over and over again, and meticulously rinsing out her pyjamas or her bra or whatever he had disarrayed around her, but never feeling completely clean.

Many times she longed for a day when her mam was not working just for a reprieve, but Danny was right, she was drinking a lot again, and so even on her days off she would be too drunk by nine or ten in the evening to do anything but snore in front of the TV.

Tricia was sick with it. Sick to the core of her being. Yet she also somehow felt like he wasn't really doing anything wrong. After all he had never tried to fuck her, not like those boys had threatened, or even to put it in her mouth like Tony had done that one time before Jimmy had caught him and beaten him black and blue. 'I'll never hurt you', he kept saying. 'Trust me.' And in a way he was right, it didn't hurt. It was worse, far worse than that, far worse even than if he had fucked her, at least then she would have known what was happening, but this – what was it? It was disgusting. That's what it was. She was disgusting.

And then it ended just as abruptly as it had began.

It was a cold wintery day and Tricia had resigned herself to going straight home from school as there was really nowhere else for her to go. Danny had instantly followed her upstairs and into her room. 'Go on then', he said, 'you can get changed.' She turned her back to him and began to take off her shirt. He came up behind her. 'There's no need to be shy', he said, continuing to tease her with that stupid word-game that she never had a hope of winning, 'it's only Danny.' He turned her around by her shoulders so that she was facing him and then reached behind her and unfastened her bra. He pushed her into a sitting position on the edge of her bed and undid his pants.

Tricia clamped her eyes closed, trying to shut herself away from Danny and his slimy penis rubbing against her skin.

Downstairs her mam opened the front door and saw Tricia's bag hanging on the banister. The house was eerily quiet, no TV, no stereo blaring. If the pair of them were out she would have time for a drink to console herself for being sent home early before they got back and she had to explain herself.

Her boss had said she had had too much already to carry on the shift, but she felt fine. She had barely started. She thought she heard a noise from upstairs and thought she should check if Tricia was in or out before she settled down with her bottle. Danny had probably taken her somewhere. It was great how well the two of them got on, made her life so much easier.

If she had thought she was sober when she arrived home, she was certainly stone-cold sober seconds after she had stepped into the open doorway of Tricia's bedroom and had seen what was happening. For a few seconds she could not believe her eyes, and she blinked and blinked again. But there was no mistaking it. If she had had the bottle in her hand she would have smashed Danny's head with it. The dirty, lying, cheating, filthy bastard was rubbing himself all over Tricia like a dog in heat.

There had been such a commotion. For a moment Danny, unsure how drunk Caitlin really was, tried to confuse her. But she could not be fooled. Her rage had driven him quickly out of the house. He had taken of his belongings only what he could grab on the way. The rest disappeared into the back of the bin-lorry in anonymous black bags two days later.

'Might you be pregnant?' Caitlin had screeched at Tricia after the door was closed behind Danny.

'No, no', Tricia mumbled. 'He never did *that.*'

'Thank God!' Caitlin had sighed, genuinely relieved. 'Thank God you're all right then, and no need for anyone to know about it.' And that had been all she had to say on the subject.

Tricia did not feel allright. In fact, even though Danny was now gone from the house she didn't feel any better. She didn't want to be there at all. Caitlin had cut back her hours at work, and also supposedly on her drinking, and was around all the time now it seemed, but that only made Tricia feel worse. It felt like Caitlin was constantly cornering her, just to reassure herself, that Tricia really wasn't pregnant and that everything was allright. 'Not like when me da did that to me', she told Tricia on one of the nights when she had allowed herself a few cans. 'You're lucky you didn't have to go through what I did, an abortion in England and everything, you're lucky you got away with it and no one has to know. We can just forget about it now and get back to you and me again like the good old days', she had slurred.

'Lucky', 'trust', 'nothing happened'. Tricia didn't even know what those words meant anymore. She didn't know anything. But she constantly felt Danny rubbing himself against her, his hard wet penis grinding against her skin, the grunts and groans he made, and the shudder when he came on her. It felt as if he had left a trail of putrid slime in her skin that she could never wash away. A stain that would mark her out forever, that would show the world exactly what she really was. She couldn't sleep in her bed anymore. She would lie fully clothed on the sofa for most of the night slipping into and out of confusing dream-filled sleep. Eventually she stopped going home at night at all whenever possible. It was like an unspoken deal between her and Caitlin; Caitlin no longer had to pretend that she wasn't drinking and Tricia just stayed out of the way. Sometimes she even slept rough, but only on good nights and if she was with a crowd, or sometimes she just wandered around through the small hours. Then she would go home and wash and change in the morning and head out to school like a normal teenager. Some of the kids she met used the emergency out-of-hours service and they showed her the ropes, how to register at the Garda station and giving her the low-down on the different places they got sent. The odd time, if the weather was really bad, Tricia had tried it for herself, but it had meant talking with social workers and that frightened her. She couldn't get the lies right and she knew they could see through her.

But still she could not get Danny out of her head, the way he looked, the feel of him. He had seemed to get right inside her somehow even though she kept repeating to herself that 'nothing had really happened'; he hadn't hurt her, but it still wouldn't go away. She scrubbed and scrubbed at herself in the shower, but still she could not get rid of the feeling. One morning she noticed the bottle of bleach on the side of the bath. Her mam must have been doing some cleaning, or more likely thinking about doing it. It didn't look much like there had been any bleach used in there very recently, or in any other part of the house for that matter.

Tricia picked up the bottle of bleach and squeezed it out onto her wash-mitt. She rubbed it against her chest and stomach, carefully scouring all the places that Danny had left his mark. It stung. It felt good. Clean at last. It made each day a little easier to face, her body a little more comfortable to live with.

When the bleach ran out she found oven cleaner in the kitchen and tried that. It hurt like hell, it must have been stronger than the bleach, and also her skin was pretty raw by then. The pain was almost too much; it brought tears to her eyes. It frightened her for a moment, her heart racing and her skin sweating with the adrenaline of it. But, then, as it began to subside she felt amazing, high almost, and more clean and more alive than she had done in ages.

Caitlin hadn't been in work much and there had been social workers at the house a few times. It made Tricia nervous. She stopped using the out-of-hours service and tried to go home more often, but it was getting harder and harder. Tricia did not know what to say or how to behave around the social workers and she hoped that with Danny gone if she said nothing it would be fine, just her and her mam. The less said the better always seemed to be the way. It surprised her then, when she came in from school one day and found her mam deep in conversation with two social workers. The trio were sitting in the kitchen as if they were all very at home there and it was Tricia who was the outsider. Caitlin, it transpired, had been persuaded to go into alcohol treatment and Tricia was going to be taken into temporary care. Tricia stared dumfounded at her mam, and a cold wave of betrayal washed over her. Why had she not said anything to her before, she demanded to know. 'You're never here love', Caitlin replied in a tired voice. The tide of betrayal turned to ice in Tricia's body. She couldn't believe her mam would say that in front of the social workers, were they not supposed to be keeping things just between the two of them? She desperately protested she was sixteen in a few weeks, could they not just wait until then and she could stay home. But her mam had been going on about the worry of her as if she was still doing it all the time. It was the final blow. Had she told them about Danny too? And was that really why she was going to be put away somewhere? What must they think of her now? Her life was falling further and further apart.

Tricia had been placed in Teen-Link, allegedly lucky to get a placement fast-tracked for her at this new and progressive project. But it didn't feel lucky to Tricia. It was awful. She felt severed from everything she knew and cast adrift. None of it made sense. Not why she was there; not the rules and regulations; not the weird kids she was housed with who were an endless stream of noise and chaos and dirt and sullen rage and resentments. She hated it. But she kept telling herself she just had to hold on for a few weeks until her mam was out of treatment and then she could go back home and everything would be back to normal again. Still it felt like the end of the road, as if now that she had inhabited Teen-Link she was unmistakably marked for life and would never be normal again.

Then she had found out her mam was back home, early: she had left the treatment centre without finishing the programme. Actually, without getting even halfway through it. But she had not asked for the Care Order to be reversed. Tricia was frantic. How come she was still in this alien world with the street kids and the junkies and her mam was back at home? Surely she wasn't going to leave her here!

Finally, after what felt like endless one-way unanswered calls between Aoife, her Teen-Link keyworker, and her mam's social worker she got them to agree a time when she could go and visit her mam at home. This was her chance to persuade her mam to get the order overturned so she could go back home again. It would be such a relief, even to be in her old room, the room she had grown to hate so much. She would happily stay there all day and all night if only they would let her back. She was full of nervous tension as the day of the visit approached, her whole future and the only possibility of escape from the hell-hole project now hanging in the balance.

Tricia arrived home early on Thursday evening. The front door was ajar and she walked into what smelled like a brewery and looked like the scene of a riot. Caitlin was passed out on the sofa, and sitting in the chair smiling at her was Danny. 'Well Tricia, long time no see. How are you?' Tricia started to back towards the door but somehow Danny got there before her. 'There's no need to be like that', he said with a hard edge of sarcasm cutting into her. 'Do you not have one of those special hugs for Danny for old time's sake?' He laughed. Tricia felt sick. 'Come on', he said in a mock-coaxing voice, let's have a look what you're hiding under all those layers. He backed her against the wall, and began fumbling at her clothes. He smelt strongly of alcohol and his co-ordination was poor, muddling his attempts to undress her. He was getting angry, frustrated with his own clumsiness, 'Get your top off', he growled through gritted teeth. Tricia had no choice. She let her hoody fall to the floor and then began to lift up her t-shirt. 'Jesus Christ,' she heard him mutter, 'that's fuckin' disgusting!' He stepped back repelled by the state of her skin. Grabbing her hoody in one hand Tricia had seized the opportunity for escape and ducked away from him and out of the door. She hadn't stopped running until she had made it all the way back to Teen-Link.

No one saw her come in, aside from Margie who was doing the door, and Tricia had slipped quietly up to her room and lain down on her bed, trying to catch her breath and take it all in. Danny was back. That was why her mam didn't want her home again. She had chosen Danny. She could feel herself smarting with a betrayal so immense it felt like it would kill her. Great convulsing sobs began to rise from the core of her being. It was over. Her life was really over now. She started to weep, but realised that someone would only hear her if she cried in there. So she lay on her bed swallowing back her tears. She fingered the scabs beneath her t-shirt. It had got very bad lately and it didn't seem to be healing up.

Then, all of a sudden, and with an intensity that took her by surprise she made a decision. She got up off the bed. She needed help. She needed to talk to someone. She couldn't do this anymore and she had nowhere else to go. There was nothing left. She needed someone to help her make sense of what was going on and to find out what would happen to her now. Everything was ruined and her skin was worryingly sore. The infection was deep and she was becoming afraid of what it would do to her. She needed to talk to someone. Ciaran seemed nice and she had seen him around earlier; she made herself get up and find out if he was still there. She would try and talk to him. She stepped out of her room and into the corridor and there he was, like a genie that had appeared just as she thought of him. 'Can I talk to you?' She had asked before she had time to regret it or to even figure out what it was she was going to say or how she would say it. All that she knew was that she needed to talk and in private. She couldn't deal with any of it anymore. She turned instinctively towards her room, trying desperately to think of words that would explain everything that had happened and what she had done.

When they were in her room she looked at Ciaran standing in front of her, he looked a bit tense and that scared her. She was getting very confused. She started to speak, 'I need to tell you something,' she said. 'I can't explain, I don't have really anyone I can trust.'

'You can trust me', he had replied.

She looked at him, 'It's like ...' she tried to find words but didn't even know where she could begin to explain it all. How could she put it all into sentences? How could she find words for everything that had happened? She didn't even know how to say it to herself. She was acutely aware of the stinging throb of her skin under her clothes. She knew it was bad, it had got really out of control. She needed help. Perhaps that would explain it. Perhaps that was the right thing to do. They were in her room, it must be the right thing to do. 'I need you to see this', she said, thinking it would all suddenly become clear. She stepped back from him and automatically perched on the bedside locker in front of him and unzipped her hoody. Ciaran was looking more and more confused. 'I need you to know something', she had said and lifted up her t-shirt.

She didn't even know how long ago that was now. Back then she had thought her life could not have got any worse, but she had been wrong, so wrong. She had even thought that her skin could not get any worse than it was then and she had been wrong about that too.

HELP AND RESOURCES

Full contact details can be found in Appendix Three: Resources.

UK
- AA (Alcoholics Anonymous): 12-step recovery group for problem drinkers
- Al-Anon: 12-step recovery group for friends and families of problem drinkers
- Alateen: Part of Al-Anon (above) but especially for 12–17 year olds
- The Basement Project: Information and resources about self-injury for people who hurt themselves and those who live and work with them
- The Bristol Crisis Service for Women: Telephone, text and email support for women and girls who self-injure and also wide range of self-injury resources and publications
- 42nd Street: Free and confidential support for young people in the Manchester area
- The Hideout: Online support for children and young people affected by domestic violence and run by Women's Aid
- One in Four UK: One-to-one and helpline support for females and males who have experienced sexual abuse

- Rape Crisis England and Wales: Support for women and girls who have experienced sexual violence
- Scottish Women's Aid: Scotland branch of Women's Aid
- Shakti Women's Aid: Support for Black and Minority Ethic women who are experiencing domestic violence
- Women's Aid: Support and campaigning organisation for women who are experiencing domestic violence

Republic of Ireland
- AA (Alcoholics anonymous): 12-step recovery group for problem drinkers
- Al-Anon: 12-step recovery group for friends and families of problem drinkers
- Alateen: part of Al-Anon (above) but especially for 12–17 year olds
- Dublin Rape Crisis Centre: Helpline and one-to-one therapy for females and males who have experienced rape or sexual abuse
- One in Four: Support and therapy for females and males who have experienced sexual abuse
- Pieta House: Free one-to-one therapy for people who hurt themselves
- Women's Aid: Support and campaigning organisation for women who are experiencing domestic violence

Northern Ireland
- Women's Aid Federation Northern Ireland: Support and campaigning for women who are experiencing domestic violence
- Zest: Free one-to-one therapy for people who hurt themselves

RESOURCES, REFERENCES AND FURTHER READING

Cutting the Risk: Self-harm, Self-care and risk reduction. Originally published by the National Self-Harm Network and now available as a free download from www.kreativeinterventions.com and harm-ed.co.uk

The Hurt Yourself Less Workbook. Originally published by the National Self-Harm Network and now available as a free download from www.kreativeinterventions.com and www.harm-ed.co.uk

The LifeSIGNS Self-Injury Awareness Booklet: Information for people who self-injure/self-harm, their friends, family, teachers and healthcare professionals. FirstSigns Self-Injury Guidance and Network Support, www.firstsigns.org.uk

BROKEN

I don't remember much about who found me and called the ambulance aside from being utterly mortified by the whole thing. It's all really blurred which is kind of good in one way, but really embarrassing in another. I don't really want to know the details of that night, but then part of me thinks maybe it would be better if I did know so I can stop tormenting myself about who was around and who did and saw what.

My memory gets a bit clearer when they pumped my stomach, mostly 'cos it hurt like hell, but also 'cos it was kind of a relief too, feeling the pain and getting a bit more clear-headed. They kept me in overnight– what bit of the night that was left by the time they had done – and told me I would have to see the shrink in the morning. It didn't seem like I had a choice in the matter and I was still too wobbly to get up and leave or I probably would have done. I hadn't meant to end up in hospital and I just wanted to go home. Pat must have gone by then, though I'm not sure I remember Pat actually being there at all.

I slept pretty deeply after that, probably partly still 'cos of the pills. They woke me up in the morning with slops for breakfast and the offer of a shower in a filthy bathroom, both of which I declined. I'd wait till I got home and have a nice hot bath with the radio on. Then a nurse led me up a couple of corridors to a waiting area and told me to sit there till my name was called. When the nurse was gone I thought about legging it, but I was a bit disoriented and thought I'd probably only get myself into more shit if I tried to do a runner. Probably better to just wait and get it over with and then go home. That's all I really wanted to do, just get out of there and go home. I went to look at my watch and realised I didn't have it on, they must have put it somewhere, and then I realised I didn't have my wallet and keys and stuff either. There was defiantly no escaping then. Thank God I hadn't done a runner; I wouldn't have been able to get home anyway! It was a bit like being a hostage. It felt like I was waiting for hours – it probably wasn't hours, it's just like you're in a different time zone and there's something about the smell of hospitals that makes me feel really sick and anxious. It's like you're expecting someone to drop dead right there in front of you or something.

Finally, after about ten years, one of the doors across the way from where I was sitting opened and the psychologist, or psychiatrist – I never really did figure out which she was, or what the difference is anyway – called me in. She didn't look that much older than me, late twenties probably, she had a white coat on over a grey blouse and black skirt. She told me her name was doctor something or another; I didn't really hear her properly, and didn't get chance to ask 'cos she was already saying that she was going to do some kind of assessment on me. She indicated for me to sit in front of her desk and she took her place behind it and pulled out a stack of papers. She started by asking me my name and date of birth and all that kind of thing, and then, just when I thought this was looking like the easiest assessment I had ever had to take she started on the deep shit. It totally threw me, I had no idea what she was on about to begin with. She was asking me all this weird stuff about death and depression and whatnot until I finally realised she thought I had been trying to kill myself. God, as if it wasn't bad enough already ending up in hospital, brought in by ambulance and all the drama and fuss that must have gone along with that, when I twigged that was what she was thinking, well then I was totally mortified. I figured that was why they had kept me in; they thought I was a gonner. I didn't know what to say: would it make it worse or better if I told her the truth? And what could I say anyway? Tell her that it was just a bit of a mistake, I misjudged it 'cos I don't normally do it with pills? I don't think so! I couldn't figure out any words that wouldn't sound totally crazy, and if she was some kind of shrink I knew I'd have to be really careful not to make myself look completely mad, 'cos things were already looking pretty bad as it was. It was really confusing and I kind of felt like she was starting to get pissed off with me, and whatever I said I just seemed to be digging bigger and bigger holes for myself.

Finally, thank God, I managed to convince her that I wasn't trying to kill myself, that I just took too many pills; that I had thought I would be allright; that I didn't realise it would be that bad. For a long time it seemed like she wasn't going to believe me and she had kept asking more questions about what had happened leading up to me taking the pills. She wanted to know if I'm married, and I said no, but I live with my partner. So then she started asking if we were having difficulties, if we'd had a row recently. She didn't seem to want to believe that everything could be going along fine, and that actually this is kind of normal for us. I suppose it didn't really help that Pat wasn't there to back me up and I was getting kind of nervous about the way it was shaping up in doctor wotnot's mind. And then when it came out that we live in a shared house with four other people she started writing furiously on her assessment sheet, as if that would make me want to die or something! I don't know. I guess it just wasn't possible for her to accept that Pat is pretty much used to what I do by now, and so are the others as well. Well, except for the pills and the ambulance – that's not how it normally goes at all. So I guess it was all a bit unusual in that way and I suppose I was kind of out of my depth, but still it didn't add up in the way she seemed to be implying.

Anyway, one thing that I did eventually find out from her that was useful is that if you take pills you never know what kind of damage it's going to do to you. It's not like when I do the glass and I know just how deep and how much to cut, how far and where to take it. With pills you might just take a few and end up dead, or you might take a ton of them and just have a stomach pump and a sick belly for a few days. I hadn't known that, I thought by measuring the amount of pills I could be doing pretty much the same to the inside of my body as what I do with the glass to the outside. I thought it would be kind of like swallowing glass but without actually having to do that, 'cos obviously I knew if I actually did that I'd be seriously fucked.

To begin with, when she had started on about the pills I wasn't too sure if she was just trying to scare me, but then after a bit I believed her. And it was kind of good to know that, even if it did make me feel even more stupid at the same time, 'cos at the end of the day, I certainly don't want to die, and nor do I want to end up back there again in another endless assessment interview! So I made a mental note of that information and I definitely won't be making the same mistake twice.

When she finally did believe that I wasn't trying to kill myself I found out that there was a name for what I do, and that apparently a lot of people do it. News to me, but then, seemingly, I never was the quickest on the uptake. 'Deliberate self-harm', she called it. With the 'deliberate' really emphasised so that there was no mistaking that 'cos I did it on purpose, I must be mad, or bad, or both. When she got on to the whole 'deliberate self-harm' thing she got all excited and wouldn't stop talking, to start with she was asking me a whole load more questions and then she went on about some course or programme they run.

She was interrogating me about my family and childhood and stuff, just like shrinks on TV, for what felt like forever. I don't know what she was looking for but I didn't have anything special to tell her. We're just a normal family: two parents, four kids, three boys and one girl, all went to school, all did OK, all got jobs, no violence, no abuse or alcoholism or anything else like that which might explain why I am the way I am. I was starting to feel more and more uncomfortable the longer she went on. Like I don't even have a reason for it, I'm just fucked I suppose, a freak of nature or something.

It reminded me of one time when Pat got really angry with me about it and accused me of using it to manipulate people. I have to say I honestly have no idea where that came from, 'cos even though I do kind of need people to know, like Pat and the guys in the house, it's not like I want them to see it or to do anything. I just need them to accept it and leave me with it. It's like a secret, but a special secret, that I have to share to let me know if I'm really OK with them or not. To be fair, though, I know it must be hard for Pat coming home week-in week-out never sure if this is going to be one of the days where I'm under the sheets covered in blood, too sore to move and not wanting to talk, raw and ragged like one big open wound. At the beginning it kind of brought us together, but right now, to be honest, I don't know how much longer we're going to last. Pat wants to travel and I just don't see the point. I'd only end up working in another kitchen in some other part of the world, and one hot, aggressive kitchen is pretty much the same as any other to me regardless of whether it's Dublin, Sydney, Toronto or New York.

But, back to the hospital, and just when I was finding it really tough, all the questions and what it was making me think, and worrying how to get myself out of there, then the shrink got on to even harder stuff. She wanted to know if I'd done it before and when did I start. I wasn't sure if she meant the pills – which was only the second time, hence making such a balls of it – or if she meant cutting with the glass 'cos I think she had copped onto that by then, or maybe I had said something just to get her off the suicide trip, and they must have seen all my scars when they did the stomach pump. It was all getting very confusing at that stage anyway, and then I was wondering, God, does she mean the other stuff as well? Like, I've always had something that I do for as long as I can remember. When I was really little I used to bang my head, not always against really hard things, sometimes just against the arm of the sofa, but I'd do it over and over again, and I just remember liking the way it made me feel. Once or twice I got caught and got a right bollocking for being stupid, and my brothers took the piss out of me something rotten over it. After that I used to pinch myself really hard on the thighs. I'd do it slowly and carefully for ages, making patterns of blue-black bruises. I liked the slowness of making the bruises, deciding where they should be and what kind of shape I would make, and then holding on through the pain till I knew they would appear. I liked the way the soreness lasted for days after too, a bit like I do with the cuts now. But even then, and that was about age six or seven from what I can remember, I was really careful to keep it above the line of my PE shorts. I knew I'd be in shit if anyone found out. In my teens I put my fist through a door a few times and once or twice through a window in one of the derelict houses at the back of the village. I had to go to hospital one time with that, I told them I'd been in a car accident and managed to get away with it. I must have lied about my age – and my name too come to think of it – 'cos my parents never found out. I think that's what eventually got me into cutting, the windows, the glass, but most of it is quite hazy and I know I've forgotten a lot of it.

I knew I couldn't say any of that to the shrink though. I couldn't tell her the truth, that the answer is 'always', or she'd think I'm a total head case and God knows what would happen then. They'd bring out a straightjacket and cart me off to the funny farm, and that would be me banged up for life. It's like it's just a part of me and I don't know why. I don't have any answers or explanations for her or for anyone else, except that maybe I'm just not quite wired up right or something inside me is a bit broken. Anyway, since I clearly wouldn't have been doing myself any favours to mention any of that, but I still had to say something, I just thought about the cutting and told her the truth; that it had been going on for about four years.

She asked me how I felt when I did it. 'Great!' I wanted to say, but of course I didn't. Actually, I don't really know what I feel like when I'm doing it. It's like I'm in a different zone altogether and I'm not sure I really feel anything at all. It's afterwards I sometimes feel stuff, and that can be kinda weird. The best times are when I'm just totally spaced afterwards. I'm exhausted and I don't care about anyone or anything. I just haul myself off to bed and flake out. I think those are the times that Pat gets the most pissed off, which is kind of ironic 'cos that's when I'm actually doing grand. But still, I guess it can't be nice to come home and find bits of glass in the bathtub and then to pull back the bed sheets and find me all carved up. I guess it probably is too much to expect that anyone could just leave me alone in that state. But I hate all the questions and anxiety. I just want to sleep till the next day and then, when everyone has gone to work, I'll get up and phone in sick to the job and have the house to myself for the day. I'll stick on the TV and watch any old crap, drinking pots of coffee and rubbing Savlon into my arms and legs. It stings like hell but I almost like this bit the best, when the cuts are still red and raw and hurting and I can see what I've done and kind of take care of it at the same time. Yeah, these are definitely the days I like the best, and this is when I like myself the best too. It's like a holiday from everyday reality, just me, the TV and my sore arms and legs. It's like a pause, like life has stopped for a while and I can just rest in the space of the soreness and breathe free for a bit.

I know I'm pushing my luck at work with all the sick days I've had, but I don't care, I hate my job anyway. And it would be easy enough to find another. No one stays long in one place in catering, unless of course you're the head chef, and the chances of me ever getting to that are about a million less than zero.

It's not always like that though. There are other times that are much harder to handle, especially if it ends up with other people around, then it's a complete fucking disaster and I might as well want to kill myself just to get away from them. The worst thing is that there's no way I know when it's going to happen like that. I will have begun just like I always do: wait till night-time, make sure everyone is out or in bed and I have the house to myself before I start. And it will all be going fine, and I'll have got to the point where I know I have done enough – and I never go on for more than an hour anyway even if I want to – and then everything just falls apart. Out of nowhere something just takes over me. I don't know what it is, but suddenly I'll be crying, and I mean really crying: blubbing my eyes out, hysterical like, uncontrollable. And truthfully I haven't cried since I was three, not when my dog died when I was nine, not at my best friend's funeral when I fourteen, not at the movies, nothing, never. And then suddenly I'm just this blubbering wreck. Crying and crying and I can't stop, and I don't even know what it's about, like I've totally gone off my head and completely lost it. It makes me feel so stupid 'cos it's about nothing really, all emotional for no reason, like suddenly being pissed drunk and talking stupid, but crying instead. A bit like the way some girls get when they've had a few: all laughing one minute, and then the next in a big serious huddle, with one of them crying her eyes out and the whole crowd taking her off to the toilets for hours on end. I stay well away from that kind of thing, even when it's my own mates, I just go to the bar or chat to one of the lads or something, try not to notice it happening.

I think that's why it freaks me out so much when it happens like that with me. And of course Pat or one of the guys in the house will inevitably end up coming home in the middle of it, and it's all panic and questions and concern, and I just feel even more fucked up with them seeing me like this, crying like a baby, totally out of control, especially when I'm normally so cool about it. Like I've worked really hard to get them to just accept that it's me and it's fine and I can handle it, and then they see me in a complete mess over it and I feel ridiculous. It's better when they just have the basic facts in the cold light of day, no drama, no fuss, this is who I am and that's it. The only question is can you handle it, 'cos it's not a problem for me. And then suddenly it has started to look like a really big problem. Though, Pat has just about given up on giving me the third degree when it happens now, finally realising that loads of fuss and attention and questions just make it worse and that it's best to just leave me alone to get over it. 'Cos there's nothing that anyone can say or do that will help anyway. It's funny, thinking about it like this, 'cos I've thought recently that Pat might be getting a bit pissed off with it, and I can sort of understand why. I mean I look at those girls off for a good cry in the toilets every Friday and Saturday night and I think do they not notice that every weekend they're getting all dressed up for a good night out and they're going to spend half of it in floods of tears in the bathroom? Hardly the highlight of the week! And I wonder, is that what Pat might be starting to think about me: why the fuck do I keep doing it if I can't handle it? But I never really expect that, I mean I'm always intending that I'm going to be OK afterwards, but it's a risk I suppose, and one that I take every time I do it without really thinking, just like the girls on their sixth vodka and Redbull on a Friday night.

I knew I had to say something to the shrink though – she was waiting for an answer. So I said the first thing that came into my head after thinking all of this, and I ended up telling her that I feel sad when I do it. And that's when she got all hyped up about the course or the programme or whatever they call it that they have in the hospital. Once she started on about the course it was like she had stopped assessing me, which was a relief to be honest, except that now it felt like she was trying to overload me with information instead. A lot of which, it has to be said, was totally weird. She was rattling on about how this was a new specialist programme they had just started running and that she could refer me to attend on an outpatient basis. She said it was designed for people like me, whatever that means, 'cos I thought the reason I was being assessed was 'cos I wasn't normal, like there was something really wrong with me, and that I wasn't like other people at all. I wasn't really sure if I had a choice either, but I was getting really anxious to get home, to be able to use a clean bathroom and just sort myself out. She was really starting to do my head in by then too. I mean I never even knew there was a proper name for it up till then, and then suddenly it was like there's this whole school for it as well! And God, she was really loving the whole idea of getting me on this programme and laying it on really thick. And then, just when it seemed like it couldn't get any more nuts, it got weirder still. She told me that before being accepted onto the programme I would have to sign something called a 'No Harm Contract'. Basically, an official agreement stating that I wouldn't harm myself while I was on the programme. That made me laugh! I thought it was a joke to begin with and was about to laugh out loud but then I realised she was dead serious. Like she just couldn't see that what's the point of having a programme to stop doing it if you can just sign a piece of paper and not do it any more?! And anyway, if it was that simple does she not think I would have done that myself, and years ago? By that stage I was really beginning to think that she might be a bit mental, or maybe this was some kind of sci-fi trip or parallel universe where instead of having doctors and hospitals you just went to a mind programmer and signed a bit of paper agreeing not to be sick: 'I promise not to have anorexia anymore', 'I solemnly vow that my cancer will not return', 'I promise not to be a schizophrenic from now on', 'I swear I'll never get heart disease', 'I promise not to take too many pills or cut myself again' – sorted!

Funny, when she was talking about the programme I noticed that her nails were bitten really low. I wondered if she thought that was 'deliberate self-harm' too. She noticed me staring at her hands and picked up her pen and started to fiddle with it like she might just write something really incriminating down on my form if I didn't knock off that train of thought.

Anyway, the whole thing was turning into a bit of a nightmare and I just wanted to go home and it was beginning to seem like I was never going to get out of there. But I had kind of copped on by then that the more I said, the more difficult it got, and that I just kept talking myself into deeper and deeper shit. So I decided it was probably best to just shut up and agree with her. Thankfully it turned out there was a six-month waiting list for the programme anyway – which is kind of funny too if they think people are at risk of killing themselves, or maybe there is a piece of paper to sign to say you won't kill yourself while you're waiting to be made feel better! Anyway, in the end I just let her put me on the referral list and reckoned it would be easy enough not to go when the time came. It was a bit freaky though 'cos she wanted my GP's details, and I still use the doc back home the odd time I need anything and I was a bit worried about him finding out. Like what if he said something to my folks or anything? I know there's supposed to be confidentiality and all that but there's no such thing in rural Ireland, like Pat says, if you sneeze on the train on the way home half the village will be preparing for an epidemic by the time you get there.

I have to admit though, the shrink did kind of spark a bit of interest about it all, especially now I knew there was a name for it and that apparently there were lots of people like me – God help them! I went into an Internet café the next day and did a Google search on it. There are millions of sites, and tons of different names for it: self-harm, self-mutilation, self-injury, deliberate self-harm, non-suicidal self-injury, delicate cutters syndrome, self-inflicted violence, and fucking hell they make it sound really nasty. Well, apart from 'delicate cutters syndrome', which sounds a bit like something that refined English ladies might do at tea parties. But seriously, I'd never seen anything like it before and it was kind of scary, especially when it started going on about all the mental disorders it was attached to. Borderline personality disorder, depressive illnesses, post-traumatic stress disorder, all kinds of shit that I swear I don't have any of. And then there were so many different sites too: sites for people who called themselves survivors and who seemed to have been locked up in hospitals for years; sites all about how to stop it – using anything from medication to God; sites that celebrated it, where people put up pictures of themselves all cut up. It was crazy stuff, all of it, and nothing like me at all! If I had thought I was losing it, then some of this stuff is really off the wall. Totally nuts. Then I started thinking, I wonder is that what that shrink was thinking about me, that I was like that? 'Cos really that shit is nothing to do with me. Nothing to do with me at all. I don't belong with any of that, no way.

At the same time, I do know that from the outside it must look a bit like I'm crazy. It does even to me sometimes too. It's like two different worlds. There is the one where I'm doing it, and I know it's kind of weird, but at the same time I'm not stupid. I only ever cut the backs of my arms, never the front or my wrists where the arteries and tendons are, and my legs, the fleshy parts – that always seems safe enough. And I only ever cut in vertical lines so even if I do hit an artery or something I won't do irreparable damage. I don't want to die, and I don't want to seriously mess up my body either. Sometimes I cut my chest too, but never far enough up to get too close to my neck or low enough to get my nipples. Like I say I'm not stupid. I know I have to keep it under my clothes too, and even though I wear long sleeves more than most people, it's not that obvious. And it's defiantly not like I get into a mad big frenzy and just randomly slash myself up all over the place. I'm always slow and careful and I take my time. I know what kind of edge will make what kind of cut, and how much pressure to use to go through the skin to the right depth. Mostly I don't even do it as deep as I want to the first time, I prefer to go over it till it's deep enough and feels just right. Like I say, I know what I'm doing. I'm careful.

But, even so, sometimes afterwards I kind of freak out at myself. It's like I wake up and see what I have just done through totally different eyes, and all the soreness and the blood are no longer a relief, a necessity, the reward for the days, sometimes weeks, all pent up since the last time. Suddenly, even to me, it looks crazy, insane, totally inexplicable and incomprehensible, and part of my head starts going mad asking myself why I have just done that. Why in God's name have I spent the last hour with pieces of broken glass, sorting through the sizes and shapes of the pieces, utterly engrossed in being able to make exactly the right depth and width of cuts? Why have I been sitting on the edge of the bath tub totally wrapped up in slowly carving up the surface of my skin so that I look like a deranged red zebra and thinking it is OK?! Then I am sick at myself and I know I have to get it all cleaned up and get to bed before anyone gets home.

There was another time recently that it got a bit weird too, but in a different way. For some reason lately I have been really thinking a lot about wanting to cut my face, and I'm not sure why. One night I looked in the mirror and just thought about doing it for ages. I really wanted to. Like it would be the final relief; that once and for all it would bring me where all of this has been heading – even the balls-up with the pills I guess. And I ended up stood in front of the bathroom mirror fighting with myself for nearly two hours over it, getting so close to doing it but never quite getting there, until it finally got too much and I did my stomach instead. I'd never cut my belly before and I was so wound up I ended up going really deep, much deeper than I normally would. It kind of scared me. It looked like it might need stitching and I started to panic a bit. There were bits of glass in it too and I started to think about infections and tetanus and stuff like that, I was probably just overreacting, but still, it was a worry and it looked really bad. Anyway, I got my act together. Fortunately one of the guys in the house had left a packet of thick sanitary pads on the side of the bath. I didn't think anyone used them anymore especially not girls my age, but thank God they did, 'cos they were a life saver! I packed three of them against my stomach and zipped my jeans over them and went out in search of a late night chemist. I managed to get some steri-strips and dressings and antiseptic and stuff to patch it all up. And I managed to get it pretty well sorted. Actually, since then I've always kept a supply for emergencies, 'cos I don't want to be ever get caught out like that again and be left wandering the streets of Dublin looking for a late night chemist and hoping I find one before blood starts seeping through my clothes and I look like something that has just escaped from a horror movie.

It was such a relief that night when I got back home and got myself all fixed up and the bleeding finally stopped. I gave the bathroom a good clean too, I really didn't want anyone finding out about that one. Thankfully Pat was on nights for the week so I could keep it totally out of sight till it looked a lot better. Taught me a few things though, that did. And I have to say I feel much better knowing I always have a proper supply of stuff now for afterwards, not just the Savlon cream; it's like I'm a bit less crazy and a bit more in control. It also made me think some more about the glass, and cleanliness and stuff, and since then I've always washed the bits that I'm going to use in antiseptic first, and sometimes I even swab my skin with it too. I really don't want to end up in hospital again with any of it, 'cos I don't know if I'd be able to talk myself out a second time, and then God alone knows what would happen to me. I just need to keep it under control for now, maybe one day I'll figure it out, or stop, or something. But I doubt it, I can't imagine it, I think it must just be the way I am.

When I was finally on my way out of her office the shrink gave me a list of numbers that she said might be helpful before I started the programme. I looked at the list, the Samaritans were at the top. So I guessed she never really did believe that I wasn't trying to kill myself after all then. I chucked the list in the bin and went to find my keys and stuff so I could finally get the hell out of there and get back to my life.

NOTES

Any response to someone who has hurt themselves is shaped by a whole range of factors including assumptions and judgements that are made unconsciously or automatically. This story is deliberately written without any gender identifiers. Did you read the protagonist as male or female? And what assumptions did you make on the basis of that? What does it feel like to re-read the same story and substituting an alternative gender to the one which you assumed? And what did you assume about the person's sexuality, did you see them as gay, lesbian, straight, bisexual? Does reading a different orientation into the character impact on your response to them and your assumptions about what is going on?

Supports and information for people with non-normative gender and/ or sexual identifications and those interested in raising their awareness in this area are listed below.

HELP AND RESOURCES

Full contact details can be found in Appendix Three: Resources.

UK
- FFLAG: Support for parents of people who are lesbian, gay and bisexual
- The Gender Trust: A charity which supports trans people and their families

Republic of Ireland
- BeLonG To: Dublin-based youth project for LGBT young people
- L.inC (Lesbians in Cork): Resource and community centre for lesbian and bisexual women
- OutHouse: LGBT community and resource centre
- TENI (Transgender Equality Network Ireland): Support, campaigning and resources by and for trans people

REFERENCES AND FURTHER READING

Alexandra, N & Clare, L (2004) You still feel different: The experience and meaning of women's self-injury in the context of lesbian and bisexual identity. *Journal of Applied and Community Social Psychology, 14*, 70–84.

Babiker, G & Arnold, L (1997) *The Language of Injury.* Leicester: BPS Publications.

Bornstein, K (1995) *Gender Outlaw: On men, women and the rest of us.* New York: Vintage Books.

LifeSigns (now FirstSIGNS) (2004) *The LifeSIGNS Self-Injury Awareness Booklet: Information for people who self-injure/self-harm, their friends, family, teachers and healthcare professionals.* FirstSigns Self-Injury Guidance and Network Support: www.firstsigns.co.uk

Pembroke, LR (2007) Harm-minimisation: Limiting the damage of self-injury. In H Spandler & S Warner (eds) *Beyond Fear and Control: Working with young people who self-harm* (pp. 163–72). Ross-on-Wye: PCCS Books.

Rothblatt, M (1996) *The Apartheid of Sex: A manifesto on the freedom of gender.* Pandora: London.

RESOURCES

Belonging. Produced by the Swedish Federation for LGBT Rights. www.rfsl.se

Cutting the Risk: Self-harm, self-care and risk reduction. Originally published by the National Self-Harm Network and now available as a free download from www.kreativeinterventions.com and www.harm-ed.co.uk

The Hurt Yourself Less Workbook. Originally published by the National Self-Harm Network and now available as a free download from www.kreativeinterventions.com and www.harm-ed.co.uk

FLASHBACK THREE

Her voice is straining through the greasy milk-chocolate-brown receiver of the public phone by the nurses' station. I hate having to use this phone. It smells and it makes me feel dirty. But I'm not allowed my mobile in case I use it to hurt myself. A girl in here tried to swallow the battery out of her phone a while back and since then we've all been banned.

Mam's voice is high-pitched with worry and she is talking very fast. She's having trouble with the bills again, and she's been back to the moneylender that she got into trouble with before. I've been in here for nearly three months now and she just can't cope when I'm not around to sort out the money stuff for her. I don't know why she always gets it in such a mess.

I can see her now sitting at the kitchen table, full ashtray beside her, hands trembling as she looks at the sheets of paper all demanding money off her when there are just a few coins left in her purse 'til giro day, and the next two months' child benefit are already taken up with paying off the loan. I feel her need for me to sort it out, and I can't, I'm stuck in here. It's as if her fear snakes down the phone line from her to me and takes me over. My chest feels tight and my mind is beginning to race through all the possibilities of what I can do or say to fix this. I curl a lock of my hair around two fingers of my free hand and pull it tight. I can feel the roots of the hairs beginning to snap away from my scalp.

***

I am hurrying home from school, phone pressed to my ear, while my mother's anxious voice trills me along. They have come for the TV and the DVD player, she wails, it might be the washing machine next. What should she do? She doesn't know what to say to them. I must get home fast so that I can deal with them. She can't think straight with them in there and Kerri and Ben screaming 'cos they want to watch the TV that the men are trying to take. I am scuttling along, I hate this part of the walk home, past the sex shops and the grubby pubs and the trucks and cars pulled to the side of the road in the archways where the street-women work. I'm always getting comments and shouts that scare me and make me feel sick and I don't know what to do about it. So I'm glad to have my phone in my ear and mam's voice giving me a reason to rush along, head down, and not having to notice what is going on around me.

**

Suddenly I feel a weight of bodies pressed against me. I am lying on my back on the floor, the receiver is bouncing forlornly against the wall which is streaked with grime, grey finger marks and blobs of chewing gum. I feel sick. I am being pinned to the ground by three or maybe four people. I don't know why this is happening. I think I might be shouting or trying to get up. I haven't finished talking to mam. I haven't sorted anything out yet. I don't know what is happening and I need to get away from this so I can help mam. Then there is a crushing weight on my chest that is so intense I can hardly breath. I close my eyes. I am spinning now, everything has gone fast and slow at the same time and I can't feel anything anymore. It's like being in one of those dreams where you're falling backwards and then wake up with a sudden jolt. Except there is no waking up part here.

**

I turn the corner, I'm nearly past the arches and just four streets from home now and I tell mam I'll see her in just a few minutes. Then all of a sudden I am on the floor, my phone flying out of my hand and skidding across the street. Everything is suddenly very slow and very fast. As I watch my phone sliding away from me I can see every detail of the tarmac as if I'm looking through a magnifying glass. It's like my mind photographs each and every millimetre of the surface and the change in texture: a blob of oil; the wads of chewing gum squashed into the rise and fall of the lumpy surface and the small puddles of spit that shine like putrid Christmas baubles melting on the black. There is litter everywhere here, crumpled cigarette boxes and butts, used condoms, and decaying dog shit covered in hungry flies in the gutter. I can't believe I'm on the floor in all this filth and I struggle to pull myself up.

It is only then that I cannot avoid what is really happening to me. I am being held down. I think there are maybe three or four people. There is a smell of unwashed men's armpits and stale beer. Things seem to be happening in two different time zones, like alternate realities where my brain is in slow motion and everything else is speeded up and then, at the same time, the other way round. I'm not sure where I am. Part of me is right there, too much there, and part of me is very far away. I try to call out for them to stop, to leave me alone, I don't want this, but it seems to take such a long time for my breath to reach my lungs that I don't know how many years of time it will take for me to make a sound that will go out into the world of this smelly, dirty pavement and the cruel weighty bodies that surround me. There is so much pressure on my chest I think someone must be crushing me. My arms are pinned down on either side and my head is held fast to one side so I cannot properly look at or see them. The realisation that I am utterly powerless and can do absolutely nothing forces its way through my body, and pushes me away from myself.

I feel them forcing my legs apart.

I focus on the dog shit for a long, long time.

***

'OK, c'mon, you can get up now', a voice from somewhere tells me. I realise the pressure on my body is gone and the receiver is no longer dangling against the wall. I'm not sure what just happened. Two sets of hands are placed under each armpit and help to pull me to my feet. Things are coming back into focus. I'm by the phone at the end of the ward. I look at the floor where they had been holding me. Grubby grey tiles with blue speckles that a thousand dirty feet must have trodden. I need to take a shower, but they lead me back to my bed and pull the curtains around it. 'Right, let's get you out of those pyjamas and examine you', one of the voices says. 'What?' I falter, they can't really be telling me I have to strip off in front of them now? Why, what for? 'We just need to be sure that none of your ribs are bruised', the voice explains. 'It's normal procedure after this kind of episode.' An episode, is that what it was? Like from the sick soap opera of my life that no one would believe? I lie naked on the bed and they press their fingers into different parts of my body – hurting me to see if they have hurt me. I look at the ceiling. Two flies are crawling around the light fitting. I wonder what it is like in here if you are a fly. Is it better or worse? It couldn't be worse. I'd like to be a small, hard, black, winged creature looking down, not the soft, naked, pink girl on the bed. When they finally leave me alone I no longer have the energy to go and wash myself. I just pull my dressing gown around me and slip under the bed covers and close my eyes.

***

A long time after they have gone I finally manage to get up. I hurt between my legs more than I ever thought possible, and there is slimy stuff coming out of me and all over my thighs. I think I am bleeding too. It's hard to move. There is a pain in my back too, and it is only when I have finally managed to stand up that I realise that it was the buckles of my school bag that had been piercing my flesh. I balance myself against the wall and look around me. My phone is still lying in the street but it has been crushed as if something has driven over it. My torn knickers are in the gutter. I quickly pick them up and put them in my bag, desperate to hide anything to do with what had just happened. I lumber forward and grab my phone. It is destroyed. Tears flood down my face.

When I get home the flat is quiet. The men have gone and Kerri and Ben are watching TV next door. Mam has been crying. Her face is all blotchy and she has mascara smeared around her eyes. She looks at me with daggers, 'You said you were coming home hours ago', she accuses. 'You're just like your Da was; always letting me down when I need you!' She eyes me closely then, 'And look at the state of you! What in God's name have you been doing?!' But she doesn't wait for an answer. 'Go and get changed and then you can stay in your room. I don't want to have to look at you again tonight.'

***

There are ward rounds the next day and they make a point of stopping by to see how I am after the 'episode' yesterday. Apparently Ma had been on to them too, wanting to know why I was suddenly cut off from her. 'You were disassociating', they told me, and presumably Ma too, though I don't think she would really understand what that meant. 'You had disassociated and were pulling your hair out. We had to intervene to prevent you from harming yourself, you understand that don't you?' I want to tell them that I was doing OK until they pinned me down, until they crushed me, and made me lie there naked while they poked at my body to see if they had busted my ribs. I want to tell them I was doing OK on my own, I was always doing OK on my own; if everyone would just leave me alone then I would be OK. But I can't say any of that. I have never even told them what happened before. Sometimes I think that I should, that maybe it would help. There was a student here once who was nice and I nearly did tell her, but she was gone after a few weeks and I don't think the others would understand, and definitely not now, I couldn't say it to them after this.

So I just wait for them to go away.

***

Ma is furious about the phone, but I manage to salvage the sim card and eventually get an old handset from Patsy at school. I'm so glad when my period comes, even though I know I might still have diseases, and there is no way for me to go to the doctor about it without Ma knowing.[1] That will have to wait till I'm older.

***

The ward is quiet and I take the pink padded journal from my bedside locker and open it at the back. I peel back the sticky paper lining from the cardboard and prize open the layers between it and the fabric cover. My treasure trove: an old-fashioned ring-pull from a can of God-knows-what that I found behind the trays in the dinner room. It might have been there for years but it was like a gift waiting just for me. I had put it into my slipper so that I could get it back to the ward. I was hardly able to walk normally with it cutting into my foot. I cleaned it in the hand steriliser in bathroom and I have cherished it ever since. I do try not to use it though. I keep it just for emergencies, the times when I can't get clean or right in myself again. And I have been doing quite well lately, thank God, and especially that there were no very recent ones for them to see yesterday. That would have only made things worse. But still it's so hard not to, especially in here where I have nothing else. I go to the toilet farthest away from the nurses' station and check if anyone notices me going in. No one is looking, that gives me a bit of time. I lean against the cold ceramic sink feeling it press into the back of my thighs. I can feel all the dirt and the tension and the fear in my body, building and building, desperate to be set free. With one hand I hitch down the waist of my pyjamas and with the other I begin to slowly carve the first of a neat row of Vs down my stomach. I feel like I can breathe again. Each millimetre of pain is like purification, and the blood is washing me clean. I feel strong and safe again, like I have found my one true love who won't let me down.

---

1. Mandatory reporting and the lack of confidentiality for minors accessing statutory services are strategies which were adopted with child welfare in mind. However, both of these practices can be counterproductive and prevent young people from accessing services when they know that their confidentiality may be breached. This was something which had been particularly detrimental for a number of my research participants. Some non-statutory organisations such as the Bristol Crisis Service for Women (which provides support for women *and* girls) and ChildLine have protocols in place to enable support to be accessed without running risks of subjecting their young service users to unwanted breaches of their anonymity and confidentiality or enforced interventions.

HELP AND RESOURCES

Full contact details can be found in Appendix Three: Resources.

UK
- Bristol Crisis Service for Women: Telephone, text and email support for women and girls who self-injure and also wide range of self-injury resources and publications
- ChildLine: Confidential telephone and email support for children and young people
- DA (Debtors Anonymous): 12-step recovery group for people struggling with compulsive debting
- 42nd Street: Free and confidential support for young people in the Manchester area
- MABS (Money Advice and Budgeting Service): see Irish listing
- One in Four UK: One-to-one and helpline support for females and males who have experienced sexual abuse
- The Patients' Association: Support and campaigning organisation focusing on the concerns and rights of patients
- Rape Crisis England and Wales: Support for women and girls who have experienced sexual violence
- Victim Support: Confidential support for victims and witnesses of crime

Republic of Ireland
- ChildLine: Confidential telephone and email support for children and young people
- DA (Debtors Anonymous): 12-step recovery group for people struggling with compulsive debting
- Dublin Rape Crisis Centre: Helpline and one-to-one therapy for females and males who have experienced rape or sexual abuse
- Irish Patients' Association: Support and campaigning organisation focusing on the concerns and rights of patients
- MABS (Money Advice and Budgeting Service): Free and confidential service for people struggling with finances and debt
- One in Four: Support and therapy for females and males who have experienced sexual abuse
- Victim Support: Confidential support for victims and witnesses of crime

TRUST ME 3
(THIRD TIME LUCKY)

Tricia feels the train slowing down and knows that they must be nearing Klandurk station. She prepares herself for the dash from the toilet onto the platform and out of the station before she gets caught without a ticket. If she only had a real address she could change her giro to Klandurk and not have to make this precarious journey back to Dublin every week to sign on and pick up her dole with the rest of the NFAs.[1] But it's worth the anxiety of the journey, and even the humiliation of being ejected from the train the couple of times she has been caught, just to be away from the whole scene in Dublin, the drugs and the violence and the girls who sell themselves in the dirty back streets and the boyfriends that get them to do it so they can get a few cans or a fix or whatever it is that they want. She'd easily risk another run-in with an angry guard just to get back up to Klandurk and stay in the Patrick Street hostel. It's considered rough, but it's got nothing on the Dublin hostels. At least there are just four women to a room here and most of them are pretty harmless. Tricia usually tries to share with the older women; they might be a bit crazy but at least they're not strung out or arguing with errant boyfriends on stolen mobile phones through the night. It's also much cleaner than the places in Dublin she has stayed in and there is a washing machine they can use, as well as a kitchen to make their own food. Tricia has stolen a few things from the kitchen sometimes, food and bits and pieces, and she feels bad about it, like she has betrayed the closest she has to a sanctuary and which will only inevitably lead to more shit for her. But she had to do it really, just to stay alive, just to get the things that would help her cope with the day-to-day struggles of existing. There was a whole big fuss made over the missing knife. It was not supposed to have been left unsupervised in the kitchen anyway, but one on the relief workers had forgotten to lock it back in the office after someone had been cooking, and so everyone was really wound up about it. It had been getting to the point that they were about to

---

1. NFA means no fixed abode, the term used for people who are without a home and receive welfare payments on a different system to those with permanent addresses.

search rooms and bags, but then Andrea's boyfriend had started throwing stuff at the windows and by the time that had been dealt with and the gards[2] had left the knife had faded into distant history.

Tricia didn't know where the idea came from. The knife had just been there, its clean shiny blade glinting at her in a rueful smile, and she had instantly known what she needed it for. She had slipped it up her sleeve and then waited out the commotion, her mouth dry and heart pounding, knowing that if she was found out she would be barred from there and worse off than ever. But now that she had it in her grasp she could not give it up. So she held on, and it paid off.

She kept it with her for the train ride back to Dublin the next day, and then it became her permanent travelling companion as well as her night-time friend. She got the morning train to Dublin because it was busy and also because early in the day there wasn't time for the toilets to have got too manky. The commuter rush also made it harder for the guard to get down the train collecting tickets so she could usually get to Dublin undetected. Then, when they arrived in Connolly station, she would slip through the exit to the Luas terminal and out on to the pavement. However many times she executed the plan perfectly undetected, each journey remained a knot of ever-growing anxiety. But once she had the knife it was different. She cut long slow lines in her arms, her own train-tracks making inroads to the tightness in her body. It felt like her heart slowed down a bit; it felt like everything slowed down just enough to breathe and to hold on for the next cut. It felt like the pain was seeping from inside her chest and out of her skin in the thin lines of blood that criss-crossed all around her arms.

She always made a point of getting one of the busy evening trains back, but the toilets were often pretty gross by then. Mostly, however, unless she was still feeling really bad she didn't need to do it on the return journey and she usually made it back to the hostel OK. There she'd wash her arms and put some cream on them. But one time the woman at the welfare office had given her a really hard time about having proof that she was looking for work. It seemed kind of stupid to Tricia 'cos who would employ an eighteen-year-old girl who had been out of school and out of home for more than two years? What job could she do anyway? She couldn't think of any job that she would be capable of, and even if she did, it wasn't like she had anything that she could wear to go to work or even an interview. Her clothes were cheap or second-hand, and even when they were clean they were still bald and sagging from their endless rounds in the industrial-strength washing machine at the

2. An Garda Síochána, Ireland's national police service, literally translates as 'guardians of the peace'.

hostel. It had frightened her, though, that a person just like that could tell her that she wasn't complying with the rules of her benefit and could just as easily take it off her without warning. It made her feel like the bottom had been pulled out of the last bit of security that she had; that she would be cut loose and cast adrift to slip unnoticed from the surface of the world. A world that she only maintained a tentative grasp on at the best of times.

She had managed not to cry in the welfare office, but by the time she got to the station later that day it was almost uncontrollable. She had flung herself into the toilet of the first carriage, not even caring about the state of it. She had never been more thankful of the means to ease her panic and tension, and the increasing soreness in her arms seemed to reassure her that things might be more solid after all. But then the train had lurched unexpectedly just outside Klandurk and come to rough halt. She stumbled and the knife went right into her arm, cutting through the skin way deeper than the marks that she usually made. She looked at the gash and could see through the thick layer of sliced flesh to the inside of her own body, like a cut of meat on a butcher's slab. It scared her, and it would not stop bleeding. She bound what was left of the toilet roll around it but it soaked through almost immediately, and pieces of the wet tissue broke off and slipped into the wound. She took a jumper out her bag and tried to bandage it but the blood was still pouring out. She was beginning to feel very sick and dizzy. By the time they got to Klandurk she knew she had to get help. She staggered off the train and, in pure survival mode, got into the back of a taxi and asked to be taken to the hospital. The roads were fairly quiet and the driver sped her to the small hospital. He didn't even ask for a fare, but Tricia didn't notice that, or how he kept glancing anxiously in the rear view mirror at her, acutely aware of her draining complexion and her blood-soaked arm. Her vision was blurring by the time they arrived and she would have collapsed in the doorway of the small Accident and Emergency department had a vigilant nurse not stepped forward and caught her in the nick of time. They rushed her through. She was given her a blood transfusion and then taken her into surgery to carefully repair the layers of damaged tissue and partially cut artery.

Hours later, when she came round there was a nurse was beside her. She saw Tricia's eyes blink open and smiled and squeezed her hand, 'Welcome back', she said softly. 'You're in the hospital and your arm is all fixed up now, good as new.' She smiled again and helped Tricia sit up. Tricia blinked. It was dark, sometime in the middle of the night. Her mouth was dry and tasted of chemicals. She licked her lips. 'Here, let me get you some water', the nurse said, and poured a beaker from a jug on the bedside locker and helped Tricia to drink it. 'Probably best to just have a few sips for now. The anaesthetic can make you sick if you rush too much down on top of it.' Tricia acquiesced and let the nurse take the beaker away from her again. 'My name's Carol', she said. 'I'll be here until the morning, so if you need anything you just let me know OK?' Tricia nodded still dazed, her brain only seeming able to very slowly put the information together. Carol continued, 'When the day shift come in a special nurse will come and have a chat to you about your arm.' She sighed. 'You must have been feeling rotten, you poor thing', she said softly, peering sadly into Tricia's unfocused gaze. 'You'll be kept in for a couple of days to build you back up again and to make sure that's healing up OK, you had lost a lot of blood.' Tricia's eyes were heavy and the lids were starting to close shut again. 'I'll leave you to get some rest now', Carol said, plumping the pillows and letting Tricia lie back down again. 'There's a buzzer just above your bed, if you need anything give me a call.' She smiled and squeezed Tricia's hand again and then slipped off into the night ward. Tricia, still fuddled with anaesthetic, stared after her briefly before her eyes completely closed again and she slid back into a deep sleep.

The noise of the morning finally drew her back out of her sleep, which had been thick with intoxicated dreams, and it took her a few moments to work out where she was and how and why she was there. Her arm was throbbing. It was bound tight with a pure white bandage that held a thick dressing in place. She was in a ward of just six beds, and only two of which besides hers were occupied. Each bed had a chipboard locker to the right-hand side of it and above it, suspended from a high ceiling, was a metal rail on which pale blue curtains were hung. Tricia's bed was closest to the double doors that opened out onto the corridor. At the other end of the short ward was a large window which looked across a thin strip of grass to a concrete space that was increasingly filling up with cars. The double doors to the corridor beside her were wedged wide open allowing the noise of the day to tumble through. Tricia tentatively pulled herself to a sitting position and carefully leaned over to the locker and reached for the still half-full beaker of water. The inside of her mouth and throat felt like they had turned to sandpaper. She took a couple of glugs and waited to see if she felt sick. Nothing happened so she poured two more beakers and drank them down. She was still adjusting to her surroundings when a middle-aged woman in a grey uniform pushed a tea trolley through the open space of the doors. She looked at Tricia and smiled, 'Morning, love', she crooned. 'Would you like some tea?' Tricia nodded. 'Milk and sugar?' She nodded again and was soon sipping hot sweet tea from a thick pottery mug that felt like the most beautiful thing she had ever tasted. Then, to her surprise, Carol appeared through the doors just to see how she was and say goodbye before she went of shift.

A nurse came round with some meds for the other patients and some painkillers for Tricia, and then there was breakfast of porridge with banana and soda-bread toast and jam and more tea. It was lovely and warm in the hospital and there was a comforting smell of bleach. Tricia felt like she could just lie down and sleep there for weeks.

At about eight thirty a woman in a long emerald green dress with a wrap-around cardigan and flat shoes swished through the doors and came straight over to Tricia's bed. She had glossy brown hair cut into a bob and the biggest chestnut-coloured eyes Tricia had ever seen. She looked a bit like a woodland pixie or an elf out of a kid's story book. The woman smiled. 'Hello', she said in a sing-song Belfast accent. 'My name's Brigit and I'm the psychiatric liaison nurse. It's my job to look after everyone who has hurt themselves.' It wasn't even a question. Still Tricia knew that the map of ridges, scars and cuts on both her arms couldn't possibly be explained away as anything other than self-inflicted. It scared her. Now they knew, what would happen to her next? But the big cut, she really hadn't meant to do that; that was an accident. She swallowed, her mouth was suddenly dry again. Despite her encounter with Carol the previous night, all that her body seemed to remember was what had happened in Teen-Link and she was terrified. What were they going to do this time? Would they find that she had stolen the knife and put her back out on the streets again?

'Do you mind if I take a seat?' Brigit asked, indicating the chair beside the bed. That was not what Tricia had been expecting next, and bemused, she shook her head. Brigit smiled, 'Thanks', she said. 'How are you feeling this morning?' Tricia shrugged. 'Tired', she said, and couldn't think of anything else to say, or how to even begin to explain the silent turmoil inside her. 'Well', Brigit smiled, 'I'd really like to have a chat with you, and it's not very private here, do you think you'd be OK to come down to my office – it's just on the next corridor – or would you prefer to stay here? I can get a chair for you if you're still a bit wobbly on your feet.'

Wrapped in a thick powder-blue hospital blanket which smelt of strong detergent and which covered the standard-issue pyjamas, robe and slippers that she had been provided with, Tricia found herself being wheeled down the corridor by the elfin Brigit. They turned a corner into a cream-coloured corridor with a horizontal blue stripe down the middle and navy blue doors at regimented intervals standing erect like a silent army awaiting command. They came to a halt outside one of the doors and from somewhere in the folds of her dress Brigit produced a bunch of keys and unlocked it, she held it open with a foot and steered Tricia and the wheelchair inside. The door closed behind them. It was a small room, painted dusky pink. There were shelves and a desk and two chairs, a grey filing cabinet, and a glass fronted medicine case which had a kettle and a tea tray on top of it. Brigit parked Tricia by the desk, where there were some stacks of paper, a laptop and a wilting begonia jumbled together, along with some framed pictures of two children at various different ages. 'Can I get you a cup of tea?' she asked. Tricia nodded. 'Please', she said.

They sipped their tea and Brigit made a bit of small talk, checking every now and then to be sure that Tricia was feeling OK. Tricia mostly just listened, trying to fathom this woman and what on earth she was going to do or say next. She was not like anyone Tricia had ever met before and this was like nothing she had expected, even when Brigit finally got down to the business of their meeting. 'I'm the psychiatric nurse here', she explained for the second time that morning, 'and anyone brought in who has hurt themself in any way is assigned to me. It's my job to see how you are and what we can do to help you. The psychiatrist will be in later on, and he will probably want to go through an assessment checklist with you, but I wanted us to be able to have a proper chat first and see if there is anything that you want to talk about.'

Brigit went on to explain that she was there for people to talk to her about whatever was going on for them, anything that they might be finding hard to cope with, and then she would try and help them to find ways to understand what had been happening and ways of dealing with it. She didn't seem to find anything shocking or bad about the fact that Tricia cut her arms, and she also believed her when she said she hadn't meant to do it that badly, that it was an accident 'cos of the train. But it was also like she wouldn't have minded if she had done it that badly on purpose, or even if she had deliberately tried to cut her hand off! She was very calm about it all. She didn't freak out or get angry or scared. She acted like it was a perfectly natural way of dealing with something. After a while Brigit asked her if there was anything else that she did, and Tricia found herself telling her about what she used to do with the bleach and stuff and how she had got thrown out of Teen-Link because of it. Tricia couldn't believe how much she was suddenly talking. It was like years of saying nothing had all become unleashed, pouring out of her like they had put something in the tea to make her talk. She ended up spending two hours with Brigit that morning and big chunks of time the subsequent days that she was in the hospital, so that soon Brigit pretty much knew everything about the last few years of her life and the circumstances that she was in. Brigit immediately began working hard to stall Tricia's discharge and to keep her in for longer than would be usual without having to have her transferred to the psych ward. Brigit had a plan. A new residential project had opened to the south of the town for women just like Tricia who needed somewhere safe to go to get back on their feet again. 'Just like Tricia', however nicely Brigit said it, Tricia knew that meant girls who did things to themselves, girls who had nowhere to live. Was that really the sum total of what she was? Was she really anything like other people that did that? It was not really who she was, it just kept happening because things had gone wrong and she didn't seem able to make it right again. And what would it be like in there? She remembered Teen-Link and the strung-out, violent kids and the noise and chaos. 'It's a really nice place', Brigit continually reassured her. 'Brand new and really not like the Patrick Street hostel or anywhere else you have been. This place is something else, it's really special.' Brigit's eyes would light up when she talked about it, as if she really did like it. 'It's called Solstice House, and it is totally different to anywhere else. I know there are two vacant places there at the moment, so I'm just trying to persuade them to fast-track your referral. It would be great if you could go straight there from here and not to have to go back to the hostel and struggling up and down to Dublin.'

A week later when Tricia was still on the now full small ward with her arm covered by a much lighter dressing, two women from Solstice House came to visit her. Brigit brought them in and introduced them as Elsie, the project leader, and Grace, one of the key-workers. Elsie was blonde with an English accent, and Grace sounded like she was from Cork. She had thick black hair and red-rimmed glasses. Just like Brigit both Elsie and Grace seemed to find it totally normal that she would have been cutting herself, and Tricia wondered if Brigit had told them about the other stuff and what they thought of that. But they were very friendly and relaxed. They told her that in Solstice House everyone was accepted exactly as they were, and the aim of the project was to help people to stay safe and to support them in working out their own life in their own way and time. They said they were there to interview her about a placement, but they never did anything that felt like an interview to Tricia. mostly they just asked her practical stuff like did she have a social worker, and where she had been living, and how she had been managing – nothing that seemed designed to test her or catch her out. They gave her a leaflet with some pictures and information about the project and asked her if she wanted some time to think about it, or to have a visit before she made a decision. There were some words on it like 'self-injury' that made Tricia feel ashamed of having to be associated with it, except that Elsie and Grace seemed so nice and the pictures made it look beautiful. The brochure also said she would get her own room and there were only five or six residents in the whole project. That seemed an unimaginable luxury, she was used to sharing one room with almost as many strangers every night. There were other words on it that Tricia didn't really understand, like 'harm reduction' and 'person-centred' and she didn't feel brave enough to ask. But at the same time she was beginning to feel like maybe she could try and trust that what she was being shown was real, and that it might be OK, even though she had no idea really who all these people were, and could not make sense of the way they were behaving towards her. It was like she had fallen off the train and landed in a parallel universe: there was Carol who worked at night who always made a special point of paying her attention and looking after her; then there was Brigit who spent hours listening to her and putting complicated schemes into action so she could stay in hospital until she had found her a good place to go; and now Elsie and Grace whose idea of an interview was to see if Tricia thought what they were offering was good enough for her!

'No', she said, almost afraid that if she left any more time to try and work it out the bubble would burst and she would wake up back in the Patrick Street hostel and find out it had all been a dream. 'No, I'd like to move in, definitely!' she said looking at Elsie and then Grace. 'Well, we'll be very happy to have you with us', Elsie smiled. 'Grace will come and collect you when you're discharged and she'll be your key worker.' Grace smiled too, 'I'm really looking forward to getting to know you better', she said and seemed to really mean it. 'I'll be in touch in the next day or so.' Then they said their goodbyes and left, leaving Tricia with just a folded A4 brochure to reassure herself that this was really happening.

It was the following Monday that the taxi pulled up outside the large Georgian building on a tree-lined street overlooking a park. Tricia couldn't quite believe this was where she was going to live. She had seen the pictures in the brochure but it didn't seem real that some kind of hostel, or 'supported housing' as they called it, was really located somewhere like this. She felt embarrassed by her shabby appearance and her wrecked arms in comparison to the surroundings, almost expecting that at any moment the mistake would be realised, the decision reversed, and that she would be told that she couldn't stay there after all. But Grace lifted Tricia's small bag out of the boot of the taxi and bounced up the slope to the front door, smiling and beckoning her to follow. 'Welcome to Solstice House! Your new home!' She beamed as the door swung open revealing a wide hallway painted bright yellow and with a huge painting of sunflowers on one wall and a potted plant almost the height of Tricia beside it. Opposite there was a row of coat pegs with a different jackets and coats hanging on them and a wooden bucket with an assortment of umbrellas. The hallway stretched backwards with number of doors leading off it, and there was a wide wooden staircase about halfway down with a chair-lift folded up against the rail that fixed it to the wall.

Grace strode to the end of the corridor and opened the door which led into a huge bright kitchen, also painted sunshine yellow and with a large, chunky pine table and eight chairs in the centre. 'Have a seat and I'll put the kettle on', Grace crooned. She was plump, curvaceous, and she wore jeans and a rich burgundy-coloured hippyish blouse. Today she had straightened her thick mane of hair which fell halfway down her back. Tricia liked her already; she seemed earthy and safe and a little eccentric. Tricia found herself smiling as Grace made the tea, as if she wanted to laugh and cry at the same time. 'We have the place to ourselves for a bit', Grace explained. 'Two mornings a week we do group work up on the top floor so everyone's in there until about half twelve, and I can show you around and get a few things organised before everyone comes down – they're all dying to meet you!' Tricia shifted in her chair, suddenly nervous, but Grace leaned across the table and touched her fingers, 'Don't worry, everyone's nervous when they first get here, but we're a really good crowd and you'll be fine, really.' Tricia swallowed the mixture of smiles and tears still worryingly close to the surface. 'Now', Grace continued, 'there are two things we have to get done today, one is to show you around so you know where everything is and get you settled in, and the other is a whole stack of paperwork that we need to get done. We need to register you here and sign the contract, but I also need to get all your benefits transferred here and I want to make sure you're getting everything you're entitled to – there's a few bits and pieces we can get to help you set yourself up, like a clothing grant and a moving-in allowance. But, it's up to you, which you would like to do first, the guided tour or the paperwork?' She smiled.

'Can you show me around please?' Tricia asked, needing to get a sense of where she was before she could focus her attention on anything official.

'Sure', Grace smiled. 'And we'll bring some tea with us', she said refilling the mugs from a large orange teapot. 'It's a big place and we might need a bit of sustenance on the way!' She laughed and got up. She opened the door at the far end of the kitchen into an outdoor space. 'Well, this is the garden, she said waving her hand across a half-slabbed, half-grassed square of land with a high wall around it. It's pretty basic at the moment, but a friend of mine is interested in coming in as a volunteer and doing some work on it at the weekends if we can get any of you guys interested in giving her a hand. She's thinking about doing a bit of landscaping and starting a vegetable plot, which would be great 'cos we have a house dinner together every Saturday night, so who knows, in a few months we could be eating our very own home-grown veggies!' She smiled at Tricia and then turned back into the kitchen. 'Everyone has a press for their food and your own pots and plates as well if you prefer them to the communal ones. There are two fridges, the one with the green stripe on it is for vegetable and dairy products only, to keep things separate for the vegetarians. At the moment we have a vegan with us, Joan, and so she uses the top couple of shelves in the green fridge so that nothing can get spilled on her stuff.' Grace turned from the fridges where she had been directing her attention and looked at Tricia. 'Do you think we're completely bonkers?' she laughed. 'Don't worry, it will all seem normal very soon!' She moved towards the door that led back to the corridor. 'Here is something important', she said, stopping and indicating a noticeboard on the wall by the door. 'This is the staff rota and it always shows the next four weeks, so you know who is in when. Oh, and we also have Anne who comes in three times a week and cleans all the communal areas and the offices, and she can do one of the bedrooms once a week as well, though mostly everyone prefers to do it themselves. And we all still do our share of tidying up around the place after ourselves too.' From the hallway they went into two offices, both containing two desks and four chairs, but one much more clinical in appearance than the other with tiled walls and floor and a wash basin beside what looked like a large medicine cabinet. 'We have a nurse, Deirdre, who comes in on Wednesdays and she uses this room when she's here. She's great. Most of what she does is help people take care of any injuries they have but she's also a bit of an agony aunt and she does sexual health and smear tests and all that kind of thing too. You'll get to meet her this week – she can show you how to look after your arm and order in all the supplies you'll need.' Grace turned around in the room, as if checking there was anything else she needed to explain. And then she looked at Tricia, and said, 'Don't worry about trying to remember all of this straightaway, it's loads to take in at the beginning, so just ask whenever you get confused or need anything. We're all a bit overwhelmed when we first get here. When I started I spent the first two weeks walking into the wrong office and sometimes even into the sitting room!' She turned and walked out of the office leaving Tricia to close the door behind them. 'And here is the sitting room.' She smiled and opened the door into a huge bay-windowed room with polished wooden floors and a large dark red rug. There were three sofas and matching beanbags in dark red baize and a huge ornate red and black tiled fireplace in the centre of the wall opposite them. The walls were painted cream with framed prints mounted at intervals along them. There were pots of lush green plants and a widescreen TV and DVD player in one corner and a bookcase against the far wall. 'There's books, and magazines and CDs and stuff here that you're free to help yourself to, and we leave things back or add to the collection whenever we feel like it', Grace explained. A book caught her attention and she put down her mug and picked it up as if in demonstration. It was an old well-thumbed paperback copy of *Wuthering Heights,* and had something barely legible written inside the front cover in faded red ink. Grace frowned slightly at her foiled attempt to read the inscription and then placed it back on the shelf. It must have been something that one of the girls had picked up in a second-hand shop. 'Right', she said, turning back to Tricia, 'I'll show you the next floor and your room, but we'll leave the top floor till later so we don't disturb the group. There are two group rooms up there and one bedroom that we don't use at the moment. We do lots of stuff with the group rooms, there's the two sessions a week that a woman called Marie always facilitates which is therapy kind of stuff and then we have different people come in and do all kinds of different things: art, creative writing, yoga, massage, maths and

budgeting, we even did face-painting one week which was loads of fun!' Grace
stopped at the bottom of the stairs. 'You OK with stairs?' Grace asked. Tricia
didn't understand the question, but Grace was already elaborating anyway.
'Sarah, one of the gang you'll get to meet a bit later on has cerebal palsy and so
she can't always manage without this', she tapped the stair lift, 'but you're OK?'
Tricia nodded and followed Grace's swinging hips up the long wide staircase.
'So this is where all the bedrooms are, and you're in number three', she said
turning to a door with a key in the lock and opening it. She handed the key to
Tricia. 'That's yours, it opens the top lock of the front door too and I'll give
you a key for the bottom lock later. The bedroom locks are all on a master key
system, just so you know that in emergencies we can get in if we need to.' They
were inside the room and Grace was still talking but Tricia was not really listening
anymore. She was staring in disbelief at the room she had just been handed a
key for. It was the most beautiful place she had ever seen. The walls were
painted alternately lilac and cream and there was a huge window with sunlight
streaming through it and bouncing off a mirror made up of a mosaic of tiny
glass tiles on the wall opposite. There was a sturdy pine bed with lilac bedding,
and on a bedside table a huge vase of fresh flowers. Tears sprung to her eyes.
Surely this couldn't be for her? There was a pine wardrobe and a desk and chair
with a table lamp, and pine shelves fixed to the wall above. It was all brand new
and beautiful. Grace had opened a door in the wall beside the wardrobe. 'This
is your bathroom', she was saying and pulled a cord that switched on the light
and ceiling fan. 'There's a small first aid box in here with the basics in, but do
let us know if there is anything in particular that you need, or if you run out of
anything, and Deirdre of course can help sort that out too.' Grace turned
around and saw Tricia standing in the centre of the room, still staring at the
vase of flowers, with tears streaming silently down her cheeks, 'Hey, it's OK',
Grace chimed moving gently towards her. 'Would you like a hug?' Tricia nodded
and very carefully Grace put her arms around her, softly rubbing her back. 'It's
OK', she whispered, 'you have a good cry if you need to.' Tricia leaned into
Grace's soft warm embrace soaking her with what became a hurricane of tears.
It was a long time later that she had no more crying left inside her. But Grace
stayed right there with her all the while holding her and letting her cry. Finally,
spent and exhausted, she fell asleep.

Later Grace called back up to her, tapping gently on the door of her
room with a tray of tea and toast. Then, when she was feeling restored, she
brought her back downstairs to meet her new family of peers and to sign the
papers that would confirm that this strange and beautiful place really was
where she was going to be spending the next part of her life. 'Trust me', the
very walls of the building seemed to whisper to her, and this time she knew
that she could.

HELP AND RESOURCES

Full contact details can be found in Appendix Three: Resources.

UK
- The Basement Project: Information and resources about self-injury for people who hurt themselves and those who live and work with them
- Bristol Crisis Service for Women: Telephone, text and email support for women and girls who self-injure and also wide range of self-injury resources and publications
- 42nd Street: Free and confidential support for young people in the Manchester area
- harm-ed: Self-injury training and resources

Republic of Ireland
- DisABILITY.ie: Information and support for people with disabilities by people with disabilities
- Kreative Interventions, free downloads of *The Hurt Yourself Less Workbook* and *Cutting the Risk: Self-Harm, Self-Care and Risk Reduction*
- Pieta House: Free one-to-one therapy for people who hurt themselves

Northern Ireland
- Zest: Free one-to-one therapy for people who hurt themselves

REFERENCES AND FURTHER READING

Arnold, L & Magill, A (2007) *Getting It Right* (2nd ed) Abergavenny: The Basement Project.

Bristol Crisis Service for Women (2006) *Good Practice Guidelines.* Bristol: BCSW.

Brontë, E (1847/1992) *Wuthering Heights.* Hertfordshire: Wordsworth Classics (with introduction and notes by JS Whitley).

Spandler, H & Warner, S (eds) (2007) *Beyond Fear and Control: Working with young people who self-harm.* Ross-on-Wye: PCCS Books.

RESOURCES

Cutting the Risk: Self-Harm, Self-Care and Risk Reduction. Originally published by the National Self-Harm Network and now available as a free download from www.kreativeinterventions.com and www.harm-ed.co.uk

The Hurt Yourself Less Workbook. Originally published by the National Self-Harm Network and now available as a free download from www.kreativeinterventions.com and www.harm-ed.co.uk

CATHY AND HEATHCLIFF 1999

Martina pulls her coat around herself and steps out of her red Nissan Micra and straight into a greasy puddle formed in the indent of a pothole in the hospital car park. She tuts as she feels the cold dirty water instantly seep through the seams of her increasingly careworn brown boots. These were her weekend boots, only recently relegated to her work wardrobe, and accelerating into an alarmingly rapid decline as a result. She slams the car door closed behind her and it echoes accusingly in the grey afternoon drizzle. It is only Tuesday and already her nerves are jangling with what feels like a year's dose of stress and anxiety which she has absorbed from her workload since just yesterday morning, and which she is now under pressure to transform into workable care plans and manageable goals and targets. These are futile gestures in this no-budget world, for people and services whose prospects of longevity are about as realistic as her boots seeing out the end of this dreary winter. She sighs and with her arms folded tightly across her chest and her head dipped in a protective scowl against the elements she sets off through the drizzle to the hospital entrance.

The foyer is hot, loud and chaotic, and for a hospital it is also remarkably dirty. It smells too, of sickly disinfectant and human debris and an aroma of cheap coffee which wofts intermittently from the machine by the barred reception counter. Martina can never understand how people can consume anything in this environment. She had always felt bad anytime she was here to see Tara and Tara had offered her coffee from the ward machine, trying to normalise their situation somehow, yet all the while with Martina conspicuously perched in front of her, fully dressed in her outdoor clothes, swilling the brown liquid round the flaccid plastic cup and hoping she would be able leave without Tara having noticed she hadn't touched it. She would hate Tara to think that is was because she was HIV+ that she wouldn't drink from a cup she had touched, or that it was anything to do with her at all. It was just this place. She always felt like she needed to shower when she left. Then she realised she wouldn't be back here after today – or not to see Tara anyway. All she had to do was pick up her things and get the paperwork sorted out and Tara's case was closed for good. Martina suddenly felt an intense loss; she had not realised how far Tara had slipped under her skin, and how much her visits here had actually touched her. She never would have thought she would miss those strained twenty or thirty minutes, tension thick in her body, as Tara sat across from her in her cheap nightwear, all lace and silky fabric clinging to her wasted frame, looking like a macabre hybrid of a child and a middle-aged woman kitted out for some low-budget peep show. The last time she had seen her, the bags under her eyes had darkened and her skin was paler than ever. Even the freckles across the bridge of her small impish nose looked blanched of colour, as if the life was literally fading out of her. Tara had seemed particularly small that day, and the gold jewellery and her one golden tooth glistening amidst its methadone-decayed neighbours, looked more like weights than decorations on her body. Martina always found it strange how Tara could persist in maintaining these outer frivolities while neglecting the fundamental basics of her well-being, but then Martina had always felt at a bit of a loss to understand Tara at all. She was a myriad of contradictions all bundled up in one small frame, so hard that she was fragile, and could shatter at the slightest touch. Whenever they met Tara would be by turn silent and sullen, or animated and full of promises and dreams, high as a kite on the lies she told to herself. Martina had learnt quickly that underneath either of those exteriors was the same hard-edged aggression, the foulmouthed violence and chaos that ruled her life in the outside world, which she nursed and fed with more attention than she had her own child after he was born.

Martina begins the long walk to the HIV ward, located at the far end of the longest corridor leading away from the main building. It might have once been the isolation area for TB, which would have been rife when the hospital was designed, but now the two units in the basement of the building house the HIV and the psychiatric wards. She had felt ashamed the first time she had come here, then on placement and still full of all the world-changing ideals of taught social work practice, only to witness for herself the stark contrast between values and reality. She had been incredulous at the blatant way in which the most stigmatised and undesirable patients were lumped together and consigned to this invisible dungeon as far as possible from the rest of the hospital as if not to contaminate it with their incurable and unwanted ills. She had not realised then that her role would not be so much about enabling change, about saving people or freeing them, as simply picking up the pieces of an endless procession of broken lives and tidying them away to be discarded. She had tried to let the bright yellow walls of the psych ward and the pink flowery curtains on the HIV wing console her, but she had been lying to herself. Nothing could compensate for this place, the dirt and the shame, the human lives left to turn sour and rot in this drab no-man's land.

Now, however, she rarely thinks in those terms. Her mind is permanently overcrowded with custody orders, court cases, care placements, addiction, violence, and even death. And that is before she even gets to her own life, and the growing anxiety that has inhabited her from the abdomen upwards every morning for the last three weeks when she wakes and finds her period has still not come. Each day of the last seven she has told herself that if it has not come by tomorrow then she will tell Mark. And every day she gives herself another twenty-four-hour reprieve. She does not want this to be true, and she keeps believing that just one more day will make a lie of her fears. She knows that she has to say something very soon though. Mark wants to book them a special summer holiday together, and a baby will change all of that. She tries to think of the summer as it must still appear in Mark's imagination: carefree, indulgent, just the two of them. She sighs, she needs some sunshine more than anything right now.

THURSDAY WARD ROUNDS

A random Thursday morning towards the end of 1999, and Sorcha lies on her bed. She's confined to the ward now until after the doctors have been round, and that could be two or more hours. All the visitors have been unceremoniously swept away in preparation, not that Sorcha generally has visitors anyway, so their exclusion becomes a weird kind of social levelling between her and the other patients on the psych ward. She closes her eyes. Until she came here she had never known how much time it was possible to spend daydreaming. But now it has become a regular passtime to stave off the mind-numbing boredom that slowly eats away at the hours. She found that daydreaming could be quite fun at times and, she hoped, would even help to keep her imagination alive for the books that she would one day write.

Lately, however, her mental flights have taken her no further than her own recent memories, which she has begun to cherish like scattered crumbs of hope in a love-starved world. Today she travels back to the time, only a few weeks previously, but which already feels like an age, to when she and Tara first began to get really close. Sorcha had been nervous of Tara to begin with. Well, she still was in many ways, nervous of her temper at least, and the rapid changes of mood that sweep through her should someone look at her crossways or make a comment that riles her. She could be vicious, dangerous even, but from the first day she had arrived, Sorcha had also sensed something else in her. Picking her moments carefully, she had eventually managed to befriend her. Still, she had been surprised how easy and open Tara was the first time they had a real heart-to-heart, sitting on the bench in the drafty smokers' courtyard. Tara had been talking about the meds she was on, triple therapy, saying how much she hated it, and how she would often go for periods at a time without taking it at all. The staff were always livid with her for that. They told her over and over that messing with her medication was why she was getting so unwell so fast, and it was only going to get worse if she didn't get her act together, but Tara didn't seem to care. They tried every means to gain her compliance, working hard at pulling her emotional strings. But for every reason they gave her to acquiesce to the treatment regime, Tara had an instant and pitiful rebuttal. They mentioned her son, but he was not hers, she insisted, he belonged more rightly to the foster family – they would be so much better for him. They said she should stay well so that she could get married, but, she would retort, why would Darack really want to marry her, when he could surely choose from any number of women? They even tried to make her want to stay well for herself, but what was there left to care about she would ask, and truly when they looked at her, they had no reply.

Sorcha guessed that really Tara enjoyed this attention, the opportunity to lament her life, to prove that she was really not worth the medication they tried to ply her with. And that this depressing lose-lose argument was probably the closest Tara got to feeling properly cared for. So, one day, when Tara was repeating the list of woes that she had already recited to the nurse earlier on, Sorcha took advantage of her mood and risked the question she had been longing to ask, 'How did you get it, AIDS I mean, was it the drugs?' The question hung in the air just long enough for Sorcha to begin to think she had misjudged it. But then Tara matter-of-factly broke the impasse, 'No', she said calmly, 'I got it when I was working for Darack.' Sorcha frowned. She didn't understand, but was already wary of further showing her ignorance or pushing her luck with more personal questions. Tara could flare up at any moment and this special intimacy could be shattered for good. Tara noted Sorcha's incomprehension and sighed exaggeratedly, as if having to explain something painfully obvious to a small child, but clearly enjoying having Sorcha's rapt attention – her own thoroughly captivated audience. 'After Ronan was born I was really strapped for cash. I had been wanting to keep him then, so Darack said I could go and work with some of his girls for a bit to get some money together.'

'Work?' Sorcha interrupted, still not understanding.

'Work, *the game*, you know!' Tara said beginning to sound dangerously frustrated. Sorcha swallowed, hoping not to betray the shock and revulsion she felt that the guy who Tara had a baby with would send her out to work as a prostitute, and then Tara getting AIDS because of it. As if reading her thoughts Tara added, 'It paid more to begin with because I was young and new at it and I'd do it without a rubber.' She sighed, 'It was all a waste of time in the end, 'cos the social workers were always on top of me to take Ronan anyway, and then Darack said it would probably be better for Ronan to get fostered. After all, what kind of a life would I give him? I was pretty strung out by then too.' She paused for a moment, looking off into the middle distance, perhaps awaiting a particular response. But Sorcha had no idea what she could say in the interval after such shocking information so nonchalantly revealed, and decided it would be best to keep quiet. Tara shuffled on the bench and pulled a box of cigarettes from the tattered red bag which lay beside her: John Player Blue Kingsize, probably the harshest brand in the hospital shop, and definitely the cheapest. She lit a cigarette and inhaled deeply, and then, back in the present, she said, 'I have been pretty much clean now for eighteen months', and then, smiling proudly, 'and I get to see Ronan every week. He even recognises me now and calls me mammy.' She smiled more broadly still, betraying a softness and depth of love that was usually a million miles beneath the hard exterior she presented to the outside world. Sorcha was still reeling from the pieces of Tara's life she was putting together, but that deep, raw love was unmistakable and she felt her heart pull away from her and offer itself irrevocably to Tara.

Tara had talked a little about Darack before and since that day, telling how she had met him when she was fifteen and they had been going out off and on since then. He was much older than Tara, and Sorcha had not liked the sound of him to begin with, but the more she discovered the more incomprehensible it all became. Why would Tara stay with someone like that? There was Ronan of course, his son, but he had even wanted her to have an abortion and tried to push her into going over to England. Only the fact that Tara was still sixteen and didn't have a passport had saved Ronan from that fate – and brought him into this one. Sorcha thought that surely it was illegal for a man of that age – whatever it was, but at least twenty-seven from what Sorcha could gather when Tara had first been with him – to be having sex with a sixteen-year-old girl. And it was pretty obvious what was going on because Ronan had been born only five months after Tara's seventeenth birthday.[1] But Tara had just laughed bitterly in Sorcha's face when she had said that, and had not spoken to her for two days after. Sorcha had had to learn fast what she could and couldn't say.

But that day, sitting side by side on the rickety bench in the smoking yard, Sorcha had been utterly thrown off balance by the nonchalant way that

---

1. In Ireland the legal age of consent for sex is seventeen.

Tara could talk about experiences which were, for Sorcha, the most horrific things imaginable. It might have been Tara's lighted cigarette that made her think of it, especially with all these conflicting feelings churning around inside her, or it might have been that she wanted to change the subject back on to her own territory and something that they could share. It might have been that Sorcha wasn't allowed cigarettes in here, and would have only got Tara into trouble if she asked her for a smoke, but still, she needed something to relieve the tension inside her, and that would bring them back together. 'Look', she said, not even thinking clearly about what she was doing, but placing her arm alongside Tara's and pulling back the sleeve of her cotton pyjama shirt, so that their flesh was side by side, 'I've got the same as you.' She smiled indicating the light pink round scars which were dotted all the way up her arm, formed by the lighted cigarettes she pressed into her flesh, and comparing them with the intermittent and lighter sprinkling of them on Tara's skin. She had noticed them on Tara's upper breasts too, revealed below the lace of her nightdress. 'When did you do that?' she asked innocently. This time Tara frowned and did look offended. 'I didn't do that! I'm not a crazy!' She huffed indignantly but then, still moved by the tenderness she felt towards her son, and realising she was probably upsetting Sorcha, she quickly added, 'Sorry, I didn't mean it like that, it's just that I'm not like you, I don't do stuff to myself.' Sorcha looked at her uncomprehending, and Tara paused and took in a deep breath. 'Sometimes', she said, 'sometimes I can be a real bitch and I wind Darack up. He never means it, and he's always really sorry afterwards. I just push him too far sometimes.' Sorcha felt tears well into her eyes at the thought of someone hurting Tara that way, and instantly a barrier descended between them. 'You wouldn't understand!' Tara snapped. 'What would you know about men anyway?!' She looked Sorcha up and down, who, even in her pyjamas and fading robe, carried an unmistakably lesbian air about her. In fact, with her floppy, ear-length blond hair, her tall gangly frame and small gold-rimmed glasses framing inquisitive grey eyes she looked more like she belonged in a 1930s smoking room of an Oxbridge men's dorm that a female psychiatric ward. Perhaps that was why the nurses didn't seem to like her very much, as if her natural state was somehow a deliberate affront to their femininity. At the beginning some of the nurses had tried to persuade Sorcha to pluck her eyebrows and to, 'Do her hair up nicely', telling her it was important that she made an effort to look well, especially for the ward rounds. They had wanted to feminise her in their own carefully cultivated display of womanhood to convince the world she was really a nice normal girl who could get well and go back to school if only she would do as she was told. Sorcha had only felt mortified by their attention and more estranged from the world around her than ever. Finally they had left her alone.

Sorcha opened her mouth to say something, but Tara got there first. 'How old are you anyway?' she demanded, as if trying to deflect from having drawn attention to the obvious issue of Sorcha's sexuality, perhaps not wanting to admit, even to herself, that it was one of the things she liked Sorcha for. 'Seventeen', Sorcha answered by rote, and immediately realised that Tara had a baby, a drug habit, and God only knows what else by her age, and the chasm of their life experiences opened between them. Tara felt it too. 'You're way too young to be in a place like this, and especially talking to someone like me. Piss off back to your crazy's ward and your school books.' Her tone was hard, but there was a sadness in it too that seemed to come from a far-off place, rather like her love for Ronan: a place that was mostly inaccessible, even to Tara herself. She stood up and snatched her bag from the bench and strutted back inside, wobbling indignantly on her bedraggled pink mules.

A MUNDANE WEDNESDAY

It's quiet in there today. There don't seem to have been any visitors for anyone in this end of the hospital all morning, and there is a stillness, a deadness, in the air, despite the TV rattling away to itself down the corridor. Sorcha has been reading all morning. They are doing *Macbeth* for the Leaving Cert[2] and she's trying to keep up, though her concentration is not so good now because of the medication. She thinks she will stop taking it. She doesn't feel right with this fog between herself and her brain, even if it does damp out the worst of the feelings. She looks at the clock, she's done an hour and a half on *Macbeth*, so she decides she has earned a treat, and there is one treat that is always fail-safe despite her foggy concentration. Squatting down on the floor she opens the door of her beside locker which reveals her treasure trove of well-worn paperbacks. Without even looking she knows which one she will select, and exactly where it is. *Wuthering Heights*: her favourite book in the world, which she has read so many times she could recite from beginning to end without pausing for breath. The other books in the pile face outwards, staring resentfully at her for never being her chosen one. Kate O'Brien's *The Land of Spices* and *The Oscar Wilde Anthology* eye her accusingly for her constant privileging of an English writer over her queer Irish compatriots. She apologises to them in her heart, but still there really is no competition. She feels so safe when she is with Emily Brontë, in a world that she intimately knows her way around, and where everything is carefully orchestrated. It is

---

2. The Leaving Cert are the exams which students stay on in school from age sixteen to eighteen to complete and which lead them into higher education. The UK equivalent is A levels.

incomparable to anything else she feels, except of course, for Tara. And then she has an idea, she could share *Wuthering Heights* with Tara! They could read it together! They could share it. It could be a special place for them together. Without even closing the locker door she rushes barefoot up the corridor to Tara's ward. Tara is lying on her belly on top of her bed flicking through a crumpled women's magazine that she probably took from the day room. She turns as Sorcha approaches and smiles at her. Her hair is pulled back in a ponytail high on her head and she has her knees folded back with her ankles crossed behind her, appearing that strange mix of very old and, at the same time, very young that she always seems to embody.

'I have an idea!' Sorcha announces waving the copy of *Wuthering Heights* in the air between them, 'Let's read together! Let's do *Wuthering Heights*!' She is so caught up in her own enthusiasm that she fails to register the procession of feelings that march across Tara's face. At first curiosity, then uncertainty, then as she looks at the book in Sorcha's hand, shame, and finally anger. She jumps backwards on the bed, throwing the magazine to the floor and dives under the sheet pulling it tightly around her, glaring at Sorcha from the cocoon of her bed. 'Fuck off!' she hisses. 'Take your pissy book and fuck off!'

Sorcha opens her mouth to speak but she is so floored by Tara's response, so devastated by her horrible rejection of this precious offering, that she does not know what to do or say. She looks at Tara who continues to glare at her, waiting, hoping that something will change. Finally she flops down in the chair beside Tara's bed, fighting back tears and feeling as if she has been kicked in the heart. Without thinking she leans forward and picks up the magazine Tara has thrown on the floor, refolds it, and places beside Tara on the bed. Tara looks from the magazine to Sorcha scowling, trying to think of something nasty to say. She wants to hurt Sorcha for showing her up; to make her feel as shitty as she does right now. But then she looks at Sorcha's big hurt eyes, her gentle face, contorted with pain and confusion and she cannot hurt her any more. 'I can't read', she offers through gritted teeth. 'I'm not like you.' Sorcha's pain and confusion melts away. 'Oh', she mumbles, and then as guilt and compassion and relief swirl around inside her she tries to think of something else to add. 'Would you like me to teach you? – to read, I mean', she eventually suggests.

And so began their reading lessons together. Sorcha has to tell and retell the whole story again and again before Tara will even try and look at the words on the page, but Sorcha is deliriously happy to do so. She embellishes and performs, she revels in each nuance of the story and the complexities of the characters. She tells Tara that she is Cathy and Tara loves the role. She finds her flounciest nightwear for the days when they are to read and strikes dramatic poses, instantly becoming the words she does not believe herself capable of understanding. Darack hangs in the air between them as the unsaid Heathcliff, but that is not the way it is in Sorcha's heart.

On many occasions they don't read at all. Tara's attention span is short and she gets quickly frustrated and ashamed at her own slowness in learning, and Sorcha can never placate her however earnest or creative her reassurances. Tara often diverts Sorcha with questions, personal questions, and even though Sorcha is partly aware that this is a ploy to detract from her reading skills, she can't help but feel delighted that Tara is taking such an intense interest in her.

One day Sorcha senses a slight tension in the air between them when they meet. Tara obviously has something on her mind, and as soon as they are settled in their regular spot in the day room she looks straight at Sorcha and says 'What's wrong with you?' Sorcha is taken aback. Her mind races; surely she has not done anything in the few minutes since she collected Tara from her ward that would make her angry? She panics, she must have done something, perhaps she can't remember. Maybe the pills have permanently messed up her head. She looks at Tara with a stricken expression, feeling the day falling apart and without her even knowing why. 'I mean why are you in here?' Tara asks again, explaining this time. 'Like you're really smart and everything, and you don't seem like a crazy.'

Sorcha feels relief and shame crash through her all at once and an avalanche of tears roll up behind her eyes. 'I don't know', she falters. 'There's something wrong with me, I don't feel right, but I don't know what it is.' She begins to cry. 'I don't know what's wrong with me but I feel worse and worse all the time.'

'Is it 'cos of what you do to yourself?' Tara asks, trying to ignore Sorcha's grief for long enough to get a satisfactory answer out of her.

'It's 'cos of ME!' Sorcha sobs angrily. And then, for the first and only time in the short interlude in which they will know each other, she gets up and walks away from Tara.

SATURDAY AFTERNOON

It's hard to tell the days apart in here, and the only way Sorcha knows for sure it's a weekend is that there are no social workers, support workers, case managers, or anyone else visiting any of the people on the ward. They are all off now, for two whole days of normality and regular life before they return to the endless merry-go-round of crazies, psychos and junkies on Monday. Sorcha is particularly restless today. It would be so nice to get outside, to be able to walk for an hour or two in the open air, rather than pace the corridors or stay trapped in the confines of the smoke-filled courtyard. She can't concentrate on her books today either, though she is still determined to sit her Leaving Cert this year and to get enough points to go to college. She wants to study English and Philosophy. She wants to write.

The nurses seem in good form today, so she decides to take a walk over to Tara's ward and see if she is back from visiting with Ronan in the family room. It's nice that he doesn't have to see his mammy in bed in the ward. Tara gets to put on a tracksuit for his visits and to spend a couple of hours in the office that has been converted to a family room. It's nice they have done that, with toys and cushions scattered around to make it a bit more normal. Though 'nice' and 'normal' are both relative concepts.

Sorcha turns into Tara's corridor and then freezes. Darack is there beside the bed. Rage and hate and jealousy pound through her, freezing her to the spot. Tara is propped up on pillows, a low-cut tight silky black nightdress visible to where her waist disappears under the sheet. Darack leans over her and takes her chin in his hand and tilts her head up towards him. Then he runs his hand down the front of her body, over her breast and then under the sheet. He squeezes between her legs, and says something that Sorcha cannot hear. Tara looks at him with a pasted-on submissive adoration that makes Sorcha feel sick. Then Tara sees Sorcha in the doorway behind Darack and her expression changes. Darack instantly notices the deflection of Tara's attention and spins around. He is a big man, still sturdy despite his years of heroin. His face is lined and set in a permanently nasty scowl. He registers Sorcha and looks her up and down with disgust, 'What are you looking at, dyke?' He spits the word with a venom so acrid it that could burn through rock. 'Fuck off back to your lesbi-friends.' He pauses and then a nasty sneer arrives on his face. 'Unless of course you've come for a bit of this!' He gestures at his crotch, 'Is that what you want? You want some of this to sort you out? You fucking queer!' He moves a step towards her as if to carry out his threat. Sorcha is shaking with fear but still manages to hold her ground. She looks over at Tara in solidarity, in support, to show her that she is strong enough to take her away from this. But Tara is looking down at her hands placed neatly on the white sheet that covers the lower half of her body. She acts as if she cannot see her. Sorcha feels something plummet inside her. She swallows and then turns forlornly away. Crushed, she begins to walk very slowly back in the direction she came. She is only a few steps of the way when she is confronted by an angry nurse. 'What's all the shouting about? Ah you, I might have guessed! What are you doing up here? Trouble again', she accuses, and then answers her own question. Taking Sorcha by the arm she leads quickly her away. 'Can you not just keep out of trouble for once? You're worse than a child! Back to your bed. If I catch you up here again today it'll be obs for you.'

When the shift changes and the evening staff are on Sorcha wanders up to the TV room and hopes that Tara will make an appearance. Fortunately, she doesn't have long to wait long before her wish is granted. Tara flounces in on a cloud of perfume, sniffing at her wrists flamboyantly and announcing to the room that it's Chanel that her fiancé brought in for her. Sorcha's jaw tightens, she hates it when Tara calls that man her fiancé: it makes her sick the thought of her marrying him. Tara flops down in a vacant chair beside Sorcha and Sorcha is relieved and grateful that Tara is not ignoring her after what she did today. But even so she still can't let it go. 'I don't know why you put up with him', she whined. 'He's horrible, he treats you like shit!' The words are out and she can't unsay them and she knows instantly from the cloud that descends on Tara's face that it was the wrong time to bring up Darack. 'What would you know?' Tara spits at her. 'You're just a stupid little dyke full of your fucking school book stories and your fucking stupid exams.' She jumps up out of the chair, the octaves rising in her voice, 'What would you know? Dyke! I'm a junkie, and I sell myself, and I've got the virus, and I'm lucky to have someone like Darack at all. And he's the father of my kid! Get it? Oh no! I forgot: your type don't do things like kids, unless you're molesting them! You should learn to fuck off and mind your own business! Keep out of things that you don't understand and are nothing to do with you!' Everyone in the room is staring them, Sorcha's skin is burning with shame, but she is rooted to her chair. It seems to go on forever, Tara screaming into her face, leaning over her, showing her with angry spittle. All the while Sorcha can't stop thinking about the way Darack touched her and how sick it made her feel, and her head is pounding and pounding with shame and regret and how stupid she is and she hates herself more than ever and it feels like she is going to die from it.

Finally she is alone and it is quiet aside from the buzzing in her head. She is in the toilet on the corridor by her ward. She pushes her head against the cool tile wall. The pressure in her head is immense, she needs to get it out: those words, that memory, the feelings, the bile and the hatred that seem to have burnt their way into her skull. With her hands level to her chin she pushes her forehead harder against the tiles and then draws back. She brings her head forward, hard. There is cold and pain and relief. It feels good. She does it again. At last the badness is coming out.

Sorcha wakes on an unfamiliar bed. There are voices above her. 'She was building up to it all day, misbehaving and causing trouble everywhere: on the HIV ward, the TV room, and when that didn't create enough attention she locks herself in the toilet and knocks herself unconscious!' Another voice sighs, 'That's the trouble with these personality disorders, there's not a lot you can do with them, they just act out all over the place, manipulating, attention-seeking, its constant with them. We're fighting a losing battle really.' The voice lets out another long sigh and then, 'Make a report in her notes anyway and see if her consultant will have another look at her in the week. He might have something new he wants to try.'

NEW YEAR'S EVE

It is nearly midnight on New Year's Eve 1999: the end of one millennium and the beginning of another. Yet in here it is much the same as any other night. The patients have all ingested their meds, served up like a colourful array of deserts from a macabre sweets trolley, and have fallen into the pharmaceutically induced slumber that passes for rest. Sorcha takes out a red pen and her favourite book and writes quickly inside the well-worn front cover and then slips it into the pocket of her burgundy corduroy robe and tightens the belt around her waist. She pulls on her socks and then pushes her feet into her moccasins and slips quietly up the corridor to the next ward. Most of the staff here tonight are agency nurses, working for the triple-time that eve of the new millennium pays, and who don't really know enough about any of the patients here to be certain who is a troublemaker and who they can trust. Agency staff always provide Sorcha with the opportunity to be liked for just a little while before her diagnosis becomes known and she is once again consigned to being borderline personality disorder incarnate. She pads softly towards the HIV ward. Tara's bed is right on the corner by the door and she has the curtain pulled round the inward-facing sides so that it is easy for Sorcha to slip in unnoticed. As Sorcha approaches her heart sinks. Tara's eyes are closed. Did she change her mind and swallow her meds after all? Did she abandon their plan as if it was nothing to her? Despite her disappointment and hurt, Sorcha's heart still swells hopelessly with love when she looks at Tara lying there. She looks so sweet and quiet and angelic without the mask of her waking guard. In this light she is young and vulnerable, despite her twenty-three years and the ravages that heroin, HIV and the hard edges of life have inflicted on her. Sorcha squats down at the head of her bed and gently slips her treasured copy of *Wuthering Heights* under Tara's pillow, an offering from her consistent and unshakable love, even if it is forever unrequited and their plan abandoned.

Tara's eyes immediately bat open and she grins a wide-awake smile. 'Fooled you!' she mouths mischievously, and then silently turns back the sheets and slides out of bed. She is swathed tightly in a floor-length, blood-red nightdress with a long slit at the side front which reaches almost to the top of her right thigh. The neckline plunges low and is trimmed with lace.

She pulls a gown of matching fabric from the nightstand and wraps it around her as if it would afford some warmth or protection from the cold night air. Her toenails are painted a matching red and each foot sports three gold toe-rings. She pushes her feet into new fluffy pink mules and stands up smiling. 'I got this specially', she whispers seductively. 'Do you like it?' Sorcha nods, speechless. She wants to reach out and touch her but, as always, is turned to useless, lumpen sludge in Tara's presence. Tara smiles revelling in the impact she can still create and the power it affords her. She flicks her hair back over her shoulder. 'Come on,' she hisses, 'Let's get out of here!'

They hurry up the corridor to the day room and Tara tries the door. It's open. She grins and they slip inside. Sorcha follows, a mix of admiration and fear curdling in her belly. They go over to the door that leads to the small smoking courtyard and it too is miraculously unlocked. Tara smiles again; her pride at being able to bring their plan to fruition is palpable. She had told Sorcha she had given the night security man a blow job and he was now obliged to do anything that she demanded. Sorcha desperately hopes this isn't true, that it is just another of Tara's stories. She prays that really it was one of lads from the flats Tara had grown up in who was working as security here and happy to do a local girl a favour on New Year's Eve. She didn't want to think of Tara on her knees sucking on some hairy, smelly oaf for the two of them. She knew what Tara did for drugs, and cash and to appease that bastard of a boyfriend of hers, but she desperately didn't want her to have done it for them, for tonight. She knew she couldn't ask her either, she'd only get an endless cruel teasing of graphic details to shock and wound her for her questions, or a rabid outburst of anger harnessed in a violent attack or in days of silent sulking and rejection, none of which Sorcha could bear.

'Come on!' Tara's voice hisses from the courtyard. 'It's nearly midnight!' Sorcha steps outside into the cold night air. The sky is patchy with clouds and stars and Tara is looking upwards, her hair falling gently down her back. She looks so much younger, so much softer, with it loose around her, rather than scraped tightly back and fastened into her regular ponytail, high on the back of her head. She turns towards Sorcha, and smiles, her face open, no teasing or anger this time. 'Hold me', she whispers. Sorcha steps towards her and encases her with her own body. Tara feels so small and fragile, so precious, she leans forward and buries her face in her hair. It is sleek and soft, and smells of floral shampoo. She could hold Tara forever – if only she would let her. Tara whispers something that Sorcha does not quite hear. Still with her own body wrapped tightly around Tara's she leans her head back to look at her face. Tara stares into Sorcha's eyes, her gaze is intense and serious but alight with some kind of magic. 'Kiss me', she said simply. Sorcha leans forward, her heart exploding, her body light and fizzing. She brings her lips to Tara's. It is midnight.

MANIC MONDAY

Sorcha had kept away from Tara on Sunday evening. Darack had been in during the afternoon and the last few times he has visited Tara had been very strange afterwards. Dozing, incoherent, acting almost like Sorcha's brain had felt when she had been on the really intense medication. At the back of her mind Sorcha had a suspicion about what was happening but she dare not voice it, even to herself. After all, what did she know about it, and what could she do? Saying anything would only mean risking losing Tara and she couldn't bear that, not now. Tara had never mentioned what happened between them on New Year's Eve, but it lay quietly within their friendship like a deep-sea pearl waiting for the chance to be rediscovered.

It was about three o'clock in the morning when Tara was found. The commotion was immense. It woke everyone as far back as the men's wing, and brought an army of pyjama-clad spectres to the women's HIV ward, moving along the corridors in formation to the shuffle-rhythm of their night-time medication. Sorcha had pushed her way to the front but she need not really look; her heart already told her what her eyes were about to witness.

The curtain was half pulled around Tara's bed, the sheet was back and her body exposed, gaunt an almost blue-white. Her eyes were closed and the only movements in her limbs came as her body was hooked up to a range of dumpy machines that stared outwards, each bearing a useless collection of electronic beeps and squiggles. One of the nurses lifted Tara's arm for inspection and then shook her head knowingly. There were fresh pricks into the veins in the front of her elbow. Another nurse returned from the ward bathroom brandishing a syringe and a tiny plastic package. 'This was taped on the inside of the cistern', she said and now it was obvious to everyone what had happened.

The machines relentlessly pumped energy through Tara's body. They shook her limbs so hard that Sorcha really believed it could not fail to wake her from her coma, or to even bring her back from the dead.

But it was too late.

Tara was gone.

Sorcha fell to her knees and began to wail, keening an uncontrollable lament as her heart exploded into pieces.

She scratched at the floor, she beat her fists into the ground. 'Cathy is not supposed to go first!' she screamed. 'It doesn't happen like that!' Tears and snot and spit were streaming from her in a rabid pool of grief. Grief and guilt: if she had said something, anything, Tara might still be alive. She was dead because of her, and her weakness and stupidity. She beat at the floor, at her legs, her face, at anything around her, as if she could fight her way out of this reality and back into the one where everything was properly ordered and happened only as it was destined. She needed to go back to before all this happened so that she could fix it and make it allright. She was freefalling. She didn't even know where she was anymore except that she was lost in a nightmare tornado that she had to fight for her life to get out of. She was in such a tempest that she could no longer distinguish between the knees pressing into her back and her own fists raining down on her.

There were only the straggling remains of the army of mute witnesses as the second tragic spectacle of the night unfolded and Sorcha's arms were pinned up behind her, her face pressed to the floor. Her pyjama pants were pulled roughly down and a vile of sedative jammed into the exposed soft flesh of her buttocks.

Eventually there was silence all around.

And then, not many hours later, the morning medication round began, just like any other regular Monday.

***

Martina sat for a moment on the grey metal bench which was bolted to the floor of the corridor halfway back to the main hospital and opened the meagre plastic bag of belongings. Inside were three sets of nightclothes, the fabric so thin they folded down to practically nothing. The scent of hospital laundry detergent which rose from them seemed more substantial than the scraps of lace and fabric that Tara had encased her vulnerable flesh within. There were some pieces of cheap gold jewellery, hoop earrings and a bracelet made to look something akin to an old-fashioned toilet chain. The locket which contained the picture of Ronan will go with her to her grave, after the post-mortem, along with the everyday regalia of chains and rings she bedecked herself in. After all who was there to take them? Her mother would pawn then as soon as keep them, and if either of her brothers kept them for more than half an hour before exchanging them for a fix then it would be a miracle. Perhaps her youngest sister would like something though. Out of the five of them she seemed to be the one who might actually make it into adulthood and some kind of life for herself without falling prey to the drugs, crime and destruction that consumed the rest of them – and their whole generation.

Martina put her hand in the bag to see if there was anything else that she could discretely slip to Una that might make a more worthy keepsake of her older sister. To her surprise her fingers touched the edges of a small, thick paperback book. She pulled it out of the bag and stared in surprise: a Wordsworth Classic edition of *Wuthering Heights*. What on earth would Tara be doing with that? She could barely read and write enough to fill out Ronan's birth details, and certainly not to understand the foster care forms that Martina had laboriously explained to her. She turned the book over in her hands. It was well used, the spine creased and the front cover battered with curling edges. Many of the pages were loose, precariously hanging on to the cheaply bound spine, with refolded corners singling out specially marked sections. There was no way Tara could have read this, so why was it in her bag of belongings? Had she stolen it from another patient in some petty vengeance for one of the battles of will in which she compulsively pitted herself against her peers? Maybe she had even taken it from a nurse, perhaps the ward sister who had the all-too-frequent task of reprimanding Tara for the skimpiness of her attire and insisting she cover herself more appropriately, especially in the mixed areas. For a moment she thought about turning back up the corridor to the ward and returning the book to the nurses' station and its rightful owner, but then she realised that it was most likely a nurse had packed Tara's possessions and would have set aside anything that did not properly belong to her. Even more confused, Martina turned the book over again in her hands and then looked inside the front cover. Written in small neat letters of red biro was inscribed, *To my own Cathy, New Years Eve, 1999, S x*. It made even less sense now. Martina sighed and looked at her watch, and her focus suddenly shifted. She had to be at the Murtagh's in fifteen minutes in order to drop off Tara's things, go through the necessary condolences and then be back in the office to meet with the probation officer at twelve o'clock. She stood up and dropped the book back into the bag: it was someone else's dilemma now. She strode up the corridor, her intent focused on the day ahead of her rather than all that had passed. As she stepped outside she noticed that the drizzle had finally stopped, and the clouds were thinning, revealing the hint of a promise of sunshine to come and lightening her mood at its prospect.

Behind her, being wheeled along the endless tiled highway towards the newly empty bed on the HIV ward, a middle-aged woman clutches a small bag of belongings anxiously on her lap, taking the journey to the end of her life.

On the psych ward a seventeen-year-old girl lies on a narrow bed in a small isolation room. She is dressed only in a green hospital gown and she stares vacantly at the ceiling. She has a black eye and cuts and grazes where she broke her glasses into her face; her body is covered in bruises.

In a neat, pale blue bedroom in a suburban estate a small boy sits on his bed, each fist clenched around a plastic superhero doll. He wants to be at school today, to play football with his friends and to go and see his mammy at the weekend just like normal. He doesn't want to be sat here, with serious-faced adults whispering things he doesn't understand in the rooms below him. He doesn't know what is going on, but he knows that it is bad, and that it has somehow got to do with him. He grits his teeth and then in a rage bashes the plastic figures headlong into each other, again and again. He doesn't care anymore about Spiderman and Daredevil who he has cherished in his heart like brothers up until now. He drives them together, more and more. He doesn't even care that his knuckles clash painfully as he does so. In fact, as he repeats it, he almost likes the feeling. The crack of bones and shock of the pain as his joints slam together seem like a relief, as if it can somehow cool the inferno of incomprehensible feelings which are threatening to boil him alive from the inside out. The pain is like a visit from a strange new friend with a secret promise to make it better.

HELP AND RESOURCES

Full contact details can be found in Appendix Three: Resources.

UK
* Bristol Crisis Service for Women: Telephone, text and email support for women and girls who self-injure and also wide range of self-injury resources and publications
* ChildLine: Confidential telephone and email support for children and young people
* 42nd Street: Free and confidential support for young people in the Manchester area
* The Hideout: Online support for children and young people affected by domestic violence and run by Women's Aid
* Mind: For Better Mental Health: Voluntary organisation which provides information and also campaigns around mental health issues
* NA (Narcotics Anonymous): 12-step recovery group for people struggling with drug use
* Scottish Women's Aid: Scotland branch of Women's Aid
* Shakti Women's Aid: Support for Black and Minority Ethic women who are experiencing domestic violence
* Women's Aid: Support and campaigning organisation for women who are experiencing domestic violence

Republic of Ireland
* BeLonG To: Dublin-based youth project for LGBT young people
* ChildLine: Confidential telephone and email support for children and young people
* Crisis Pregnancy Agency: Irish government agency that sponsors information and links to resources for women and girls with unplanned pregnancies
* Irish Family Planning Association: Information, support and campaigning around all aspects of sexual and reproductive well-being
* NA (Narcotics Anonymous): 12-step recovery group for people struggling with drug use
* Open *Heart* House: Dublin-based, member-led organisation for people living with HIV and AIDS

- Pieta House: Free one-to-one therapy for people who hurt themselves
- Positive Options: Funded by the Crisis Pregnancy Agency (see above); provides free information about services relating to unplanned pregnancies
- Ruhama: Supporting women affected by prostitution
- Women's Aid: Support and campaigning organisation for women who are experiencing domestic violence

Northern Ireland
- Women's Aid Federation Northern Ireland: Support and campaigning for women who are experiencing domestic violence
- Zest: Free one-to-one therapy for people who hurt themselves

REFERENCES

Brontë, E (1847/1992) *Wuthering Heights.* Hertfordshire: Wordsworth Classics (with introduction and notes by JS Whitley).

Holland, M (ed) (2000) *The Oscar Wilde Anthology.* London: HarperCollins.

O'Brien, K (1941/1982) *The Land of Spices.* Dublin: Arlen House (with preface by Lorna Reynolds).

A THOUSAND EPILOGUES

Sorcha gets up from her desk, it's 2 A.M. and starting to get very cold. She is still in her pyjamas from when she got up around fourteen hours ago and she has consumed nothing but cigarettes and two cafetiers of rough Arabic coffee since then. She opens her wardrobe and pulls out the first item from the jumbled and ever-rising pile in the bottom and slips it on. It is a man's dress coat, something she picked up in one of the local charity shops on her way home from her job. She looks at her watch. She's still wide awake and buzzing, and there's not much point in going to bed at all now as she'll have to be up in a few hours anyway to make it to her morning shift. Most of the time she is happy enough to go to work, but today she would really rather stay put in front of her ancient, second-hand pc and get the rest of this play out of her head and onto the page. Her job, as they call it, is easy, undemanding. She is a part-time administrator in a small mental-health charity office. Technically, she thinks, she is the charity. Since she was finally discharged from the hospital for the last time she has been assigned the status of being permanently disabled by virtue of her diagnosis and being incurably mentally ill. So now she works on a Community Employment Scheme for twenty hours a week at the Mind-U: Mental Health Awareness and Support office, gets her rent paid, and her medication – which she flushes down the toilet – for free. It suits her well enough. She has been doing an Open University degree in English Literature, and it also gives her time to write. And better still, if she arrives early or stays on late or over lunchtime, she can print out for free the chapters and samples of her writing that she has been sending to different publishers and agents for the last six months.

She has written mountains in the last four years. There is a complete novel and two others already more than half finished, two dozen short stories, a complete play and the one that she is now working on. And that is only a fraction of the ideas that she has had, ideas that arrive like visitations and swirl around in her mind. She lets them roam free and take life through her and transform themselves into stories and plays. Mostly she drafts them out in poem form, it feels the best way to capture the shape and texture of each piece and preserve it until she can return and flesh it out. Which she does with the all devotion of a new lover: caressing each word and sentence into its perfect form and fullness. Her physical world is small, but her imagination spans universes and keeps her where she needs to be. It seems that now she has found her gift and can use it, and now that the world has a label for her, it doesn't matter so much that she is shy and sensitive, that she feels things way too deeply for normal living, and that she doesn't seem to quite belong anywhere except amidst the pages that she fills with her own imaginings.

At work they seem to have finally got over having to tiptoe around her, as if her mental health was so precarious that even the slightest hint of a reference to any kind of mental illness would set her off and must, therefore, be avoided at all costs – quite a challenge in a mental health charity! But it is still surprising to her, the amount of creative euphemisms they managed to come up with during her first months there. Sorcha knows they mean well and appreciates their efforts at sensitivity, even if at the end of the day it still has the same effect as outright prejudice, ultimately rendering her an outsider to their normal world. But she is so used to being on the periphery that she has come to wear it well.

Nonetheless, some of the things she has heard in there do make her wary. Like the time when everyone was talking about the legislation that was being proposed in the UK which would make it possible to arrest and detain a person with a mental health diagnosis just in case they go mad and do something dangerous. It sounded like mental health internment to her and, if she was feeling Republican, she might have seen it as a typical extension of the English imperialist mentality in a post-colonial world. 'Why not just be honest about it', she had thought to herself, 'and bring back concentration camps?!' She had shuddered then, suddenly she could feel how easy it was to get swept down that road, and then she felt a story coming on.

It also made her extra-cautious about her own diagnosis. Though BPD is usually seen as relatively harmless – more annoying than dangerous – she knew that if she ever got herself labelled as non-compliant then things could get more complicated. She eventually learnt how to manage her interactions with her psychiatrist and the array of mental health workers who skimmed the surface of her life so as to keep herself on the periphery of the system. She also learnt how to hide, and in her own way to manage the strange darkness that still sometimes overtakes her, which pushes her beyond the edges of herself, and past what she can cope with. The place from where she has to fight her way back and where often only pain makes her sure she is really alive and who she knows herself to be. It happens less now anyway. Now she is free and safe, and now that she is relentlessly writing, her mind seems so much more at peace.

She gets up to make more coffee and puts two slices of wholemeal bread in the toaster and rummages in the fridge for something to put on it. She is suddenly hungry, and realises she will need something solid to keep her going if she has the whole day ahead of her. She takes out a jar of homemade apricot jam that she picked up when the school beside the Mind-U office had a bake and cake sale for them a week previously. She had felt quite self-conscious going along, as if she was on display as the tragic specimen that all their baking would redeem. Though she knew that in reality none of them would have actually known about her diagnosis, that she was just another member of staff to them. Anyway, she had told herself, people were probably much more afraid of a dyke than a nutter being in a girls' school cake and bake sale, in case she molested, or worse still, converted, any of them. She had not wanted to go at all, but it had been on a Thursday when she worked a full day, and so she couldn't really find an excuse for not joining her colleagues when they filed over to their scholastic neighbours.

She finds a jar of peanut butter and spreads it thickly on the toast, adding a layer of the apricot jam and then slicing a ripe banana on top. She brings the plate and cafetière back to her desk, already munching on her toast.

By the time she gets into work at 8:30 she is already tired, and she's on until two today. She switches on the kettle to make more coffee even though her nerves are already on edge from the pints of it she has consumed through the night. There is a packet of fig rolls on the counter and she chews on a couple while she brews the coffee.

The postman has been by the time she is back at her desk, and she sorts through the small array of envelopes. So little is done by post these days, yet she much prefers it to email, the simultaneous physicality and distance of letters add a grace to them that is lost in electronic technology. Sorcha knows that really it is the period novels which she continues to obsessively read that make her hanker after the unworldly romance of letter-writing. She drops the named letters onto appropriate desks, and then takes the ones addressed to Mind-U to her own desk. There are two for the charity – one is an electricity bill and the other is in a plain slightly battered white envelope. It has a printed address label which has been stuck over a hand-written address, clearly someone doing a bit of recycling. The top left of the envelope has been franked with what must be an organisation's stamp, but it has smudged and the only word that is legible is 'Health'. Unusually, at the bottom of the pile there is also a letter addressed to Sorcha personally at the Mind-U office. It is in a new pale blue envelope which is strewn with what looks like laboriously constructed handwriting and containing one or two spelling errors. She has no idea who it could be from and it makes her a little anxious. She decides to leave it until last.

She files the bill. They have a direct debit so she has to do no more than check the readings every now and then and make sure the figures are correct. Then she opens the white envelope. She reads through the letter quickly and laughs out loud to herself. Then she catches herself, glad that no one else is in yet. She is so used to being on her own now that she sometimes forgets to readjust her instincts for the shared office space. She is not only glad that no one is here to witness her laughter, but also that she does not have to suddenly concoct an explanation for her outburst to reassure them that she is not losing her mind. And knowing that the harder she tries to appear normal and reasonable the more cracked she would really seem. She could not have told them what she was really thinking. The letter is from a woman called Katie Smyth who is writing on behalf of a new grass-roots collective calling themselves The Lesbian and Bisexual Women's Health Network. They are starting up a peer-support group for lesbian and bisexual women who harm themselves and they want to know if Mind-U will support them by including them in their listings. At first Sorcha had laughed just from imagining how her boss would have reacted in the early days to Sorcha handling something with contained two such direct descriptions of who she was and what she did. But then, as she rereads the letter, she realises that she also laughed for another reason. She laughed because she identified with it. Those words which boldly set out the group and its purpose laid a claim to something in her. It felt right, intended for her, and for the first time in her life she felt she was offered something that finally made sense. She put the LBWHN number in her phone and promised herself that she would call them later on, in private, from home.

Feeling more poised and optimistic she turns to the mystery letter addressed to her in person. Taking a deep breath she opens the envelope. There are four pages of the same handwriting that she does not recognise. She looks at the signature at the end, and the address in the top right corner of the first page.

It takes a moment for it to make sense.

It is signed by someone called Darack, Darack Bulger, who was writing to her from Mountjoy Prison.

She folds the letter and puts it back in the envelope, a tidal wave of emotions crashing through her. 'I can't read that here', is her first thought, quickly followed by an overwhelming sense that nor could she take it home with her either. She does not want to bring that into her own space, unaware of what it contained, but very unlikely that it would be anything that she would want polluting her own private world. She takes it out of the envelope again and looks at the clock. It's not quite nine yet, and it will probably be another half an hour before anyone else gets in. She unfolds the letter and takes a deep breath begins and to read.

Dear Sorcha,

I know I am probably the last person you expect a letter from. Or who you would want a letter from. But please read this and I will tell you why I am writing to you. I am in Mountjoy, doing ten years for a whole rake of things that finally caught up with me. I won't write them down here. I am not proud of what I did and who I was and I think you know about some of them anyway. In the last four years I have been in NA (Narcotics Anonymous) and I have been clean now for the last thirty-two months. NA is all about changing and learning to live differently. There are twelve steps in NA that we work through to help us change and we have a sponsor to help us. A sponsor is a person that has already done the steps and who then helps the next person. I have a sponsor from the outside who comes into Mountjoy to run meetings and who is helping me work through the steps. I have come up to step nine which is where we make amends to people we have hurt. Obviously one of the people who I hurt the most is Tara, but she is dead, so that is why I am writing to you.

It's funny after all this time, but I still know your name from Ronan, from when you and Tara were in hospital. After his visits he used to tell me that mammy's new friend Sorcha had been teaching her to read. When he visited Tara would spend time writing out all the names she knew and getting Ronan to do the same. So he always used to talk about Sorcha O'Brien, saying each letter of your name one by one so that he could show off that he knew how to write it. It used to drive me crazy at the time. But now I know there was a reason for it. My sponsor says there are no accidents, it is God doing His work. So I knew your name and my sponsor was able to find where you work.

I am writing to you because I want to make amends in the best way I can and especially because I cannot make amends to Tara. I was horrible to you at the time and I am truly sorry for that and if there is anything I can do I would really like to. You were good to Tara and I know she really liked you. I know you meant a lot to her and helped her like no one else ever did. I didn't care about her then but I wanted to keep her away from you. She was always happy in herself after she had hung out with you. That made me angry then, especially because you are gay. But now I know how good you were for her and I am sorry I was so bad to you. I think you treated Tara better than anyone else in her whole life and I am glad you were friends. I know I did so much wrong back then that a letter cannot really change it, but I still wanted to write to you to say that I am sorry and that I know you are a good person and that you were good to Tara.

I pray for God's forgiveness everyday and that I can do something better with the rest of my life. When I get out I want to start trying to be a father to Ronan and to try and make it up to him. I hope it's not too late. He is nearly sixteen now and he can get pretty wild at times and it's hard for him to stay in one place. I think he hates me and I am afraid he will turn out just like me. But I will do anything to give him the life that he and Tara really deserved and I pray for God's grace and direction for him. I will pray for you too. If there is any way I can ever make amends or help you I would be happy and thankful to do it.

God Bless You,

Darack Bulger

Sorcha just manages to put the letter down and make a mad dash to the toilet before she is violently sick, her stomach wrenching and heaving in turbulent spasms. She is so intensely sick and for so long she is almost afraid she might bring up her intestines as there must surely be nothing else left insider her. She is still on her knees, shaking in front of the toilet wondering if she will ever be able to get up when she hears the front door open and footsteps in the office. 'Hello?' her boss's voice calls out from above the footsteps, 'Sorcha, is that you?' Sorcha flushes the toilet as if in answer and leaning on the handbasin she pulls herself to her feet. In the mirror she sees that she has gone completely white, even her lips have lost their colour. She takes off her glasses and splashes cold water on her face, hoping to pinken her complexion and muster some semblance of normality. She looks at her reflection blurred in the mirror and wonders how she is going to make it until two p.m., but she will, she tells herself, she will.

***

Martina jumps into her new, silver Mitsubishi SUV and throws the bundle of paper bags onto the back seat. They land in a messy pile and she tuts at the disorder but decides to leave them be for the moment as she'll have to move them again anyway when she gets to the school and she's already running late. It took much longer than she had expected to pick up enough treats to satisfy the requirements of a birthday party of a dozen nine-year-old girls and a handful of five-year-old boys. She smiles to herself. The nine years since her eldest was born have flown by, and in a direction she would never have imagined. She remembered how worried she had been when she had first found out she was pregnant, about how they would manage, her with just a social worker's salary, and realistically only part-time after the birth, and Mark still on his IT internship. They had not known then, that just as their child was gestating so too was a whole commercial relationship that was going to bring Mark into a very lucrative partnership and change their quality of life forever. She thinks back to their hasty wedding, her bump barely camouflaged under her carefully chosen dress, and unmistakably visible on the honeymoon photos from their week in Morocco. She drives up the hill into Dun Laogharie and looks out over the sea. She never had imagined a life quite as charmed as this, and nor has she forgotten how charmed it is. Now the kids are both in school she has gone back to college and is doing a Master's in Applied Social Research. She can't quite bring herself back to social work, but she still needs to do something that feels like it has a meaning or purpose in the world.

She turns up onto the road that will bring her to the school, and before long she arrives at the gates. The crowds of children are thinning now and it makes it easier to find a parking space among the glistening array of SUVs, Mercs and BMWs. She can see her two long before she is close to them, and she cherishes them from afar, relishing an opportunity to see them fully immersed in their own world, totally unaware of her presence. They are animated, laughing and smiling with an ease that makes her heart glow. They are loved and safe and thriving. She has got out of the SUV and is walking towards them before they spot her and come bounding over. Her daughter and her son: Tara and Jake. Tara hugs her instantly and Martina wraps her arms around her and plants a millionth happy birthday kiss on top of her head. She has light brown hair and freckles across her nose and blue eyes that sparkle with light.

The instant Martina knew for sure she was carrying a girl, she knew that she would be called Tara. Mark had been happy to indulge her, relieved that at least there was something in his power that he could do to make her feel inexplicably secure and happy in the midst of their suddenly uncertain future. And she had never doubted the choice or, rather, that it was chosen for her: a strange memorial to someone who she barely knew and whose life was lost among so many others. But here, this time in a life where she finally had the chance to make a real difference. She hugs both of her children close to her. If they only ever have half of the love and gifts that she dreams of for them their lives will be richer than the heavens themselves.

***

Dermott places the wad of now well-thumbed papers on his desk and scratches his head. He has that sensation in his gut that he always gets when he has found something special – a dead cert. He savours the feeling, his own private victory for a moment and then presses the quick-dial to his editor-in-chief's extension. Johnny picks up the receiver instantly. Dermott only ever buzzes through if there is something really important, and that is just what he needs right now. He has been looking at their budgets and it's not a pretty picture.

'Dermott,' he croons, 'what have you got for me?'

'A new writer, actually.'

Johnny sighs. He didn't know what he was hoping for, but it wasn't a new writer, not at a time like this. He wanted something more solid, more certain. His hesitation speaks volumes and Dermott quickly fills the sagging void. 'No really, this is something really special. I haven't come across anything like this in a long, long time, not since Thelma Barton in fact.' Thelma Barton had been Dermott's first big find; she had been pitching her manuscript around all the publishing houses and getting no takers. But Dermott had instantly spotted the raw new talent and had signed her to the Rathgar Road Press immediately and they had never looked back since. Thelma's first book had been a movie within two years, and the subsequent five novels were all best-sellers. Johnny had half been hoping that the movie rights for another of those books might have been in the pipeline. But anyway he knew Dermott would never use Thelma's name in vain, so he sat up and got ready to listen. 'Go on', he said encouragingly.

'It's a first novel, very dark, haunting actually. Bit like a text version of a Dali painting, mostly incomprehensible but captivating, and you know it's telling you something about yourself even if you don't exactly know what. It has a very intriguing and twisted eroticism about it, controversial, but which will definitely keep the publicity up. I could see an art-house movie out of this too, definite cult-status potential.'

'Title?' Johnny interjected.

'A Thousand Epilogues.'

'Hmm.' Johnny paused for a second and then continued the interrogation, 'Name?'

'Sorcha Earnshaw.'

'For real?'

'Why not?'

'Doesn't sound very authentic to me, Sorcha Earnshaw: Earnshaw's a bit too Wuthering Heights for someone whose first name is Sorcha don't you think? Cathy Earnshaw wasn't it? Mind you I suppose that adds a nice literary ring to it. Is it a whole manuscript you have or just sample chapters?'

'Just the first six chapters.'

'OK drop them on my desk and I'll take a look, and you get back to this Sorcha Earnshaw and tell her we'd like to see the rest of it.'

Dermott carefully replaces the receiver and looks at his watch – eleven-thirty a.m., the perfect time for an espresso and fag break before he gets back to this woman. He wants to savour this moment as he feels the axis of his career turning and also to digest the profound effect that Sorcha Earnshaw has already had on him.

HELP AND RESOURCES

Full contact details can be found in Appendix Three: Resources.

UK
- FFLAG: Support for parents of people who are lesbian, gay and bisexual
- Mind: For Better Mental Health: Voluntary organisation which provides information and also campaigns around mental health issues
- NA (Narcotics Anonymous): 12-step recovery group for people struggling with drug use

Republic of Ireland
- L.inC: Lesbians in Cork: Resource and community centre for lesbian and bisexual women
- NA (Narcotics Anonymous): 12-step recovery group for people struggling with drug use

RESOURCES AND FURTHER READING

Alexandra, N & Clare, L (2004) You still feel different: The experience and meaning of women's self-injury in the context of lesbian and bisexual identity. *Journal of Applied and Community Social Psychology, 14*, 70–84.

Bristol Crisis Service for Women (2006) *Self-Injury Support and Self-Help Groups.* Bristol: BCSW.

Brontë, E (1847/1992) *Wuthering Heights.* Hertfordshire: Wordsworth Classics (with introduction and notes by JS Whitley).

THE HOUSE OF SMILES

'Welcome to the house of smiles', a young woman announces as she steps forward on the stage in the converted lecture hall at the back of the maze of buildings in the rapidly expanding College of Visual and Performing Arts. She is barefoot and dressed only in pyjamas: a figure hugging vest and shorts in pink and white cotton jersey with a silky pink robe slung loosely over the top. The sleeves of the robe flop down over her wrists and hands, flowing away from her in movements like melting icecream.

The blood-red curtains shudder slightly and then draw back on their makeshift pulleys and reveal a set which has been recreated as a bedroom. It has soft white and pink walls and a light wooden floor. To the front-right of the set is a double bed with a dark pink candlewick bedspread pulled over it, and lying between the bed and the edge of the stage is a thick cream sheepskin rug. On the same side of the room as the bed, white doors are set into the walls as if to house built-in wardrobes. On the opposite wall stands a tall mirror and a book case. The wall to the back of the set has a door in the left-hand corner, so that the overall impression is a room which is clearly inhabited and easily identified as belonging to a teenage girl but also oddly spacious, as if something fundamental is missing – symbolised by the absence of clutter that would normally make up such an environment.

The girl-like woman moves around the room, tracing her hand over the walls, the doors, the bed, before she faces the audience again and begins to speak. 'This is where I lived for a long time,' she says, 'and I was indeed a very lucky girl.' She looks deliberately coy; she is small and thin with a helmet of short dark hair cut jaggedly around her face but which today she has pulled up into two small pigtails on either side of her head, a parody of a young teenage girl. 'In the house of smiles all is calm and quiet and peaceful. We all get along with each other and we love each other. We are the perfect family. We have no secrets and we have nothing to hide. My parents love me very much.'

She moves around the room again, but this time she dances, pressing her body against the surfaces of the walls and the floor and the bed, as if to sink herself into them, to mould herself into the reality she speaks of, to make it real and alive in her flesh. The soles of her feet are audible, the soft pad and scrape of skin against wooden floor, followed by the gentle rush of the fabric of her robe as it trails behind her movements. She looks less fragile, less girlish, as she moves and the muscles and sinews of her calves and thighs become apparent, her tight flat stomach now athletic rather than childlike, her body exquisitely dextrous as she forms herself into the twists and shapes and turns of her dance. But still, her body conveys a story of compliance, of submission and powerlessness, despite the strength that articulating this vulnerability requires. As her movements finally begin to wind down, the first bars of *Hurt* by Nine Inch Nails are becoming audible in the back ground. She faces the audience once again, and frowns. 'And yet I do have a secret, I have a shadow. He follows me everywhere, he can see right inside me, he even knows what I am thinking. He knows what I am.'

The music is now getting louder and as the song enters the first of its crescendos the door at the back of the bedroom opens and a looming figure steps in. He is dressed from head to foot in black combat gear, boots, pants, jacket and artillery belt. He has a black motorbike helmet with black tinted visor pulled down and heavy-duty gloves. His entire body, his huge physical frame, is covered in a hard black armoury, and as the white door shuts gently closed behind him a palpable tension of fear emanates from the set. The woman/child, is suddenly excruciatingly vulnerable, her tiny body afforded no protection by the small soft fabric items that she wears. 'I have a shadow', she says again to the audience, tears sparkling in her eyes. 'I have a shadow', she whispers and then turns to embrace the dark figure who is now looming right behind her. She clings onto him, her head reaching only as high as his chest. She is miniature in comparison to him, a fragile china doll. He takes her head in his gloved hands and spins her around so she faces the audience again and then clamps her against him with one arm around her waist. They move in a violent path, a cruel shadow-dance in which the shadow leads. And while she follows him, she also seems to be subtly trying to break free, as if to comply and submit to his movement and control without ever fully accepting her fate.

Finally she pulls away from him. The force of the movement flings her against the wall and the shadow moves after her, close behind her, about to regain his control over her. She scrabbles and scratches at the wall, tearing at the paper with her fingers. The shadow reaches forward, surrounding her with his body spreadeagled and then he grabs her shoulders in his gloved hands and rips the soft robe from her back. As he does so she tumbles backwards between his legs in a neat head-over-heels roll and, for a moment is free. But her body is now more vulnerable and exposed than ever. She springs against the other wall and begins to tear at it once again. The shadow is close behind her, but before he reaches her she tears a chunk of the wall away. An avalanche of cameras descend upon her and she sinks to the floor amongst them. The space in the wall is filled with a camera eye that stares out at the scene taking place. The shadow lifts her and spins her and then pushes her face down. All the while the contrast of her near-naked vulnerability and his hard, thick, black armour are accentuated by the violence of the contact that is choreographed between them. His gloved fingers sink into her skin, his booted feet close upon her tiny bare toes, the metal artillery belt pressing into her abdomen grazing her skin as he lifts and spins her. The music is loud, distorting through the speakers. The frenzy on the stage appears violent and uncontrolled, but repeats each intricate frame over and over again as the girl re-escapes her shadow, throwing herself desperately at the wall, tearing and ripping at them, only to reveal once again the watchful eyes that freeze her into the set, and to be captured and flung back into her own submission. Each time the shadow takes her he does so with an increasing edge of brutally. Her pigtails are gone. Her hair is a tangled mess around her head, her vest is scrunched, her body revealed in red welt bruises.

Eventually, the music quietens and the frenzy begins to dissipate, the walls are spilled open of their contents. The room is a hideous parody of a child's nightmare populated by camera-monsters. And finally, the girl once again begins to move in controlled harmony with her shadow.

'This is the house of smiles', she chants over and over again as their movements gradually synchronise and they are finally moving in perfect unison: she with her back to him, her legs inside his, her arms moving only as he chooses to command them. 'This is the house of smiles. In the house of smiles all is calm and quiet and peaceful. But I have a secret, I have a shadow. I cannot escape from my shadow, I belong to my shadow.' The shadow turns, lifting her off her feet and carries her now-limp body over to the wardrobe doors. He pushes her to her knees and stands behind her. 'I belong to him', she says again. He takes her arms and holds them above her head, holding both of her wrists together with one of his hands. He pulls her momentarily to her feet, as he drops her back down again he tears her vest from her leaving her naked at his feet aside from her thin pale pink shorts. He pushes her forward with his boot. 'But he has a gift for me', she says, turning her head to the audience and smiling. 'He has a gift for me which will make everything allright. He has a special friend for me, who comes out to be with me when I cannot bear it any more.' She crawls to the wardrobe and the shadow slides open the door. For a moment it looks as if he is going to push her into the dark space. But instead, he steps inside himself and he lifts out a bulky object and hands it to her. She sits back on her haunches, arms open wide to receive her gift like a toddler at an Easter party and lovingly takes her prize into her arms. The wardrobe door slides shut. The shadow is gone and she is alone with her gift in the devastated silence of the pink and white room.

Slowly and carefully she gets to her feet and moves to the front of the stage, facing the audience, so that for the first time the gift is clearly apparent. A collective gasp escapes from the crowd. She is very carefully holding a medium-sized toy dog which is made almost entirely of knife and razor blades.

Smiling tenderly she says, 'This is my pet who comes to comfort me.' Still carefully holding the dog she moves over to the bed and lies widthways across it, tipping backwards so that her head and shoulders stretch over the side and face the audience upside down. She has her fingers placed carefully between the blades of the dog's body, and she holds it high in the air above her chest. She speaks again, 'In the house of smiles, I have a shadow, and I have comfort. When I hold my special pet close to my heart I know that he loves me and all is well.' With these words she slowly brings the dog downwards towards her body. These seconds seem like hours. There is a tense silence, as the dog of blades descends towards her naked flesh. She watches the expressions on the upside-down faces of the audience in their slow-motion trans-formations. She absorbs the intricacy of the changing expressions as they register what she is doing: eyes widen and jaws drop in fear, pain, shock or upset. She brings the dog to rest between her breasts against her skin and wraps her arms tightly around him. A cacophony of human emotions are visible as the blades begin to penetrate her skin. Some people have turned away, eyes closed or wincing in a tight frown, others have tears in their eyes and look raw, exposed by their own grief. In her own body she has an intense feeling of calm, as if she has dived five hundred meters below the sea and everything is mute, slow and timeless. She has practised carefully to know exactly what pressure is too much or too little, to be sure that none of the blades are placed so that they cut into her breasts or nipples, so that she knows exactly where and how deep each fresh cut will be.

The depth of stillness that emanates from her seems to cleanse the raw emotion that pumps through the room. It is as if the audience are having her feelings with her, for her, as if she has given them a whole turbulent well of emotion and she is now free of the gift she has offered to them. In those intense and precious moments of inarticulable intimacy she feels as if her soul has expanded to include the whole of humanity and that they are all one in the experience. There is no denial or explanation, it simply is. It is a moment of primal witness and she feels something lift from her and float away, released.

After what seems like an eternity she finally releases her grip on the dog and he rolls from her arms, off the bed, and clunks forlornly onto the stage. She spreads her arms wide open and outwards in cruciform on the edge of the bed. She feels the sting of the new cuts and the warmth of her own fresh blood on her skin as it runs over the flat white scars that ladder her arms in their own unspoken history. She closes her eyes. The silence holds her. She feels light and free. For the first time she has no secrets and no fear, just a deep acceptance and a peace which engulfs her in a gentle bliss. A drop of her blood sinks into the deep pile of the sheepskin rug and scars the surface of another creature's flesh with a memorial of her own journey.

The curtains finally close.

The show is over: her MA in performance art is now complete.

REFERENCES AND FURTHER READING (AND VIEWING)

McNiff, S (2004) *Art Heals: How creativity cures the soul.* Boston and London: Shambala.
Miller, A (1995) *Pictures of a Childhood.* London: Virago.
Pembroke, LR (2007) *Dedication to the Seven; Catatonia* [DVD]. London: Mind Publications.

RESOURCES

Cutting the Risk: Self-harm, self-care and risk reduction. Originally published by the National Self-Harm Network and now available as a free download from www.kreativeinterventions.com and www.harm-ed.co.uk
The Hurt Yourself Less Workbook. Originally published by the National Self-Harm Network and now available as a free download from www.kreativeinterventions.com and www.harm-ed.co.uk

APPENDIX ONE

HARM REDUCTION

INTRODUCTION

This appendix is structured as a response to the most common questions regarding the harm-reduction approach to self-injury (also here referred to as self-harm). These questions are usually raised by service providers, professionals, carers, loved ones, friends and family members of people who self-injure. As such, the key themes are largely oriented towards this audience. However, the information provided, the discussion of central issues and the experiences of the people who participated in my research are also intended to provide validating and informative resources for people who hurt themselves (especially 'The Kit' and 'Slow It Down'). They also provide a vocabulary towards addressing barriers to appropriate support.

Harm reduction has only relatively recently begun to gain recognition as a viable intervention for self-injury. As such, the harm-reduction ethos and practices are continually evolving and developing. What I have set out below is by no means a claim to a definitive or exhaustive account of these practices but is, rather, a guide to some of the key principals and practices which I have drawn from my research, the training workshops I facilitate, and related publications.[1] It is intended to be used in conjunction with, rather than to duplicate or subsume, already existing resources in this area.

---

1. Where quotations from individuals are used which include both first and second names these are real names, usually of service providers speaking in their professional capacity about their work and/or organisation and its ethos. Where first names only are used they are pseudonyms for individuals who shared their experiences with me in my research and who wished to remain anonymous. The exceptions to this are Clare Shaw and Rachel Friere, both of whom asked me to use their real names. Clare works and publishes in the area of self-injury (which I also cite) and she draws extensively on her own experiences in all of her work. Rachel believes that choosing anonymity perpetuates the shame and stigma around self-injury. She said, 'I think it's quite important to stand by your actions and not be ashamed of them and I'd encourage that in anyone really given the opportunity.' Thus, as befits a harm-reduction approach I have adhered to the wishes of each individual regarding what feels safest and most appropriate for them rather than applying a blanket, pre-set policy.

175

WHAT IS HARM REDUCTION?

[Harm reduction] is an alternative to preventative approaches which aim to prevent people from self-harming. Harm-minimisation approaches accept that someone may need to self-harm at a given point and focus, instead, on supporting that person to reduce the risk and the damage inherent in their self-harm.

Clare Shaw (in Shaw & Shaw, 2009, p. 6)

Harm reduction (also called harm minimisation) is an alternative to prevention. It originated in sexual health and drug services where policies based on prevention and abstinence were not only ineffective and counter-productive in terms of stopping the behaviour, but also failed to meet individuals' health and care needs. Harm reduction is increasingly being applied to self-injury, largely as the result of the pioneering work of survivors and user-led organisations – notably Louise Pembroke, and also Clare Shaw and Terri Shaw of 'harm-ed' – as well as survivor-centred organisations such as The Basement Project, the Bristol Crisis Service for Women and 42nd Street.

A harm-reduction approach, instead of focusing on ways to prevent the behaviour, accepts that the person engages in it and prioritises enabling a person to stay safe and avoid unwanted, irreversible or fatal damage to themselves. The fundamental principle of harm reduction is acceptance, and acceptance of the whole person rather than concentrating solely on the behaviour and categories or diagnosis of it.

WHAT DOES HARM REDUCTION INVOLVE?

Harm-minimisation is about accepting the need to self-harm as a valid method of survival until survival is possible by other means.

Louise Pembroke (2007, p. 166)

Harm reduction involves providing education, information and resources around self-care and safety. In sexual health, harm reduction includes thorough sex education alongside the provision of condoms, dental dams and latex gloves; for IV drug users, clean needles, swabs and distilled water are often provided through needle exchanges along with personal support and self-care services. For people who injure themselves, harm reduction entails providing reliable and accurate anatomical and first-aid information which enables people to reduce the lethality of their injuries and also to subsequently take care of their wounds. Self-care and aftercare information and resources are essential in enabling individuals to make judgements and choices about their injuries and their treatment. People are empowered to acquire the resources and skills to effectively care for themselves both during and after the injury, and so avoid injuries with unintended, irreversible or potentially fatal consequences.

Harm reduction also supports individuals in reducing the risks of their injuries and subsequent infection by enabling them to maintain special clean and sterile implements for injuries. This is sometimes known as a 'clean kit' (see 'The Kit', below). And, contrary to fears often expressed by professionals, allowing persons to maintain a clean kit for themselves – which includes provisions for both injury *and* aftercare – is NOT the same as giving out clean blades to service users and enabling them to escalate their injuries as an alternative to providing comprehensive and meaningful support. The kit functions as an alternative to preventative strategies such as the confiscation of items deemed to be 'unsafe'. In institutional settings these prevention strategies often result in treatment which people experience as violating and degrading, such as the removal of their clothing and personal possessions, and holding them in confined and closely monitored spaces. And while this approach is often used in an attempt to prevent harm, its impact is usually the opposite and certainly not conducive to alleviating distress or creating a therapeutic environment. Hilary Lindsay of the Bristol Crisis Service for Women (BCSW) explained that:

> Where people are put in seclusion, or when they're being *watched* – you know, either they have someone with them the whole time or every fifteen minutes or something like that – it's like you're keeping that person physically *safe* but actually you're not really paying attention to what's going on on the inside and they might be emotionally in a *much* worse state from being treated *like that*. But because they're physically safe, on one level it looks better, but actually what it does emotionally, it often might be worse.

In this way, the clean kit not only provides hygienic and safe means of injury, it also limits the emotional and psychological harm (see also 'Emotional Harm Reduction', below). Firstly, it relieves the forbidden nature of self-injury and the accompanying secrecy, urgency, anxiety, desperation and shame, making the process calmer and safer. It also acts as a kind of emotional safety net, providing a resource to drawn on when necessary which is no longer a shameful, or (often quite literally) a dirty secret but, rather, an accepted means of support. At the same time, it creates a window of opportunity to pause and slow down, or to intervene in the process if and when appropriate (see

'Slow It Down' below). Harm reduction reduces the emotional harm caused by punitive and pathologising approaches to self-injury which focus on the injury rather than the underlying causes of distress. Permission and acceptance create a context in which meaningful choices can be made. Harm reduction acknowledges that self-injury may be the absolute best that a person can do at this particular place and time and that it is a valid means of coping and surviving. This was true for Elaine, who said:

> I did that at the time because that was right for me at the time, and it wasn't *healthy*, but I didn't have the tools to do anything else. You know, people don't self-harm 'cos it's *fun*. And if I'd been able to do something different then I would have done something different.

Overall, then, rather than preventing the injury, harm reduction emphasises safety and self-care, while simultaneously exploring and providing support in the areas which may be currently being addressed through self-injury. Harm reduction validates people's experiences and their struggles to survive. It respects and empowers people's ability to make the best decisions for themselves in their particular circumstances, while at the same time always encouraging and supporting them to evolve with and through their experiences.

IS THAT IT?

No, that is just the beginning! The purpose of harm reduction is to accept that a person needs to self-injure to cope and survive. But the physical and emotional aspects of harm reduction are parts of a whole range of supports and interventions that need to be available in order to keep people safe and supported. As noted above, harm reduction is NOT about providing someone with the means to injure themselves as an alternative to acknowledging the issues and challenges they face and leaving them unaddressed. Harm reduction minimises the consequences of self-injury while simultaneously exploring and supporting the issues which are being dealt with through the injuries. And yet, while always working towards resolving the struggles and challenges that an individual faces, it is essential to remember that the stopping of self-injury is not the purpose or measure of the effectiveness of harm-reduction interventions. Indeed, during times of deep distress, for example, when experiences from the past are being dealt with, the self-injury may intensify as memories and issues come to the surface. Here more than ever, harm reduction is essential in supporting someone safely through these experiences, recognising that self-injury is an intervention in that distress. Harm reduction is broad and diverse, specific to each individual and their situation. Clare Shaw emphasised how harm reduction entails:

> Recognising and celebrating recovery or care-taking in whatever form that happens: it might be about somebody cutting their stomach instead of their forearm, or somebody taking care of their wounds after they've injured, or cutting themselves instead of taking a Paracetomol overdose, and celebrating when somebody *has* taken that care. Not just seeing it as a huge failure that they're self-harming.

Finally, for many people self-injury is something that will move in and out of their experience throughout their life-course, and harm reduction is essential in supporting their safety and self-care as it does so.

IS THERE A SINGLE HARM-REDUCTION RECIPE?

> Self-injury isn't the same for everyone and nor does it have the same meaning for everyone. ... It *is* intricate, it is complex, and I think it needs to be looked at in an intricate and complex way.
>
> Karl Tooher (Therapist)

> Self-harm is very complicated because it can serve many different functions for the person doing it.
>
> Emma

> It's a very deep, personal thing. ... It's one of those things that you *cannot* generalise about.
>
> Joseph

> I would see self-injury for what it is: as individual to each person, and something is being communicated.
>
> Mark

> It is personal, there might be some common things between people, but somebody who is self-injuring on one day might be completely different to somebody who is self-injuring on another day, so you can't really think, 'I *know* about this, and *this* is what needs to be

done', or 'this is what this person *ought* to be doing', it's not like that. It's about where that person is at a certain time.

Hilary Lindsay (BCSW)

Each person's life experiences, emotional pain, personal strengths and characteristics are unique and so too is their relationship with self-injury and its precise meaning, purpose and practice. Therefore, to be effective, the combination of supports and interventions must be equally unique and subjective. Service providers often attend self-injury training hopeful of being provided with a monolithic treatment plan or intervention model that can be applied verbatim to every individual, only to discover that nothing could be more inappropriate in facilitating real understanding and helpful responses. There are, however, some basic universal principles for working from a harm-reduction ethos. These include:

- Prevention, punishment and control do not work.
- The injury is not the problem.
- Balancing risk and trust.
- Slow it down.
- Clean kit (self-care and aftercare).
- Resource the staff not the diagnosis.
- Emotional harm reduction.

These principles and their practical applications are explored in turn below.

PRINCIPLES INTO PRACTICE

Prevention, punishment and control DO NOT work!

'Stopping' people self-harming isn't going to stop them doing it. ... I don't believe it's a behaviour that people just stop ... they *can't* or they wouldn't be doing it in the first place.

Elaine

That was a period of time when I actually couldn't stop injuring even though I wanted to. I mean I never wanted to injure, that's the strange thing, and I hated the fact that I did, *but* I also recognise that it was nothing I could actually control at certain times.

Mark

I genuinely believed that I'd stop doing it, because I'd grow out of it, you know, ... cos I just didn't know what else it would be. And sort of now I guess I admit that it's not going to go away.

Rachel

Being told to stop is really not a constructive or meaningful response, it makes you feel worse, and you do it anyway.

Clare

Self-injury is a coping and survival mechanism and it is therefore essential to understand that strategies which rely on prevention, punishment and control *absolutely do not work* and are often highly detrimental to a person's well-being. They make the situation – i.e. someone's level of distress and the subsequent extent of their injuries – far worse. They create an invalidating, punitive and controlling environment, often mirroring the experiences which self-injury is a coping response to. Sadly, these are often the primary policies of institutions such as hospitals, prisons, residential and 'care' centres where people who self-injure find themselves. Such policies merely create an increasing cycle of distress, injury, punishment and control. Clare Shaw poignantly details the impacts of hospitalisation and prevention on her own self-injury.

Hospital was a frightening, bewildering, upsetting place, where harassment and threat were a daily reality; and supportive conversations with staff were few and far between.

It's no surprise then that my need to self-harm increased. I became desperate to hurt myself – the only coping strategy that had consistently worked for me over the last ten years. But self-harm wasn't allowed. So what did I do?

I made it my goal. I used all the time and energy I had on my hands to pit my wits against the staff and I found new and ingenious ways of self-harming. I did it in secret; I seized the opportunities when they arose; and I did it as quickly and severely as possible, before I was found and stopped.

During my months in different inpatient units, I cut myself with razors. I re-opened sutures, I inserted objects and rubbed dirt into open wounds, I injured myself with broken glass and crockery, I gouged myself with a fork and I cut myself with a ripped open can. I punched myself repeatedly, I banged my head on the wall, I overdosed, I hung myself from the back of the bathroom door until I lost consciousness, and daily, I binged and vomited and starved. *These were all units which did not allow self-harm.*

(in Shaw & Shaw, 2007, p. 29).

Prevention, punishment and control are so utterly counterproductive because self-injury is a means of coping with intense distress and difficulty and these responses only intensify those struggles. Mark said that self-injury '*was* a way of dealing with stuff and that's just it'. He emphasised that, 'sometimes it's the very, very best one you can possibly do'. This raises very serious questions regarding the motivations behind, and the consequences of, removing people's coping strategies from them and placing them in distressing and controlling environments. What measure of harm and safety is at play here, and whose needs is it really serving? How realistic is it to expect someone to suddenly manage without the tool which has been their key survival strategy and, in many cases, for a significant period of time?

The injury is NOT the problem!

> I would have *hated* anybody to try and separate the self-injury from what was going on. ... If anybody *helped* me it wasn't because of the self-injury it was because I felt *bad*, and self-injury was a symptom.
>
> Mark

> I think that there needs to be a lot *less reaction* to self-harm in terms of physical injury.
>
> Elaine

> I would *never* talk to the actual *process* of what they're doing, I would talk to the emotional part.
>
> Colm

Of course injuries require treatment or medical attention appropriate to them. When substances have been swallowed medical attention should be sought immediately as there is no way to control lethality when medications or other substances have been ingested. Self-care, wound treatment and aftercare are always important and it is essential that individuals are resourced and supported to this end.

However, once the injury has been properly cared for there are some important things to remember. Firstly, all injuries are a response/intervention in a whole range of experiences and circumstances; they are a means of coping and surviving, and often a way to articulate or express that which is unspeakable. It is the underlying issues, the causes of the distress, which are the 'problem' and which need to be addressed with sensitive support and careful attention. These issues are many and varied, and incorporate an individual's personal experiences alongside their immediate and social context.

Personal and/or inner world factors include experiences of grief, loss, bereavement, invalidation, neglect, abuse (physical, emotional, sexual), abandonment, trauma, violence, homelessness, displacement, illness. Indeed, it is not always these experiences alone which create the kind of distress which is marked out through self-injury, but that the experiences were dealt with inappropriately, or occurred within invalidating environments where the person was disbelieved, undermined, blamed, shamed, or had their experiences and their feelings about them minimised or disregarded.

Invalidating and minimising responses can sometimes occur from genuine but misguided attempts to alleviate an individual's distress and self-injury. So that, for example, discounting an injury as 'just a scratch' or 'nothing serious' not only fails to recognise the depth of distress behind the physical wound but also gives a very confusing message about being taken more seriously if there is more extensive bodily damage. This not only increases emotional harm but may also re-enforce the expressive aspects of self-injury. This was true for Elaine who spent a number of years in a psychiatric unit for adolescents; she said:

> There were times when I would just feel really, really awful if the scar was really small because at the time self-harm is a form of communication about something. It's about something that you can't express in any other way and when it's *gone* or it's really *small*, it's not right, you know. ... I had all kinds of sets of rules: it was only self-harm if it was over ten stitches. I upped it, and I upped it, and I upped it. It was only self-harm if I was stitched, or it was only self-harm, you know, to the point where at the *end* it was only self-harm, it only mattered, it was only *worthy*, it was only important if it was *big* injury. Or, you know, a *small* scar that didn't require a skin graft wasn't good enough.

It is also essential to reduce the risks of physical and emotional harm by not making assumptions about the injuries themselves, and particularly not assumptions based on external judgements about the type and perceived 'severity' of the injury. The apparent severity of the injury *cannot* be taken to indicate the intent and purpose beneath it. Very high-risk and near fatal injuries may be a coping and survival mechanism (i.e. self-injury), while overdoses and cuts which appear 'small' in quantity or depth may actually be suicide attempts. Likewise, self-hanging and self-immolation may be either self-injury or suicide. In any case injuries cannot be simply read off as indicators of purpose and intent. Doing so not only minimises and invalidates a person's experience, but also leaves them vulnerable to increasing risk and harm.

The issues addressed through self-injury may be also connected to the broader social context in which someone lives – for many people society can be experienced as a highly invalidating and/or abusive environment. The impacts of gender norms, prejudices and inequality alongside racism, homophobia, bi-phobia, transphobia, ableism (i.e. prejudice, discrimination and marginalisation of people who physically and/or intellectually vary from the norm), the impacts of poverty, religious prejudice, ageism, appearance norms and marginalisation all need to be accounted for and understood in terms of an individual's self-relationship and the ways in which distress becomes embodied in self-injury. It is essential, therefore, that services and service providers are acutely sensitised to these issues and do not mirror any of them in their responses or in the environment they provide. An ideal response, then, as Clare described it is, 'not even specifically focussing on self-harm, but it's about just *acknowledging* that the world can be a *really difficult* place to live in, and that people get distressed, and distress exhibits itself in different ways'.

Likewise, the immediate context of a person's life may also need to be addressed. Circumstances which are controlling, invalidating, where boundaries and privacy are not respected and where individuality and individual needs are not recognised are hugely problematic. Yet, unfortunately, these features are endemic to many of the environments in which people who self-injure are 'treated', i.e. hospitals and special hospitals, care placements, the family home as well as penal facilities for adults and young people. It is essential to continually question how and why these environments contribute to self-injury rather than focusing on the apparent 'failure' or 'untreatability' of the individual. Indeed, self-injury may be precisely a response to these contexts. Lois Arnold of The Basement Project suggested that:

> The agencies concerned, the hospitals, prisons or whatever need to look at: 'What is it that *we're doing here* that possibly is driving people to [self-injure] more and more and more?' You know, sometimes people's self-harm just escalates and escalates and it's not just about the individual, it's about the context they're in. And it might be a context that they're in at home, but it might be about the context that they're in: in hospital or in prison, or in care, some sort of care situation, residential situation.

In harm reduction, then, the injury (once made safe) is not the central focus but is, rather, surrounded by a much larger person-centred philosophy of long-term and creative supports which attend to the personal, social and contextual issues related to self-injury. Harm reduction emphasises supporting an individual to stay safe and to have choices while, in their own time, and in a way which is meaningful and purposeful for them, exploring the issues and experiences which underlie their self-injury. Lois Arnold described how:

> The whole point really, is to help people who self-harm to find out what it is that's going on with them in terms of feelings and problems that are making them feel so desperate that they need to harm themselves and to work with *that* rather than to kind of make the self-harm a *massive* issue, but obviously it does need to be responded to, but in a kind of constructive way.

By not focusing on the injury, harm reduction enables meaningful and diverse supports to be accessed while keeping an individual safe as they explore their needs and issues. However, harm reduction is often highly challenging to service providers/support persons. Elaine articulated the dilemmas that harm reduction poses to support persons, emphasising not only the importance of *not* responding to the injury, but the simultaneous challenges of managing the balance between risk and trust. She said:

> I think that there needs to be a lot *less reaction* to self-harm in terms of physical injury. In that just because someone's cut their arm, and yes there is that idea that they are at risk, but they don't need to be put into a psychiatric hospital because of self-harming, that's a reaction to the *injury*. That's a big area of confusion: I can appreciate the issues that people have around is it really OK to send someone out with fifteen stitches in their arm when they'll be back in again next week? And *are we* at risk? Are we a risk to ourselves? Is that a risk to yourself? Is that a risk? And it's like *yes, technically* I can see that it would be, *but* I *don't* believe it's right to put people in psychiatric units because of self-harming. I think that actually does more damage than good. And 'stopping' people self-harming isn't going to stop them doing it. ... It's a reaction to the injury, and it would be better dealt with if people reacted [differently]. I can *understand* because one of the most fundamental, basic human things is to react to an injury, and it's kind of *wrong* in the context of self-harm. That's why it's very difficult at the minute for it to be dealt with effectively, because people react to the injury. And people don't know that I need a counsellor, *not* to be put into a psychiatric unit. 'Cos all that does is mess up people's lives and take away any reason they might have for *not* doing it: like *normality*, like their job, like relationships, friendships, and put them in an environment where they're told *they can't* do it, they're not

allowed to do it, where they're treated like they're *mentally ill* and really put them in a environment where the social acceptability of doing it is very high, you know? So they'll only come out however long later really a lot more messed up.

Harm reduction entails a more nuanced interrelationship between the individual who hurts themself, their immediate and long-term needs, and their support person than is the norm within conventional approaches. It not only shifts the focus away from the injury towards the whole person – their individual experiences, strengths and life context – but also, as Elaine described, necessitates an intricate negotiation of the balance between risk, trust and responsibility.

Balancing risk and trust

> I would like people to trust the self-harmer's ability to be OK.
>
> Emma

> Nobody, at any stage, should be treated with anything but utter respect and understanding.
>
> Karl Tooher (Therapist)

In practice there are two key aspects to balancing risk and trust. The first aspect is understanding and accepting that self-injury is a means of coping and surviving, which is fundamentally different in intention – though not always in appearance – to suicide (and para-suicide) in which self-annihilation is the intended outcome. Joseph, who cut himself and took overdoses of medications for a number of years, said:

> To me it's *very obvious*, that just because you're self-harming does not mean that you want to commit suicide. You *don't* want to do yourself deep, irreversible damage ... It's not about suicide. I *never ever, ever* wanted to commit suicide.

However, while for Joseph the cutting and the overdosing were equivalent processes of self-injury, the service providers he encountered defined them differently. This was invalidating and humiliating for Joseph, and also resulted in a missed opportunity for meaningful support. He described his experience of psychological assessment following an overdose:

> I was embarrassed – because when you swallow tablets they think that you're trying to commit suicide, and I *wasn't*. I was doing the swallowing of tablets for the same reason that I was cutting myself. ... I always associated it in the same way, but to *them* you were trying to commit suicide. And I wasn't. And I didn't need it defined or looked upon like that, so I just wanted to get out of there as quickly as possible.

Thus, only by paying careful attention to the individual and their experience can an accurate picture of the specific risks they face and the means of reducing them be established.

This acceptance of the individual's experience is integral to the second aspect of balancing risk and trust which involves trusting the individual who self-injures. The possibility of really trusting someone who self-injures is going to be massively influenced by the context in which their self-injury is understood. If they are seen as chronically mentally ill, dysfunctional or deviant because of their self-injury then it will be much more difficult to establish a meaningful and trusting relationship than if they are recognised as a human being in distress doing their utmost to survive. Developing trust requires a genuine relationship with the individual where their strengths and characteristics as well as the meaning and purpose of their injuries are recognised and acknowledged.

Service providers are often particularly alarmed by the educational aspect of harm reduction. They often fear that if they allow access to information regarding the most and least safe forms of self-injury that it may be used to cause fatal damage which they will then be held accountable for. Clare Shaw frequently encounters these anxieties when providing harm-minimisation training, she said:

> One of the biggest fears around harm minimisation is that: 'What if I give somebody information about dangerous places to cut, so they cut there, and then I end up in a coroner's court?!' And people are frightened of being taken down the legal route.

However, she went on to explain that currently in the UK:

> The RCN [Royal College of Nurses] and the Royal College of Midwives are looking at Duty of Care and they might be called upon to incorporate the harm-minimisation approach. 'Cos at the moment the code of conduct's got all these concepts like 'harm' and 'risk' and words like 'reasonable' and 'appropriate' and people *think* they

> know what it means, and they think it means that you have to *prevent* people from self-harming, but there's nothing about actually specifying what the risk is, what the harm is, what's appropriate, what's reasonable.

Indeed, the most recent (UK) National Institute in Health and Clinical Excellence (NICE) guidelines in relation to self-injury specifically recommend that professionals, 'consider giving advice and instruction on self-management of superficial injuries, including providing tissue adhesive [and] harm-minimisation issues and techniques' (2004, p. 18).

However, harm reduction is not as yet a mainstream response to self-injury, although a number of statutory and voluntary services are showing increasing interest in it having already witnessed the failures of prevention-based approaches. In the meantime many service users stumble across harm-reduction practices inadvertently, or develop their own techniques from what anatomical/medical knowledge they possess. Joseph described how he attempted to reduce the risks of his injuries by being careful about both the location on his body which he cut as well as the implement he used to do so. He described how:

> I much preferred to cut myself with glass. I used to cut myself with razor blades, but I was afraid of blades, but I had no fear with glass, I felt much more in control with glass. Because you have to *force* glass to go deeper, but with a *blade* you just cut and that was it, and you didn't know how deep it was, but if you cut with the glass you could *feel* [the depth] as you were cutting yourself.

He described how he was also careful not to damage particularly vulnerable or visible parts of his body. 'I wouldn't cut my face, I wouldn't cut my hands, but I would cut my arms, my chest, my legs, anything that wouldn't be seen in public.' And while not all of his assessment of high-risk locations is accurate (there are arteries and tendons in the legs for example, and the stomach is relatively safe), he nonetheless worked his own strategies to reduce harm, thus highlighting how essential correct information is in enabling people to stay safe. He told me how:

> This was great place to cut yourself [gesturing to backs of arms]. This isn't such a good place to cut yourself [palms of hands and undersides of arms] but here [back of arms] is a very good place to cut yourself, because, I don't know, [pauses] it's a nice space. I don't know what I mean by that, but I wouldn't cut myself *here* [front of

wrists] because I might do damage or whatever, and I would always cut myself *here* [back of arms] because it seems stronger, whereas *here* [undersides of arms] I actually wouldn't cut myself. And I'd cut myself on my chest but not around my nipples, and I would *never* touch my stomach. And your legs were an open area, you could cut yourself anywhere, it doesn't matter, but your neck and your wrists would be out.

Rachel also described her own efforts at risk minimisation through self-care. She said, 'I have always been able to look after my own cuts pretty well.' Again, this was not something that she had been provided with information around, but rather, it 'was something that I had always done, just being practical'.

Clare and Emma discovered harm-reduction resources which were produced by other survivors and service users which had powerful impacts for both of them. Emma told me how:

The first time I came across the idea of harm reduction was when I went to a conference in Manchester (in 1994?) by the National Self-Harm Network. Someone there was talking about it – possibly Louise Pembroke – and they published a leaflet/booklet from a previous conference they had done, and it had hand-drawn diagrams in it showing where arteries and veins were in the body and information about where they were more close to the surface, there was something about clean blades and aftercare, and also something about how if you cut your arm lengthways you are less likely to damage your nerves badly. It was really basic and not very medical but it was all I had at the time so I did often use this to try and minimise my chances of damage I might later regret. I felt like it gave me the option/permission to look after myself after I had cut myself and it meant that I only did the damage I meant to do which I am very glad of.

Clare also described how the discovery of harm-reduction practices was equally life-changing for her:

It was only after I'd accidentally severed the tendons in my wrist that I first came across the work of Lou[ise] Pembroke and the Self-Harm Network. It was a revelation to me ... that there were organisations who accepted that I might need to continue to self-harm; but who recognised that I still had choices; and that there were practical strategies by which I could take care of myself and to keep myself as safe as possible.

So I learnt about my own body, and about how to minimise the chances of damaging bodily structures like arteries and tendons. I learnt how to care for my wounds, and when to seek medical attention. I learnt how to minimise the risk of infection, by using a clean blade. I learnt the consequences of taking overdoses, and the importance of seeking help.

(in Shaw & Shaw, 2009, p. 8)

These experiences illustrate the immense health benefits and potentially life-saving impacts of harm-reduction information and resources. They show how just as a person cannot be stopped from injuring themselves, neither can they be kept entirely in ignorance of harm-reduction techniques and self-care. People will find their way to these practices in their desperate need to survive, and the failure to provide accurate and reliable information and support will only reduce the effectiveness of their self-caring interventions. All efforts towards self-care need to be supported and validated and failure to do so places individuals at increased risk and, only adding – on all levels – to the depth and intensity of their wounds.

Overall, then, balancing risk and trust necessitates a genuine relationship with the person who is hurting themself alongside a thorough understanding of the meaning and purpose of their injuries as processes of coping and surviving. It entails believing in them and supporting them to resource themself to stay safe, rather than leaving them without vital and potentially health and life-saving information. However, this poses further challenges to the norms of care and the structures of service provision.

Shore-up the staff not the diagnosis

They take it on as a *personal failure* ... them feeling like it's their responsibility.

Rachel (speaking about her parents)

[Service-provider] anxiety often leads to very rigid and controlling sorts of approaches.

Lois Arnold, The Basement Project

My best friend and my wife at the time were a great help to me, they were very patient.

Joseph

It's not just about 'Do I work with self-injury? – can I work with the things that lead to self-injury?' Because self-injury is *symptomatic* of other things and that's very important, … we've got to be able to work with those very, very *serious*, difficult experiences and issues that people have.

Karl Tooher (Therapist)

I don't think there is any *one* specific thing that's going to work for everybody. But the whole thing of, you know, what do you like and what makes you feel better? Those things are very important.

Hilary Lindsay (BCSW)

It should be fairly clear at this stage that self-injury is an individual and subjective experience. And while there may be underlying commonalities in terms of the issues that are connected with self-injury, there is no 'one-model-fits-all' response. Indeed, a harm-reduction approach shifts the focus of response away from pre-set diagnostic treatment plans to the qualities, skills and resources of the person who is supporting the individual in distress. Key qualities for effective responses include: acceptance, openness, love (or 'unconditional positive regard' at the least), trust, safety, listening, genuineness, respect and empathy. These qualities require capacities to be open-minded and open-hearted, aware, sensitive, non-judgemental, and to be fully present with and to each individual in their distress, and to hear and validate them and their experiences as whole human beings. This is by no means easy to accomplish – and especially not when facing the immediacy of injuries, or when working with excessive caseloads in challenging surroundings and within time and budget restrictions. Indeed, many of the basic structures of health-care services often militate against appropriate provisions for people who have hurt themselves. This is evident in, for example, the separation of mental from physical health and their severance from the individual and social factors which influence them – all of which are embodied in self-injury.

In any setting, however, for workers/support persons to be able to provide meaningful support they themselves need to be well trained, resourced and supported. Organisations and service providers must have clear boundaries, roles and responsibilities for all levels of staff and procedures. These should be clearly laid out, open and transparent to everyone, and especially to service users. Likewise, a comprehensive and up-to-date self-injury-specific policy which is consistently implemented is essential (see, for example, Arnold & Magill, 2007 *Getting It Right* or, BCSW, 2006, *Good Practice Guidelines*). Furthermore, workers can only be truly effective in their response and avoid burn-out and emotional harm to themselves if they are working with manageable caseloads and are being provided with genuine support for self-care and personal and professional development from their organisation and line manager.

Therefore, responding helpfully to someone who has hurt themself is not about focusing on the injury, nor is it about applying a pre-determined universal treatment plan to them. Rather, it requires having service providers who are open, flexible, resourced and creative in supporting the individual and their specific needs. In this way the most meaningful support which people have experienced is often connected to the quality of attention that the professional demonstrates – often despite the structures or environment they work within. For Clare it was:

> With help and with love I found my own way back. I went on to experience good meaningful support from professionals – my therapist; my housing support worker; from caring individuals working creatively within the limitations imposed on them in inpatient settings; and from other people who self-injure.
>
> (in Shaw & Shaw, 2007, p. 35)

Amanda also described the essential personal qualities of the support which she currently receives:

> The difference between her [Amanda's current psychiatrist] and the doctors I would have been under at [name of psychiatric hospital] was that she just gives you a hundred per cent, she really listens, and she *believes* you, what's going on for you. In [name of psychiatric hospital] they *don't believe* what's going on for you, they label you as an attention-seeker.

Amanda has also worked with a spiritual healer, and again she described the personal qualities that made this support so meaningful and productive for her. She told me how her healer, 'accepts you unconditionally, no matter who you are or what you have done. So it was very easy to talk to her.'

Emma contrasted the positive support she received as a child with a more negative response she experienced later in an adult psychiatric hospital. In the children's unit she described how: 'I just believed that they cared that I felt awful and that they didn't just judge me for feeling bad. They treated me as a person and not a patient. They didn't seem scared of my distress.' This contrasted sharply with the adult unit which was much more diagnostically oriented:

I think what made people mostly more OK the first time I was in hospital was that the people who worked there were there because they wanted to 'help children' and not because they wanted to 'protect society from mad adults'. I think that because it was a ward for young people its general approach was more focused on trying to understand and not medicalise than I experienced on the adult ward later.

Emma also described the personal, meaningful support she received from a counsellor:

When I was nineteen I got an appointment through my GP to see a person-centred counsellor. This woman was very patient and really seemed to care. She responded positively and truthfully to the questions I asked and really seemed to have faith that I could be OK and that I could feel positive about myself. She seemed to believe me and she seemed to respect me as a person. ... Her flexibility and her commitment to me helped me to feel safe enough to talk about, and draw, the things that I needed to.

The quality and effectiveness of the support and intervention, then, is largely dependent on the qualities of the support provider both in organisational and individual terms. Support persons in all instances need to be resourced so that they are able to meaningfully and effectively engage with someone in distress. The qualities required of support persons are not exceptional in terms of the amount of education or training required to achieve them, but are challenging in terms of the context (organisational and social) which inhibits them, alongside traditional approaches to self-injury. Moreover, preventative regimes can be equally frustrating and disheartening for staff who, Clare reported, 'feel really frustrated because they came into the work to have some sort of *caring* role, and instead they feel like they're just acting like policemen and prison guards 'cos they're working to prevent self-harm'.

Finally, one example of a quality that can be applied in any context is the technique of active listening without judgement or intervention. Indeed, Clare described listening as:

The *only* principle that is *transferable* from every individual is *listen*, and sometimes that might be listening to the fact that people don't want to talk, so listen to that. And then obviously respect what you hear! Don't listen and carry on regardless!

Active listening is something that can be easily learnt, taught and practised to everyone's benefit. Nonetheless, it is sometimes initially a struggle or culture-shock to resist offering direct interventions. However, really being heard can be powerfully transformative, especially for those who have experienced chronic invalidation. Jenny Smith of BCSW described how:

> One of the biggest journeys on the training [for helpline volunteer-workers] is that we *don't* 'rescue' people. ... It is very much [about] staying with the feelings and not trying to pull people along and ask all sorts of questions to *make it better*, but being with people where they're at. You know, that brought up a lot of stuff from volunteers about feeling quite powerless and really questioning the value of just listening, but actually just listening *is really* powerful.

Listening, then, is a simple and yet powerful means to provide meaningful support and yet it often runs counter to the structures of service provision. Another aspect of harm reduction which is also often a challenge to service providers and support persons is the kit.

The kit

> We know from work in some areas that if they're self-injuring then there is no way that they're suddenly going to stop self-injuring, so then we might look and see if there are ways that they can self-injure more safely'.
>
> Karl Tooher (Therapist)

> I think it can go so many ways, that actual physical self-harm is so much *neater*. And I think for me *that's* why I do it: because it works.
>
> Rachel

People self-injure to stay alive, to cope with and express a whole range of issues, feelings and experiences. However, individuals are vulnerable to significant risks when engaging in self-injury. These include the risk of unintended, fatal or irreversible damage (through damaging tendons or arteries, for example), or of contracting potentially lethal infections as a result of unclean wounds or of contracting blood-borne diseases from unclean or shared implements. There are, however, easily accessible resources which minimise these risks and help people to stay safe.

One of the most effective ways to reduce the risks involved in self-injury is for people to have reliable information regarding the lethality of different injuries, detailing which are the most high-risk practices, and which are particularly vulnerable locations on the body. The book *Cutting the Risk* provides all of this information in clear and accessible format and is available as a free Internet download (see Resources below).

The second element to reducing the risks of self-injury are resources which make the injuries less damaging in the first instance, and which subsequently enable wounds to be taken care of and heal to their optimum. One way to achieve this is to have a kit of special items which are used only for the purpose of self-injury. The kit should also include wound-treatment and aftercare supplies, and emergency contact numbers should they be needed. It is important to note that the kit is only applicable for external forms of self-injury such as cutting and burning, not for ingesting medications/drugs/substances as there are no predictable safe limits here. A kit may be used, however, as a safer alternative to ingesting substances and overdosing.

The content of the kit will vary depending on each person's particular method of injury. For people who cut it is important to have clean implements which are kept separately and which are not used for any other purpose or shared with another person. This reduces the risks of infections and contracting blood-borne diseases from unclean implements. Disposable items, such as blades, should only be used on one occasion and then carefully disposed of. Non-disposable items should be carefully cleaned and sterilised and checked for dirt and/or rust in between use. Sterilisation can be done using disinfectants or boiling water. In this way the kit makes injuries cleaner and safer than those created with quickly improvised and unclean implements, or which create injuries of unknown or unintended severity and consequence.

The kit should also contain aftercare supplies and be regularly restocked with the treatments necessary for the injury. Aftercare supplies can be of the conventional medical type which are available from chemists, or can be from complementary medicine and which are available from health stores. In either case, the most important factor is that the aftercare provisions are correct for the specific injury. For example, treating and dressing burns requires very different materials than used for treating cuts. And burns created with chemicals require different treatments than burns caused by flame. Both *Cutting the Risk* and *The Hurt Yourself Less Workbook* have detailed information regarding reducing the risk of injuries and the specific treatments appropriate to different kinds of injuries. They were written by and for people who self-injure and are available from the Internet as free downloads (see Resources below). They are excellent resources for putting together a kit which enables safety and self-care and should be referenced when doing so.

The kit is also an important resource in emotional terms. The kit, which gives permission for both self-injury – the coping and survival mechanism – as well as for self-care both during and after it, becomes a kind of safety net: a dependable resource that can be drawn on when necessary. It relieves the secrecy, urgency, anxiety, desperation and shame around self-injury, making the process calmer and safer. For some people the fact that they possess the kit at all actually reduces their need to use it, while others find that having it with them, especially during particularly stressful situations, provides a source of reassurance and strength regardless of whether or not they use it. As a source of support and recognition the kit allows people the freedom to make choices instance by instance, moment by moment. Some people also find they can use the kit in creative ways and avoid causing injuries altogether (see for example some techniques described in the *LifeSIGNS* (now FirstSigns) *Self-Injury Awareness Booklet*).

The kit is also really helpful when used in conjunction with the 'Slow it Down' rule and breathing exercises (below) to further reduce the risk and lethality of injuries. The kit enables preparations to be made for the injury which optimise safety but, at the same time, it also creates an additional window of opportunity to pause and slow down, or intervene in the process. Initially, this pause may only be for one or two breaths before the injury takes place, but this in itself is a significant achievement warranting recognition and support. Over time this pause may be increased, always ultimately with the permission to go ahead and use the kit if needs be, but continually opening up spaces of choice and empowerment. At each step of the process the person may choose to wait for one or two more moments before going ahead. The combination of the slow deliberate process, the paying of careful attention to the location on body, the clean implement used, and the aftercare applied, all ensure that the injury will be far less damaging than one carried out in rushed and panicked circumstances with unclean equipment and no aftercare resources to hand.

The slowness, the self-care, the permission, choices and recognition that are enabled through the kit have both physical and emotional impacts. Physically they reduce the level of damage and risk involved in the injury, while emotionally they are validating and empowering means of self-care. The kit facilitates practices in which desperation, chaos, unintended damage and shame are decreased, and the self-injury becomes cleaner and safer; its meaning and purpose recognised.

Slow it down

You're doing it as a means of coping.

Elaine

We do what we can to survive different situations.

Mark

It was a support for me, on a very *personal* level it was a support to me in a number of ways.

Joseph

'Slow it down', or the 'no one freaks out' rule applies to everyone and everything connected with self-injury. The most destructive thing for everyone involved is panic, hasty actions, rushed decisions and quick assumptions. Slowing it down is one of the most constructive interventions possible and it can be done very simply and easily by focusing on slowing down the breathing. It is really helpful for everyone to be able to pause and take a few deep breaths, breathing right down into the stomach and paying attention to the movement of the breath through the body. It's good to practise this simple breathing technique during regular periods of the day as well as when tired, stressed or lost in thought. Breathing deeply into the body in this way helps us to stay calm and to be more fully present in the moment, whereas stress and panic speed up the breathing and intensify the physical and emotional stress responses. If we practise working with our breath during ordinary day-to-day tasks it becomes an almost instinctive resource to draw on in times of high anxiety, panic or stress.

Many people (though not all) hurt themselves in a state of heightened emotion and often experience a sense of anxiety, urgency or panic with it. This urgency and panic is made worse if someone is in an environment where self-injury is prevented and/or punished, and can lead to injuries which are more lethal than they might have been had the person had space and choice around their actions. Slowing it down, then, becomes an important principle which allows them to become more present in their actions and to have the time to take steps to reduce the damage and risks of their injury.

So, when the need to injure arises it is really helpful to start to slow down the breathing as described above, and to gently and consciously breathe right into the stomach through each step of the process that leads into and creates the injury.

- Breathe through the feelings that arise.
- Breathe through the decision to create the injury/pain.
- Breathe through entering or creating the environment needed for the injury.
- Breathe through the decision about the bodily location of the injury.
- Breathe slowly through unpacking the implements that will be used, and the aftercare treatments needed (see 'The Kit', above).
- Breathe as slowly as possible through the process which creates the injury.
- Breathe through the feelings and sensations that arise during and after the injury.
- Breathe very carefully afterwards and through taking care of the physical and emotional impacts of the injuries.

Throughout this process remember that with each breath there is always both choice and permission. There is choice to slow it down even further by just staying with the breath, maybe for just one more inhalation and exhalation, or maybe for five more breaths, or perhaps even for a minute or two (or longer) on the clock. With each breath and each minute there is a choice of not continuing with the process for that moment, and there is also always absolute permission to continue on with it. A pause the length of a breath is a gift of choice and permission that everyone is entitled to provide themself with.[2]

It is important to know that breathing slowly in this way can sometimes unlock unfamiliar feelings or understandings of them. It can also eventually lead to feeling and responding very differently to difficult situations. This is because breathing in this way keeps us present in ourselves while feelings and sensations arise. It helps us to develop a different relationship with them where the feelings are not so powerful and overwhelming. We can breathe through panic, terror, rage, hate, grief, and so on. These feelings can then pass through us rather than becoming locked into our body or head. This is why breath work is often used in different meditation and therapeutic practices. It is very simple and can help us to stay present and much more in control of our actions and reactions and create space to make choices about them in all aspects of our lives as well as in safety and self-care for self-injury.

When using this kind of breathing technique for self-injury it might also be helpful to find some ways to work with or express the feelings that are associated with the injuries or which arise in the breathing process. Writing, scribbling, drawing, painting – actually just making a mess with crayons, paint or ink(!) – are really helpful ways to visually externalise some of those

---

2. This is an adaptation of the 'fifteen-minute rule' discussed in the *The LifeSIGNS Self-Injury Awareness Booklet* (2004), see below.

feelings and to develop a different relationship with them. Painting in particular is very helpful when words don't seem to fit experiences. Some people find it helpful to keep a kit of paints, crayons or whatever materials they prefer, and to keep it alongside a self-injury/self-care kit so that they have an alternative kit as well – Michael Moyer (2008) calls this a 'safe kit'. It might also be useful to reflect on these feelings and experiences in a structured way using the exercises in *The Hurt Yourself Less Workbook* or *The Rainbow Journal* (see Resources, below).

Slowing it down is also an important technique for support persons to adopt, especially in the immediacy of an injury. It is essential to slow down all aspects of the reaction to the person who has hurt themself. First and foremost, this means that the support person has to slow down themself. Don't panic or make any rushed judgements or assumptions. Try and stay calm, take a few deep breaths as described above and allow time and clarity to see what needs to be done. In some cases it might involve accessing immediate medical attention. This is essential if someone has taken pills, medications, drugs or has ingested other substances. Medical attention may also be required for other injuries including cuts, burns, broken or fractured bones, or where someone may have induced concussion. It is always very helpful to accompany the person to receive treatment and stay with them throughout the treatment if that is what they wish. The person who has injured themselves will be experiencing a whole range of physical and emotional sensations and is very vulnerable. It is not likely that they will be able to clearly state their needs, feelings and intentions at this time. To be supportive of them stay calm and solid and also ensure that all the treatment they receive is both appropriate to the injury and in the way that it is delivered. It is helpful to have established a genuine relationship with the person where you have discussed what they need when they have hurt themself, so that when the situation arises it is already clear what they require.

Once immediate risks have been taken care of, the next area to slow down is the response to the wound and its meaning. In the immediacy of their distress it is very unlikely that the person will be able to articulate what is happening for them, what led to the injury and what it is about – indeed, part of the effectiveness of self-injury is that it speaks where words cannot. Do not ask lots and lots of questions, but do show interest and concern and be prepared to follow whatever the injured person needs. This may be silence, it may be reassurance, it may be being listened to. As noted above, it is really helpful to have discussed this with the person beforehand. However, the person's needs may change over time and/or between contexts, and so listening and be fully present to them on all levels is really important in ensuring an appropriate response. Breathing slowly and carefully is an aid to this as it helps you to stay present and focused in the moment. It is also very calming to be able to mirror this breathing to someone in distress, if you are calm and breathing slowly and deeply you can become an anchor point for their own breathing to regulate.

Finally, remember that all healing – physical and emotional – takes time; it is not something that can be rushed or that there is a quick fix to. Supporting someone who hurts themselves requires genuine loving patience, allowing them to find their own route through their pain and accepting and supporting them as they do so. 'Preventing' and 'fixing' only make things worse; they create distance and distrust and a sense of urgency and panic which can have disastrous implications for the lethality of injuries. Space, time, choice and permission in the context of a mutually trusting relationship and genuine, steady patience are the most healing and supportive responses. Once the support person really slows down their own response and begins prioritising acceptance of, and reducing the risks inherent in self-injury, a space is created in which real progress can take place.

Emotional harm reduction

> It was when my distress was treated as abnormal that I felt like it wasn't OK to share how I felt, or that I was a freak, or that there was something incurably wrong with me.
>
> Emma

> I was deeply ashamed, *deeply* ashamed, if I had scars I was deeply ashamed and *deeply* embarrassed. ... It was like I was in hell and I wanted to stay there but at the same time I didn't want to stay there because I knew it wasn't right.
>
> Joseph

> I went to *so many* great lengths that nobody knew, and that was through embarrassment and shame. Not just embarrassment and shame because I self-injured, but embarrassment and shame about how I felt about myself *anyway*. And I just thought that this was just another thing that, you know, makes me worse than others again.
>
> Mark

> I refuse to beat myself up for doing it – because I did it for the reasons I did it at the time *and* had I *not* done that I might not be sat here today. ... You do pretty much what you can with the knowledge and the strength that you have at that moment. ... I perhaps wish that I had been able to do something different, but I have the understanding that I *didn't, couldn't*.
>
> Elaine

Self-injury is a complex physical and emotional experience; an intricate embodiment of difficulty and distress. Thus, in self-injury pain and damage often occur at both the physical and emotional levels: people hurt themselves because they are feeling awful, and many people also feel very badly about the fact that they self-injure.

Moreover, self-injury remains hugely misunderstood and stigmatised and this has massive consequences for people who hurt themselves and the way they are treated. Indeed, many people who become accustomed to receiving negative responses to their self-injury describe how those reactions can actually become a part of the injurious process. For Louise Pembroke the constant negative and hostile treatment she received in Accident & Emergency departments became an integral part of the process of hurting herself: 'Going to Accident and Emergency had become a form of self-harm. The judgement of staff confirmed that I really was the lowest form of life and reinforced every negative feeling I ever had about myself' (1996, p. 36). Eventually, however, Louise decided to reduce the emotional harm by no longer seeking medical help, but this increased her vulnerability to physical risks. 'At first I didn't know how to look after myself and ended up with many infections, including septicaemia' (1996, p. 36). But, after receiving the kind of support and information which she later developed into a harm-reduction practice, her experience transformed. 'I started to carry a clean blade and a first-aid kit around with me. This was liberating and I harmed myself less. I had cut out part of the cycle of degradation – Accident and Emergency' (1996, p. 36).

It is essential, then, that service providers and support persons do not respond in ways which add to the pain and damage of self-injury at any level, as this may only push someone deeper into the injurious cycle. Both Amanda and Elaine identified this in their own experiences and its immediate and long-term implications. Amanda described how:

> The act of self-harming gets a negative response as well so it's kind of negative pulling in negative. Yet if the [other] person was more positive about the situation, or more accepting, I think it would help people to deal with continually doing it to themselves.

Elaine also saw this also in, 'the negative associations through scars that you're going to have to live with, forever'. She explained:

> I remember just having that moment one day thinking, 'Oh my God! I'm going to be an old woman and *still* people are going to be asking me about them! [i.e. her scars]' And that's not really a nice thought, you know, I've had people say really unpleasant things about them

> and that's not a nice thing. It kind of carries on the negativity and it slightly carries on the being a bit unpleasant to yourself because by having the scars you're allowing other people to be unpleasant to you.

The stigma associated with visible physical difference and scarring, particularly for women and girls, is also an area where sensitive support, caring and acceptance is essential. Individuals need support in dealing with both the day-to-day implications of their injuries and scars, as well as making informed decisions about how they want to deal with the long-term effects of their injuries. All of these options are discussed in *Cutting the Risk* (see Resources, below).

Overall, any response which pathologises or stigmatises someone, which makes them feel bad, shamed or diminished in any way, is only going to exacerbate their distress. Therefore, enabling someone to stay safe and reduce risks is not just about physical aspects, it also entails being sensitised to, and taking lengths to avoid, recreating stigmatising or pathologising responses.

In some instances, avoiding emotional harm through stigma and pathology comes down to very basic issues, including how support services and the people who use them are framed. For example, Karl Tooher emphasised how, 'I don't work with self-injury, what's important is that we get a sense that self-injury is a part of the *whole* person. So what I'm actually dealing with is the person, and that's a person that self-injures.' Likewise, Jenny Smith of BCSW reiterated the importance of 'not seeing them as a 'self-injurer' but as a *person* who self-injures'.

Furthermore, both service users and service providers recognise the need for non-stigmatising services that can be accessed without having to go through lengthy medical and psychiatric referrals. Lois Arnold of The Basement Project said:

> I would like to see much better access to non-stigmatising support. For example, ... counsellors where you don't even have to go to the GP; support that you could get without having to be referred to a psychiatrist or to be labelled as mentally ill; where you could have easy access; somewhere to go; individual *and* group support; somewhere to go when *you* feel you need it.

From her own experiences – both positive and negative – Emma described in detail the kind of supports she would like to be available in a 'more home-like' environment and which included:

Counsellors available to talk to, if you wanted and when you chose, but there would also be no pressure to talk. There would be a room you could go to scream and bash cushions. ... There would be games to play, art and craft stuff so that you could be doing stuff and then talk in bits and pieces if you wanted, because this is much less pressured and can give you something to do with your hands or an excuse to change the subject when you don't want to talk about something anymore. Art stuff would also provide another useful way to express things that are hard to say.

It would be flexible and available at short notice, you would be able to self-refer without going through doctors etc., and you would also be able to get telephone support from the counsellors when you are in your own home so you could choose what support felt most appropriate at different times and you could build some trust over time if you wanted.

Finally, avoiding stigma and pathology also utilises another harm-reduction principle. So that just as responding helpfully is not all about the injury, and acknowledges that the injury is not the problem, in harm reduction neither is the entire focus on an individual's pain, struggles and difficulties. Equal emphasis is placed upon each individual's unique character, strengths and qualities and how these may be utilised for them. For Mark it was very important for people to understand that:

Even during times in my life when I *was* going through bad times and self-injuring that wasn't all of who I was in my life either, I was doing other things, I was still evolving. Sometimes I was just clinging on, but that *wasn't all*. There were some times I would go through significant bouts of self-injury then get up and go out and do some work, or get up and go out and *achieve* other things, or help somebody else, or just carry on with my daily life as normal, erm, [teasing] be a productive member of society!

Supporting someone, therefore, involves validating their strengths and personal resources and drawing on these to their best effect and facilitating each individual in finding their own path through their struggles in ways which are meaningful and productive for them. After all, anyone who has survived their difficulties by wounding themselves already has immense courage and resolve, as well as many other qualities which should be recognised, validated and used to their optimum. In this way, Amanda described how her work with her doctor and her spiritual healer enabled her to move into, 'that place where I found that strength within myself'. Karl Tooher puts this principle into practice in a collaborative and validating therapeutic approach where he recognises that his clients are:

> ... surviving; they're coping; they're doing their very best; they're struggling, they're showing *amazing* amounts of courage and huge amounts of character. ... So my job is educational; it's facilitative, and it's bringing it down to a sense where we can *collaborate* on them looking after themselves.

Overall then, an essential element of harm reduction is avoiding the intensification of the emotional aspects of self-injury through responses which are stigmatising or pathologising, or which solely focus on a person's injuries, pain and struggles. Looking beyond the injury to the whole person and enabling them to develop their own strengths and resources, on all levels, is essential. Otherwise the response only mirrors the negative, demeaning or abusive experiences which underlie self-injury and is counterproductive and often utterly illogical. Mark eloquently articulated the tragic irony of approaches which respond to distress in distressing ways.

> People go through absolutely horrendous things in their life, very difficult times, very difficult experiences and they do what they can to cope with that. Let's not make it worse by heaping judgement and [negative] responses. I mean, you know, people say, 'Well, self-injury is *mad*', but then, responding to somebody who is self-injuring to deal with very distressing things in a way that distresses them more is *completely insane*!

THE FINAL WORDS: THERE IS ALWAYS HOPE

Finally, it is *so* important to recognise that there is always hope; that people's lives and circumstances can and do improve, and that something as profound yet simple as acceptance can have powerfully transformative impacts. For this reason this harm-reduction appendix closes with words of support and hope that some of the people who participated in my research wanted to share with others who may be struggling with self-injury, or to support someone else. The messages roughly coalesce around two key themes: firstly, the fundamental importance of acceptance on all levels, and secondly, that it really does get better.

Acceptance

It's *hugely* important for people to realise that they're not the only person who's going though those things and responding to those things in their lives by injuring. That's *huge*.

Karl Tooher (Therapist)

Accept the person for who they are and what they are going through.

Hilary Lindsay (BCSW)

People having their feelings heard, it's just so basic, to be accepted for what they're saying and their experience.

Jenny Smith (BCSW)

I would like people to acknowledge the pain of the self-harmer without reacting with anger or fear.

Emma

Hope

It does get better. It doesn't hurt forever, and you don't have to hurt yourself forever. It may take time but it *does* get better.

Colm

Just to know that you're not *alone* in this, that there are ways of coming through it without having to hurt yourself over it.

Amanda

It can end. Now I'm not so silly as to believe that self-injury might *never* be a part of my life again, I don't know. It's not necessarily likely but then, hey, who knows? And then if it is, well then it is. ... But that level of *feeling bad* doesn't have to be part of somebody's life, those things *can* change.

Mark

Everybody goes through bad times and they will pass. I think that's *ever such* an important message. ... With BPD and self-harm there are so many assumptions about untreatability, and that's such an *awful, horrible, awful* message to give somebody.

So, you're going through bad times, and they can be *hideous* times, people can go through *horrendous* times, but *they'll pass*, they *will* pass and kindness and understanding and support can really help in getting somebody through a bad time.

Clare Shaw

REFERENCES AND FURTHER READING

Arnold, L & Magill, A (1998) *What's the Harm?* Abagervenny: The Basement Project (see Appendix Three: Resources).

Arnold, L & Magill, A (1998) *Making Sense of Self-Harm*. Abergavenny: The Basement Project (see Appendix Three: Resources).

Arnold, L & Magill, A (1998) *The Self-Harm Help Book*. Abergavenny: The Basement Project (see Appendix Three: Resources).

Arnold, L & Magill, A (2007) *Getting it Right* (2nd ed). Abergavenny: The Basement Project (see Appendix Three: Resources).

Babiker, G & Arnold, L (1997) *The Language of Injury.* Leicester: BPS Publications.

Bristol Crisis Service for Women (2006) *Good Practice Guidelines.* Bristol: BCSW (see Appendix Three: Resources).

Bristol Crisis Service for Women (2006) *Self-Help for Self-Injury.* Bristol: BCSW (see Appendix Three: Resources).

LifeSIGNS (now FirstSigns) (2004) *The LifeSIGNS Self-Injury Awareness Booklet: Information for people who self-injure/self-harm, their friends, family, teachers and_healthcare professionals.* FirstSigns Self-Injury Guidance and Network Support: www.firstsigns.org.uk

Moyer, M (2008) Working with self-injurious adolescents using the safe kit. *Journal of Creativity in Mental Health, 3*(1), 60–8.

National Institute in Health and Clinical Excellence (2004) *Self-Harm: The short-term physical and psychological management and secondary prevention of self-harm in primary and secondary care.* London: NICE.

Pembroke, LR (1996) *Self-Harm: Perspectives from personal experience* (2nd ed). Originally published by Survivors Speak Out and forthcoming as a free download from www.kreativeinterventions.com

Pembroke, LR (2007) Harm-minimisation: Limiting the damage of self-injury. In H Spandler & S Warner (eds) *Beyond Fear and Control: Working with young people who self-harm* (pp. 163–72). Ross-on-Wye: PCCS Books.

Shaw, C & Shaw, T (2007) A dialogue of hope and survival. In H Spandler & S Warner (eds) *Beyond Fear and Control: Working with young people who self-harm* (pp. 25–36). Ross-on-Wye: PCCS Books.

Shaw, C & Shaw, T (2009) *harm-ed.* Dublin Presentation. Unpublished paper for New Ways of Understanding Self-Injury: Ireland's National Self-Injury Awareness Day, Trinity College Dublin, March.

Spandler, H (1996) *Who's Hurting Who? Young people, self-harm, and suicide.* Manchester: 42nd Street.

RESOURCES

Cutting the Risk: Self-Harm, Self-Care and Risk Reduction. Originally published by the National Self-Harm Network and now available as a free download from www.kreativeinterventions.com and www.harm-ed.co.uk

The Hurt Yourself Less Workbook. Originally published by the National Self-Harm Network and now available as a free download from www.kreativeinterventions.com and www.harm-ed.co.uk

The Rainbow Journal. Available from Bristol Crisis Service for Women (see Appendix Three: Resources).

APPENDIX TWO

METHODOLOGY

The stories in this book are the result of an academic research project funded by the Irish Research Council for the Humanities and Social Sciences in which my remit was to use creative methodologies to develop and disseminate a harm-reduction approach to self-injury. It was to address the specifics of the Irish context but also drawing from, and applicable to, experience from other jurisdictions. The technical term for the method I employ is 'ethnographic fiction'. Ethnographic fictions are research-based stories which draw on the real-life experiences, people and issues I worked with during the research project. To carry out the research I met with individuals and service providers who had experience of, or who worked with people who experience, self-injury. I then recorded a conversation with them about their experiences and transcribed this recording. (However, organisational protocols meant it was not always possible to record conversations with people who work in statutory services. In these cases my conversations were more informal and I simply made notes of key points and themes of the discussion to refer back to in the writing process.)

I read and re-read the accounts from the conversations many times, along with other research, policy, resource and survivor publications to increase the depth of knowledge and context. I then re-wrote the experiences in a story-telling format, layering the different perspectives and understandings, but always carefully crafting them around the specific themes and issues they arose from. As such, the characters and events in the stories portray actual experiences but are re-presented in such a way that they do not reveal any single identity or experience. Nonetheless, they remain faithful to the core themes of the accounts, and are also directly applicable to real-life situations including policy and best-practice interventions. So that, for example, in the story 'Broken' I was able to combine the experiences of a research participant who had experienced psychological assessment in a hospital with the information I learnt from a professional who had developed creative ways to work around these protocols in order to avoid precisely the kind of strained interaction that takes place in this story. This is later revisited in a best-practice model in 'Trust Me 3'. In this way, many of the stories are multi-vocal, enabling the reader to enter into the range of different realities and perspectives which shape one event and, from this new vantage point, to understand the experience of self-injury alongside what are the most helpful, appropriate and supportive responses in each instance.

My use of this method was inspired by Mike Angrossino's (1998) book *Opportunity House* in which he used ethnographic fiction to address the sexual health education needs of men with intellectual disabilities. His stories are compelling and evocative narratives which vividly portray the lives of the men he lived and worked with and the issues and challenges they faced. Through story-telling Angrossino was able to convey the urgent need for thorough sexuality and sexual health education for the men and to explore the risks they were both exposed to – and that they posed to others – when this area of their life was neglected. His work resulted in substantial policy and practice developments in this area.

I chose ethnographic fiction as the method to write about self-injury for a number of reasons, and I have discussed the processes and advantages of this in academic terms in a number of publications (Inckle, 2007, 2008, 2010). Indeed, there is now an increasing cohort of researchers and academics from a variety of disciplines – including: psychiatry and medicine (Bracken & Thomas, 2005; Gray, 2002a, 2002b, 2004), communication studies (Angrossino, 1998; Ellis, 2004; Ellis & Bochner, 2000); sociology (Banks & Banks, 1998; Denzin, 2003); gender studies (Lorde, 1982; Reinharz, 1992; Richardson, 1992); anthropology (Brain, 1977) and psychotherapy (Orbach, 1999; Yalom, 1991) – who recognise the value of this kind of work and the limitations of traditional forms of research and representation particularly when dealing with sensitive issues. Here, rather than rehashing academic debate, I will simply outline the key principles which make ethnographic fiction an ideal vehicle to explore issues related to self-injury and harm reduction. These break down into four key themes which I will address in turn, also drawing from my research and the reflections of some of the people whose experiences form the basis of the stories in this book.[1]

The four key themes which ethnographic fiction address are:

- Confidentiality, safety and accessibility.
- The complexity of self-injury and its often stigmatised and misunderstood nature.

---

1. Where first names only are used these are pseudonyms which were chosen by each research participant to protect their anonymity. Where first and second names are used these are real names and are used in accordance with the explicit wishes of each person. See Note 1 in Appendix One, p. 175, for further details.

- Exploring policy, best practice and survivor politics in meaningful and purposeful ways.
- Facilitating skills development for those who self-injure and those who live and work with them.

These themes also intersect with the some of the key principles of a harm-reduction ethos, such as active listening and contextualised responses. Therefore, and as will become apparent below, the method of ethnographic fiction mirrors the ethos and application of harm reduction in practice.

Safety and accessibility

In both its nature, and the context in which it is 'treated' and understood, self-injury is bound up in a number of sensitivities which make the use of ethnographic fiction particularly salient. First and foremost, ethnographic fiction is ideal for exploring self-injury because it absolutely protects the anonymity and confidentiality of each person who participated in my research while, at the same time, being able to remain true to the depth and complexity of the experiences and issues they shared with me. Anonymity and confidentiality are often prerequisites for creating a context in which people feel safe to divulge and explore their personal experiences. In this way, not only is the research process made confidential using standard ethical and procedural protocols, but using stories to convey the experiences creates a double protection. This was particularly important for Emma who said, 'The mixing up of stories to create fictionalised stories feels quite safe to me.'

Secondly, the story-telling approach is accessible to a much wider audience than is generally reached by conventional academic reports and articles. It increases the opportunity of producing a text which is meaningful and tangible to those who have participated in my research, as well as those who self-injure and those who live and work with them across the wider population.

For Rachel using stories was an important and exciting approach. Indeed, she described how she often thought of her own life experiences with self-injury as 'a series of stories' which could not be easily communicated or understood in other formats. She said:

> I think that the most important reason I wanted to speak to you was because I wanted to say all this, because when do you ever get to say all this? It's just from talking to you that I have started to *think*, and I just think that it's so important that people *have* the option of having this knowledge. ... I mean you could put it into a case study, definitely, but I don't know what that would *be* in terms

of what I have said to you, but I love the idea that these actual experiences can become a story.

Stories, then, offer safety and anonymity while at the same time enabling a meaningful portrayal of self-injury and the experiences and issues related to it.

Representing the complexity of self-injury

The limitations of traditional forms of research and representation – in academic papers, case studies and statistics – is particularly apparent when sensitive, contentious or taboo issues are at stake. Non-traditional and creative research methods, including ethnographic fiction, have been used to explore the complexity and impacts of a whole range of sensitive experiences, including: breast and testicular cancer (Gray, 2002a, 2002b, 2004); child abuse (Fox, 1996; Ronai, 1992); abortion (Ellis & Bochner, 1992); working in the sex industry (Ronai, 1996); eating disorders (Tillman-Healy, 1996), and disability and sexuality (Angrossino, 1998; Sandahl, 2003).

Self-injury is a complex and multilayered human experience which is underpinned by multifaceted and intersecting individual, contextual and social dimensions. It has a range of meanings and purposes between individuals as well as over time (Babiker & Arnold, 1997; Hewitt, 1997; Inckle, 2007; Strong, 2000; Turp, 2003). Because it is so complex, and so often misunderstood, self-injury may seem contradictory and confusing for both the individual who experiences it as well as those around them, especially if a blanket interpretation is imposed upon it. In my project, Joseph continually articulated both the contradictory nature of his self-injury and his own confusion around it.

> It's so complicated for anybody to understand who doesn't go through it. You know, how do you help people who are willing to do that? Because where do you start and how do you know if you've ever finished?

> So *massive* contradictions, massive contradictions in every way. And I didn't realise how contradictory it was till I started speaking about it, yeah, very contradictory. [...] And confusion too, yeah confusion, that's exactly what it is, confusion.

> I thought I would have been a bit more eloquent talking about it, but it's so full of contradictions!

Likewise, Karl Tooher, a therapist who works extensively in this area, echoed the complex nature of self-injury. He said, 'Self-injury is *complex, complicated,* a whole *range* of different things: self-injury isn't one thing. It is intricate, it is complex, and I think it needs to be looked at in an intricate and complex way.' He continued, 'Self-injury isn't the same for everyone, and nor does it have the same meaning for everyone, so then the interventions with them are going to be very, very different.'

Self-injury, then, is not reducible to a single meaning, response or 'finding' and yet this is usually what is required of conventional research and practice interventions (see Spandler, 1996). Fictionalisation allows for the depth, layers and complexity of self-injury to be conveyed through the exploring of the inner worlds of the protagonists and employing narrative devices, such as metaphor (see below), which are not so compatible with the conventions of 'factual' writing. And, without re-opening lengthy debates around the merits of qualitative versus quantitative research and 'data', it is important to emphasise that those who work with people who self-injure, as well as those who self-injure, and those who have experience of both, all highlight significant problems with the use of conventional statistical, quantitative 'data' and 'findings' to understand and respond to the intricacies of self-injury. When developing an approach from which to understand and respond to each individual and their experience of self-injury, statistics and definitive categories and analysis prove little help. Therapist Karl Tooher, described how:

> When it comes down to *individuals;* statistics just break down when I'm seeing one person in a room. I can't honestly say that those larger types of trends or patterns are necessarily being seen in the clients that I have seen.

He continued:

> If we take it statistically, a group of ten thousand, and have research on them, that's fine, but the statistics only matter for ten thousand people, a similar size, or above. When it comes down to one they break down, when you have got one person coming through the door.

He emphasised how:

> I deal with *people as individuals,* and I see them as an individual, working with what's going on with them, in their circumstances, in their context, through their history, where they are now, and *that's* where my focus has been. And I suppose that's where my desire to

educate people would be around: is around getting that self-injury in broad terms is *this*; but individually it comes down to something very different, and you have to understand the individual.

Joseph, from his personal experience, also reflected on the inadequacies of generalised diagnosis of and responses to self-injury. He described self-injury as:

A very deep, personal thing. I don't think you can generalise; it's one of those things that you *cannot* generalise [about]. You cannot have a textbook and say, 'Everybody is like that, or like this'. Self-harming is such a *personal* thing.

Emma also felt it was important for people to understand the diversity of meanings involved in self-injury. She said, 'I would like people to know that self-harm is very complicated because it can serve many different functions for the person doing it.'

Likewise, Hilary Lindsay and Jenny Smith of the Bristol Crisis Service for Women (BCSW), who have more than twenty years' experience of developing and providing resources for women and girls who self-injure, recognise the importance of avoiding deterministic and generalising approaches to self-injury. Jenny described how, 'We haven't got a fixed definition of it', and Hilary explained:

We're *not* wanting to say, '*This* is what self-injury is about for people, and *this* is what people need.' It is personal as well, there might be some common things between people, but actually it's personal, and somebody who is self-injuring on one day might be completely different to somebody who is self-injuring on another day. So you can't really think, 'I *know* about this, and *this* is what needs to be done', or, 'This is what this person *ought* to be doing'; it's not like that. It's about where that person is at a certain time. It's not fixed, directional. Which is a bit frustrating, I suppose, in some ways, because sometimes that would make you feel a bit more secure if you could be, 'I know this is how it should be'. But actually, like with most things, it isn't really like that.

As a non-traditional research strategy, then, ethnographic fiction offers a route into the breadth and complexity of self-injury and the inner worlds of those affected by it. It opens up avenues for understanding and facilitating constructive, meaningful dialogue between all those involved. Using ethnographic fiction shifts the emphasis of the research from attempting to produce fixed answers and a 'one-size-fits-all' outcome or response towards a more open representation. It aims to 'encourage compassion and promote dialogue' (Art Bochner, in Ellis & Bochner, 2000, p. 748) between all perspectives involved: it can explore the complex and often contradictory aspects of self-injury in a way which is meaningful and constructive without being limiting and finite. In this way it allows points of connection between those who may have very different interpretations of self-injury, such as between conventional medical approaches and survivor and social/political models. Indeed, in the area of cancer treatment, cancer support and cancer survivor perspectives, Ross Gray has used these methods to bridge precisely such polarities of experience (see Gray 2002a, 2002b, 2004).

Furthermore, because self-injury is a multifaceted experience which engages physical, emotional, psychological, spiritual and social/cultural aspects of the self and experience (for which I use the term embodied, or embodiment – see Inckle, 2007), then it is also essential to represent it in a method which can capture all these layers of feeling and meaning. A number of my research participants commented on how pertinent creative writing is for working with self-injury in a holistic and harm-reduction context. Hilary Lindsay and Jenny Smith of BCSW appreciated the ability of ethnographic fiction to, 'get behind that sort of rationalness' (Hilary), 'And you get deeper meanings of it, and you get a deeper understanding of what it has meant to you' (Jenny). Likewise, for Clare Shaw, writing, publishing and performing her poetry has been an important vehicle for expressing and validating her experiences. She said, 'I write about experiences and I write about things I would never *talk* about, and just the very fact of putting it into writing gives me a distance from it that then enables me to present it to the outside world.'

In creative writing/fictionalisation, metaphor is a key vehicle through which to engage the imagination and empathy of the reader and to convey complex and difficult meanings. Metaphor, and speaking through metaphor, both in the body and in creative practices is also a central feature of self-injury and working from a harm-reduction approach. Clare Shaw and I discussed the importance of metaphorical forms of expression as a means to more truly capture and represent the complexity of experiences related to self-injury. Symbolism replaces literal forms of communication (and research) which divorce 'fact' from meaning and feeling, and thereby fail to capture the multidimensionality of lived experience. Clare described her creative writing as a process of 'moving the metaphor from the body onto the page'. She said:

It's such an articulate metaphor, self-harm, that's the power of it. When I look back at *what* I was trying to do, I was trying to communicate *intense distress*, that I felt I just didn't have the *vocabulary* to put into words, and I didn't have the sort of *entitlement* to put into words, and I did it through *wounds* and *overdoses*. And they were incredibly articulate ways of expressing distress, and desire and need for support and comfort. They did it *really, really well*. So it's quite a *challenge* to find ways of doing that in language, that do that *as* well. But, yeah, I love metaphor, I'm *such a fan* of metaphor, I love it. It's the only way I can think things through sometimes, is if I think of similes and metaphors.

In other contexts – from anthropology (Brain, 1977) to psychotherapy (Orbach, 1999; Yalom, 1991) – researchers have also used ethnographic fiction as a means to symbolise and convey the embodiedness of human experience which is lost in the texts of conventional clinical accounts and case studies. For example, in *The Impossibility of Sex*, Susie Orbach used her psychotherapy practice as a resource to explore issues around client/therapist relationships which she then wrote up in stories of 'imagined patients and a fictionalised therapist' (1999, p. 3). For her this was the only form of writing which could do justice to the depth and dynamics of 'the *doing* of psychotherapy' and which could fully capture the 'great beauty' and multidimensionality of psychotherapeutic relationships (1999, pp. 2–4).

Overall then, ethnographic fiction is a method which can capture and convey the complexities and multifaceted layers of self-injury, incorporating the experiences which may give rise to it, its meanings and purpose and the inner worlds and outer contexts of the protagonists and their experiences.

Meaning and purpose

The complex and deeply sensitive and personal nature of self-injury demands a method which can contain such multifaceted depths and layers of experience and convey them in ways which are also meaningful and purposeful, not unlike the actual process of self-injury itself. In this regard ethnographic fiction is a particularly pertinent strategy. Using creative (rather than academic or report) writing practices allows the visceral, emotive, unconscious and cultural dynamics to be experienced by the reader, who can then connect with, share and understand the experience. This experience can then be translated into policy and practice protocols as well as individual meaning-making and healing processes.

Purpose: policy and practice

Ethnographic fiction can impact at the level of policy and best practice interventions in a number of ways. It can also form points of dialogue across a range of different perspectives – in this book the purpose is to improve understandings of self-injury and to demonstrate the benefits of a harm-reduction ethos. Ethnographic fiction allows harm-reduction techniques and practices – which, when portrayed outside a meaningful context, may appear controversial or shocking – to be introduced and explored in an accessible and humane manner. So that, for example, Connor's story, 'Faggot', introduces the practice of the 'slow it down' rule; while in 'Broken' we see the impact of a clean kit and first-aid and aftercare provisions. In this way, the more challenging aspects of harm-reduction practice can be revealed and understood in the fullness of their meaning and the appropriate context. This enables the nature and impact of harm-reduction techniques to be explored more effectively than traditional formats or debates might allow.

For example, in her research on 'Young People and Self-Harm' Helen Spandler (1996) found conventional approaches to researching and reporting 'findings' around self-injury unable to convey the issues, needs and meanings her research explored. Conventional approaches created an impasse where, she described, service providers and researchers alike became 'paralysed by this kind of pressing need to know the causes or to find the answers' (1996, p. 117). Nonetheless, at the outset of her research Spandler had assumed that it would be possible to frame the 'results' of her research within conventional structures but, as her understanding developed, she found that trying to accurately reflect the voices of the young people in a way which maintained the integrity and complexity of their experiences impossible.

> Research findings have not been easy to grasp and write up: indeed in a conventional sense perhaps they ought not to be labelled as such! All that the study has identified is contained within the previous pages of this report and cannot therefore be easily concluded or summarised. It [i.e. the report] has tried to be as open as possible about the range of differences, conflicts and complexities which have been illuminated by the research and to cover the multitude of meanings and understandings, including their many pros and cons, offered by the young people. As far as possible this variety of meanings and the richness of the material have not been suppressed in order to make the report easier or clearer to write (or read).
>
> (1996, p. 113)

Spandler goes on to describe how the pressure for researchers and service providers to definitively 'know why', and to produce 'neat answers, conclusions and "findings" which explain why young people self-harm' (1996, p. 117) directly conflicts with the needs expressed by the young people themselves. They articulated the need for acceptance of all the ambiguities, complexities and contradictions surrounding self-injury and felt that this acceptance led to deeper and more constructive understandings and responses.

Ethnographic fiction, then, offers a means for representing the experience of self-injury in a way which is safe, meaningful and purposful not only for those who share the experience but also for those who live and work with them. In connecting with the needs and issues of all those involved it also bypasses another shortcoming of more conventional methodologies: namely, that they are usually geared towards only one particular audience – such as policy makers, for example – and, consequently, omit the core needs and issues of many of those at the coalface.

Conventional research, then, often fails to connect with and meet the needs of those whose concerns, issues and experiences they purport to address (see Angrossino, 1998; Gray, 2002a, 2002b, 2004; Pelias, 2004; Smith, 2002; Tillman-Healy, 1996) while ethnographic fiction, on the other hand, is able to convey multi-vocal perspectives, needs and issues. Furthermore, creative writing strategies allow a depth of communication which is not possible in conventional academic writing. It allows the reader to enter the inner world of each individual and to live the experience with them. Ethnographic fiction invites 'active readership' (Sparkes, 2003), where the reader 'can interact with people and come to his or her own conclusion about what's going on. The reader can do what the ethnographer [i.e. the researcher] does, immerse him or herself in the particulars and try and figure out what it all means' (Angrossino, 1998, p. 95). This enables the reader to develop a much deeper connection with and understanding of self-injury, the issues related to it, and how and why particular responses are helpful and supportive and others are wholly inappropriate and even counterproductive. This active readership and openness to hearing the multifaceted issues and experiences conveyed through each story also reflects exactly the kind of openness and active listening which is a primary mechanism for supporting and responding helpfully to someone living with self-injury (see Appendix One: Harm Reduction). Clare Shaw emphasised the importance of active listening. She said, '*do listen*' and emphasised that, 'that would stand true for every form of distress, every difficulty: just listen to each other, and respect where everybody is coming from'. She went on to describe in depth how:

Listening is not always about your *ears* listening to somebody talking, it might be listening to their *behaviour* or their other ways of expressing themselves, but, just *engage with* and try and understand where somebody is coming from, and respond to that with *caring* and *kindness*. ... Listen to what somebody is saying about who they are, and what their needs are, and what they've been through, and what they *need* from you, and what would help them, and why they *need helping*, or why they *don't* need helping.

Likewise, Amanda stressed how important it is for people to, '*believe* what's going on for the person; don't label them in any way; *really hear and listen*', and Jenny Smith of BCSW described how their volunteer training invariably highlighted how, 'just listening *is really* powerful'. Thus, by engaging with the stories in this book, readers are able to develop some of the skills necessary to understand and support an individual and their experience of self-injury.

Readers are also enabled to develop their awareness around issues which are related to self-injury – such as homophobia and sexual violence which are addressed in a number of the stories including 'Faggot' and 'Cathy and Heathcliff 1999'.

Ethnographic fiction, then, is doubly purposeful in that it both captures and conveys the complexity of self-injury and the issues related to it, and also develops many of the skills and awarenesses that are integral to responding to self-injury from a harm-reduction ethos. It facilitates active listening and empathic engagement with each individual protagonist in the specific context of their life experiences – their inner and outer worlds – and it uses creative practices to articulate and make meaning from these experiences.

Meaning: Healing and politics

Making meaning from traumatic, stigmatised and taboo experiences – especially those which attract a mental-health diagnosis in our culture (and sometimes also simultaneously medical and criminal pathologisation) – impacts in powerfully transformitvie and healing ways (Blackman, 2007; McNiff, 2004; Pembroke, 2007b; Turp, 2003). Creative practices of meaning-making have individual, social and political impacts, and transform both individual well-being and social awareness in new and positive directions. Here too, ethnographic fiction has a double function in mirroring and practising a key harm-reduction technique. Creative practices such as ethnographic fiction are not only important as a means of conveying the experience of self-injury and best practice and policy interventions, but are also vital means of facilitating individual growth and development. Writing, painting, performance art, dance, theatre and a whole range of artistic outlets connect with the expressive functions of self-injury and support someone in moving through it.

Clare Shaw described the ways in which different forms of creative practice have been important to her individually as well as for many of the women she has worked alongside.

> A thing that has been absolutely *so gigantically important* for me has been *communication*, and the *writing*, and just communicating. ... Communicating *creatively* was important for quite a lot of the women in the group, through *what I know* of their stories *beyond the group*, like: dancing, and performance art, and music, and *loads and loads* of *writing*, *tons* of writing. And I think when I look at my own self-harm and *why I did it*, and what functions it served, I *really* think that *communication* was up there at the top. So I think that moving forward for me, from that point of intense distress and intense need, *has* been about different ways of thinking, and different ways of communicating basically, which, creative writing does *both* doesn't it? Different ways of looking at the world, and different ways of expressing those different ways of looking at the world. And expressing them as impactfully and articulately as you *can*.

Jenny Smith of BCSW also recognised the multifaceted implications of the meaning-making in this project. She said, 'What *you're* doing, in terms of fictionalising the experiences, something like *that* in a writing group, where you could do that would be a great help for people, to just really creatively channel your experience.' In this way, the method that I use as a researcher also mirrors and explores one of the practices which is closely linked to exploring self-injury in a safe and meaningful way. Indeed, the process of researching and then writing this book has been an immensely powerful, moving and transformative process for me.

Creative practices are also a powerful form of social and political commentary and awareness-raising, and are an integral aspect of survivor movements, especially for those who are excluded from privileged forms of 'speech'. Writing, poetry, performance art, dance and theatre, for example, have all been used as political strategies to break the silence and to raise awareness around stigmatised experiences, including HIV and AIDS (Hewitt, 1997), the experience of 'mental illness' diagnosis and treatment (Pembroke, 2007b; Shingler, 2007) disability (Inckle, 2008; Morris, 1991; Sandahl, 2003) gender and sexuality (Hewitt, 1997) and, increasingly, self-injury (Inckle, 2007, 2010; Kenrick, 2007). In this way the use of ethnographic fiction also works in tandem with survivor movements and social activists who challenge social norms and raise awareness and advocate rights for those in marginal and/or stigmatised positions. These user-led and survivor movements have been at the forefront of developing the harm-reduction approach to self-injury, and have worked from and through their own experiences to develop alternative understandings and interventions around self-injury and the issues connected to it (see LifeSIGNS, 2004; Pembroke, 1996, 2007a; Shaw & Hogg, 2004; Shaw & Shaw, 2007; Spandler & Warner, 2007, and also *Cutting the Risk* and *The Hurt Yourself Less Workbook*).

Creative writing and especially fictionalised forms of story-telling are also important tools of social and political critique for those who occupy more privileged positions. Within powerful institutions such as medicine and academia the hierarchy often functions to prevent certain issues from being revealed and openly discussed. The psychiatrist Peter Breggin composed the novel *The Crazy from the Sane* (1971) after his supervisors prevented him from writing 'factually' about the conditions and abuses that he witnessed as a young man working in the psychiatric system (Breggin, 1991). Likewise, Andrew Sparkes (2007) uses the character of 'Jim', a university professor, as a 'fictional' vehicle to reveal the inequity of the university system under the Research Evaluation Exercise, and its damaging consequences for individual academics and students, as well as for teaching and learning practices more broadly. Ethnographic fiction, then, is a politically salient means to circumvent the silencing of dissent, and to enable the truth of experience to be heard. In this way, while based in social research and the academic context, ethnographic fiction operates in a similar vein to many other creative practices which have long been utilised towards goals of social comment and change – and this has been particularly so in 'mental health' politics (Sedgwick, 1982; Shingler, 2007).

Overall then, ethnographic fiction is meaningful in its ability to fully capture and convey the lived experience of self-injury and the myriad issues connected to it. Furthermore, it can explore the subjective and inner world of the individual, alongside the broader social issues and contexts they experience, in ways which conventional academic writing cannot. It is also an engaging and easily accessible form of writing which is open to professional and lay persons alike. Indeed, a key purpose of this book and method is that it is intended to be read by all those connected with self-injury and thereby create points of connection, dialogue and shared understandings. Ethnographic fiction is also meaningful in that creative practices are widely used in survivor and self-help movements as well as therapeutic practices as a way to articulate and make meaning from difficult experiences and in doing so facilitates healing of them. In this way creative practices can also be used to validate taboo or stigmatised experiences and raise public awareness and political consciousness.

For all these reasons, then, ethnographic fiction is an ideal mechanism through which to develop progressive understandings of self-injury and to explore harm-reduction practices. In ethnographic fiction the embodied, emotive, complex and multifaceted aspects of self-injury can be simultaneously presented along with the social, political and cultural meanings and contexts that shape it. Moreover, ethnographic fictions invite a relationship with the reader which is meaningful and productive on many levels and which enables the development of a repertoire of skills and resources for those who self-injure and those who live and work with them. Finally, ethnographic fiction allows the voices of experience to be heard in the fullness of their truth while continuously maintaining and respecting the integrity of their privacy.

REFERENCES AND FURTHER READING

Angrossino, MV (1998) *Opportunity House: Ethnographic studies of mental retardation.* Walnut Creek, CA: AltaMira Press.

Babiker, G & Arnold, L (1997) *The Language of Injury.* Leicester: BPS Publications.

Banks, A & Banks, SP (1998) *Fiction and Social Research: By ice or fire.* Walnut Creek, CA and London: AltaMira Press.

Blackman, L (2007) Psychiatric culture and bodies of resistance. *Body and Society, 13*(2), 1–23.

Bracken, P & Thomas, P (2005) *Postpsychiatry: Mental health in a postmodern world.* Oxford: Oxford University Press.

Brain, R (1977) *Kolonialagent: A novel with an appendix.* London: Faber.

Breggin, P (1971) *The Crazy from the Sane.* New York: Lyle Stewart Inc.

Breggin, P (1991) *Toxic Psychiatry.* New York: St. Martin's Press.

Denzin, NK (2003) *Performance Ethnography: Critical pedagogy and the politics of culture.* Thousand Oaks, CA: Sage.

Ellis, C (2004) *The Ethnographic I.* London: Rowman & Littleford.

Ellis, C & Bochner, AP (1992) Telling and performing personal stories: The constraints of choice in abortion. In C Ellis & M Flaherty (eds) *Investigating Subjectivity: Research on lived experience* (pp. 79–101). London: Sage.

Ellis, C & Bochner, AP (2000) Autoethnography, personal narrative, reflexivity. In NK Denzin & YS Lincoln (eds) *Handbook of Qualitative Research* (2nd ed, pp. 733–65). London: Sage.

Fox, KV (1996) Silent voices: A subversive reading of child sexual abuse. In C Ellis & AP Bochner (eds) *Composing Ethnography: Alternative forms of qualitative writing* (pp. 330–56) Walnut Creek, CA: AltaMira Press.

Gray, R (2002a) *Standing Ovation: Performing social science research about cancer.* Walnut Creek, CA: AltaMira Press.

Gray, R (2002b) Making a mess and spreading it around: Articulation of an approach to research based theatre. In AP Bochner & C Ellis (eds) *Ethnographically Speaking: Autoethnography, literature and aesthetics* (pp. 57 –75) Walnut Creek, CA: AltaMira Press.

Gray, R (2004) No longer a man: Using ethnographic fiction to represent life history research. *Auto/Biography 12*(1), 44–61.

Hewitt, K (1997) *Mutilating the Body: Identity in blood and ink.* Bowling Green, OH: Popular Press.

Inckle, K (2007) *Writing on the Body? Thinking through gendered embodiment and marked flesh.* Newcastle-upon-Tyne: Cambridge Scholars Publishing.

Inckle, K (2008) Policing the body: A conversation from the edge of normative femininity. In A Sparkes (ed) *The Auto/Biography Yearbook 2007* (pp. 75–94). Sussex: Clio Publishing.

Inckle, K (2010) Telling tales? Using ethnographic fiction to speak embodied 'truth' *Qualitative Research, 10*(1), 27–47.

Kenrick, J (2007) *Red Tears.* London: Faber & Faber.

LifeSIGNS (now FirstSigns) (2004) *The LifeSIGNS Self-Injury Awareness Booklet: Information for people who self-injure/self-harm, their friends, family, teachers and healthcare professionals.* FirstSigns Self-Injury Guidance and Network Support: www.firstsigns.org.uk.

Lorde, A (1982) *Zami: A new spelling of my name.* Freedon, CA: Crossing Press.

McNiff, S (2004) *Art Heals: How creativity cures the soul.* Boston and London: Shamabala.

Morris, J (1991) *Pride Against Prejudice: Transforming attitudes to disability.* London: Women's Press.

Orbach, S (1999) *The Impossibility of Sex: Stories of the intimate relationship between therapist and patient.* London: Penguin.

Pelias, RJ (2004) *A Methodology of the Heart: Evoking academic and daily life.* Walnut Creek, CA, Lanham, MD, New York and Oxford: AltaMira Press.

Pembroke, LR (1996) *Self-Harm: Perspectives from personal experience* (2nd ed). Originally published by Survivors Speak Out and forthcoming as a free download from www.kreativeinterventions.com

Pembroke, LR (2007a) Harm-minimisation: Limiting the damage of self-injury. In H Spandler & S Warner (eds) *Beyond Fear and Control: Working with young people who self-harm* (pp. 163–72). Ross-on-Wye: PCCS Books.

Pembroke, LR (2007b) *Dedication to the Seven; Catatonia* [DVD]. London: Mind Publications.

Reinharz, S (1992) *Feminist Methods in Social Research.* Oxford and New York: Oxford University Press.

Richardson, L (1992) The consequences of poetic representation: Writing other, rewriting the self. In C Ellis & MG Flaherty (eds) *Investigating Subjectivity: Research on lived experience* (pp. 125–37). London: Sage.

Ronai, CR (1992) A night in the life of an erotic dancer/researcher. In C Ellis & MG Flaherty (eds) *Investigating Subjectivity: Research on lived experience* (pp. 102–24). London: Sage.

Ronai, CR (1996) My mother is mentally retarded. In C Ellis & AP Bochner (eds) *Composing Ethnography: Alternative forms of qualitative writing* (pp. 109–31). Walnut Creek, CA: AltaMira Press.

Sandahl, C (2003) Queering the crip or cripping the queer? Intersections of queer and crip identities in solo autobiographical performance. *GLQ: Journal of Lesbian and Gay Studies, 9*(1–2), 25–56.

Sedgwick, P (1982) *Psycho Politics.* London: Pluto Press.

Shaw, C & Hogg, C (2004) Shouting at the spaceman: A conversation about self-harm. In D Duffy & T Ryan (eds) *New Approaches to Preventing Suicide: A manual for practitioners* (pp. 167–77). London: Jessica Kingsley.

Shaw, C & Shaw, T (2007) A dialogue of hope and survival. In H Spandler & S Warner (eds) *Beyond Fear and Control: Working with young people who self-harm* (pp. 25–36). Ross-on-Wye: PCCS Books.

Shingler, A (2007) *Only Smarties Have the Answer* [DVD]. London: Mind Publications.

Smith, B (2002) The (in)visible wound: Body stories and concentric circles of witness. *Auto/Biography, 10*(1), 121–131.

Spandler, H (1996) *Who's Hurting Who? Young people, self-harm, and suicide.* Manchester: 42nd Street.

Spandler, H & Warner, S (eds) (2007) *Beyond Fear and Control: Working with young people who self-harm.* Ross-on-Wye: PCCS Books.

Sparkes, AC (2002) Fictional representations: On difference, choice and risk. *Sociology of Sport Journal, 19*, 1–24.

Sparkes, AC (2003) Bodies, identities, selves: Autoethnographic fragments and reflections. In J Denison & P Markula (eds) *Moving Writing: Crafting writing in sports research* (pp. 51–76). New York: Peter Lang.

Sparkes, AC (2007) Embodiment, academics, and the audit culture: A story seeking consideration. *Qualitative Research, 7*(4), 521–50.

Strong, M (2000) *A Bright Red Scream: Self-mutilation and the language of pain.* London: Virago.

Tillman-Healy, L (1996) A secret life in the culture of thinness: Reflections on body, food, and bulimia. In C Ellis & AP Bochner (eds) *Composing Ethnography: Alternative forms of qualitative writing* (pp. 76–108) Walnut Creek, CA: AltaMira Press.

Turp, M (2003) *Hidden Self-Harm: Narratives from psychotherapy.* London: Jessica Kingsley.

Yalom, ID (1991) *Love's Executioner and Other Tales of Psychotherapy.* Harmondsworth: Penguin.

RESOURCES

Cutting the Risk: Self-harm, self-care and risk reduction. Originally published by the National Self-Harm Network and now available as a free download from www.kreativeinterventions.com and www.harm-ed.co.uk

The Hurt Yourself Less Workbook. Originally published by the National Self-Harm Network and now available as a free download from www.kreativeinterventions.com and www.harm-ed.co.uk

APPENDIX THREE

RESOURCES

SELF-INJURY RESOURCES:
UK

The Basement Project
Specialised service, providing support for people who self-injure, as well as training, resources and publications for those who live and work with them.
Address: PO Box 5, Abergavenny, NP7 5XW, Wales
Tel: 01873 856 524
Web: www.basementproject.co.uk

Bristol Crisis Service for Women (BCSW)
Resources, training and helpline support for women who self-injure and those who live and work with them. Have excellent range of accessible publications.
Address: PO Box 654, Bristol, BS99 1XH
Tel (Office/Admin): 0117 927 9600
Tel (Helpline): 0117 925 1119 (Friday and Saturday, 21:00 – 00:30, Sunday 18:00–21:00)
Text: 0780 047 2908
Email: bcsw@btconnect.com
Text and email support: go to website and click on Text/Email tab
Web: www.selfinjurysupport.org.uk

FirstSigns
(Formerly called LifeSIGNS) Self-injury guidance and support network for people who self-injure and those who live and work with them. Includes publications and moderated online chatroom.
Web: www.firstsigns.org.uk

42nd Street
Free and confidential emotional/mental health support for young people aged 13–25 in the Manchester area.
Address: 42nd Street, 2nd Floor, Swan Buildings, 20 Swan Street, Manchester, M4 5JW
Tel (Helpline/referrals): 0161 832 0170 (Monday, Thursday, Friday, 12:30–16:30)
Tel (Admin/enquiries): 0161 832 0169
Email: theteam@fortysecondstreet.org.uk
Web: www.fortysecondstreet.org.uk

Every effort has been made to ensure that, at the time of going to press, these details are correct.

harm-ed
Information and training for those who work with and support people who self-injure, and specialist training in harm reduction.
>Address: harmed-ed, PO Box 1045, Brierfield, Nelson, Lancashire, BB9 4BA
>Tel: 01282 698 530
>Email: training@harm-ed.co.uk
>Web: www.harm-ed.co.uk

National Self-Harm Network
The National Self-Harm Network is a UK-based survivor-led organisation (in existence since 1994) who are committed campaigners for the rights and understanding of people who self-harm.
>Address: NSHN, PO Box 7264, Nottingham, NG1 6WJ
>Tel: 0800 622 6000 (19:00–23:00)
>Email: info@nshn.co.uk
>Web: www.nshn.co.uk

SASH
Survivors of Abuse and Self-Harming newsletter and pen-friend network.
>Address: SASH, 20 Lackmore Road, Enfield, Middlesex, EN1 4PB
>Email: sashpen@aol.com
>Web: www.freewebs.com/sashpen

SELF-INJURY RESOURCES: REPUBLIC OF IRELAND

Kreative Interventions
Provides information, training, consultancy and research about self-injury from a harm-reduction perspective. Also has free downloads of *The Hurt Yourself Less Workbook* and *Cutting the Risk: Self-harm, self-care and risk reduction*.
>Email: kay@kreativeinterventions.com
>Web: www.kreativeinterventions.com

Pieta House
Specialised (free) therapeutic service for people who self-injure and those who may be at risk of suicide.
>Address: Pieta House, Old Lucan Road, Lucan, Co. Dublin
>Tel: 01 601 0000
>Email: mary@pieta.ie
>Web: www.pieta.ie

SELF-INJURY RESOURCES:
NORTHERN IRELAND

Zest
Specialised support service for people who experience self-injury or who are at risk of suicide.

> Address: Zest, The Gate Lodge, 91 Strand Road, Derry City
> Tel: 028 7126 6999
> Fax: 028 7126 9294
> Web: www.zestni.org

OTHER RESOURCES:
UK

AA: Alcoholics Anonymous
12-step group for people who experience problems with alcohol. Local group listed at the front of telephone directory.

> National contact address: Alcoholics Anonymous, PO Box 1, 10 Toft Green, York, YO1 7NJ
> Tel: 01904 644026
> National Helpline: 0845 769 7555 (Calls charged at local rate)
> Web: www.alcoholics-anonymous.org.uk

Al-Anon
12-step recovery group which offers understanding and support for families and friends of problem drinkers in an anonymous environment, whether the alcoholic is still drinking or not.

> Address (England) : Al-Anon Information Centre, 61 Great Dover Street, London, SE1 4YF
> Tel (Helpline): 020 7403 0888 (10:00–22:00 every day)
> Fax: 020 7378 9910
> Email: enquiries@al-anonuk.org.uk

> Address (Scotland): Al-Anon Information Centre, Mansfield Park Building, Unit 6, 22 Mansfield Street, Partick, Glasgow, G11 5QP
> Tel (Helpline): 0141 339 8884 (10:00–22:00 every day)

> Address (Northern Ireland): Al-Anon Information Centre, Peace House, 224 Lisburn Road, Belfast, BT9 6GE
> Tel (Helpline): 028 9068 2368 (Monday–Friday 10:00–13:00, 18:00–23:00 everyday)

Alateen
Alateen is part of the Al-Anon fellowship and is for young people aged 12–17 inclusive who are affected by a problem drinker. Alateen members share their ideas and experiences in order to gain a better understanding of alcoholism and to lessen its impact on their lives. Contact through Al-Anon above.

British Association for Counselling and Psychotherapy

Organisation for registered counsellors and therapists with own guidelines and charter. Has online information about how to find a therapist in locality as well as a whole range of other support services available throughout the country (go to 'find a therapist' page and then 'further sources of help' link).

Office open Monday–Friday, 08.45–17.00

Address: BACP House, 15 St John's Business Park, Lutterworth, Leicestershire LE17 4HB

Tel (General enquiries): 01455 883 300

Text: 01455 550 243

Email: bacp@bacp.co.uk

Web: www.bacp.co.uk

ChildLine

Run by the Society for the Prevention of Cruelty to Children. Provides free and confidential support for children and young people by telephone, text and online.

Tel: 0800 1111 (24 hours)

Web: www.childline.org.uk

CODA: Codependents Anonymous

12-step group for people who wish to develop healthy relationships with themselves and others.

Address: CODA UK, PO Box 2365, Bristol, BS6 9XJ

Email: outreach@coda.org

Web: www.coda-uk.org

Debtors Anonymous

Debtors Anonymous is a 12-step fellowship and recovery programme for people who wish to solve their problem with and help others to recover from compulsive debting.

Mailing address: BM DA Intergroup, London WC1N 3XX

Tel (leave message only): 020 7117 7533

Email: info1@debtorsanonymous.org.uk

Web: www.debtorsanonymous.org.uk (includes Irish meetings)

FFLAG

FFLAG is an organisation of parents of lesbian daughters and gay sons which seeks to promote the well-being of lesbian, gay and bisexual people, their families and friends. Has lots of useful links to nationwide organisations and groups for LGB people and their loved ones.

Address: FFLAG, PO Box 395, Little Stoke, Bristol, BS34 9AP

Tel (Central helpline): 0845 652 0311

Email: info@fflag.org.uk

Web: www.fflag.org.uk

The Gender Trust

A national charity whose mission is to improve the quality of life of trans people and their families by supporting them and working with anyone who is affected by gender identity issues. Has links to lots of local community and support groups.

Address: The Gender Trust, Community Base, 113 Queens Road, Brighton, East
Sussex, BN1 3XG
Tel: 01273 234 024 (Tuesday to Thursday 09:00–17:00; Monday and Friday
    10:00–13:00)
Tel (Helpline): 0845 231 0505 (Monday–Friday 10:00–22:00pm; Saturday and
    Sunday 13:00–22:00)
Email: info@gendertrust.org.uk
Web: www.gendertrust.org.uk

The Hideout
A website full of information and resources specially designed by Women's Aid for
children and young people who have been affected by violence in the home.
    Web: www.thehideout.org.uk

MABS: Money Advice and Budgeting Service
MABS is an Irish, free, confidential and independent service for people in debt or in
danger of getting into debt. It is funded and supported by the citizens information
board. Callers from Northern Ireland or outside Ireland can contact the helpline.
    Tel: 00 353 1 8129350 (09:00–17:00 Monday to Friday)
    Web: www.mabs.ie

Mind: For Better Mental Health
Mind is a registered charity that provides information, support, awareness raising and
campaigns around mental health issues and rights. It has branches nationwide and also
an extensive list of publications and resources.
    Address: Mind, 15–19 Broadway, Stratford, London E15 4BQ
    Tel: 020 8519 2122
    Tel (Helplines): Mind information line 0845 766 0163, Legal Advice Service 0845
        225 9393
    Fax: 020 8522 1725
    Email: contact@mind.org.uk
    Web: www.mind.org.uk

Mind Cymru
    Address: Mind Cymru, 3rd Floor, Quebec House, Castlebridge, 5–19 Cowbridge
        Road East, Cardiff, CF11 9AB
    Tel: 02920 395 123
    Fax: 02920 346 585
    Web: www.mind.org.uk/mind_cymru

NA: Narcotics Anonymous
12-step recovery group for those for whom drug use is a problem. Online meetings and
chatroom available through website.
    UK Service Office Address: NA, 202 City Road, London, EC1V 2PH
    Tel: 020 7251 4007
    Tel (Helpline): 0300 999 1212
    Fax: 020 7251 4006

Email: ukso@ukna.org

Web: www.ukna.org

Niteline

Niteline is a listening, emotional support, information and supplies service, run by students for students and open at night when few other services are available.

Address: Niteline Association, c/o London Niteline, University of London Union, Malet Street, London, WC1E 7HY

Email: enquiries@niteline.ac.uk

Web: www.niteline.ac.uk (provides local Niteline helpline numbers throughout England, Ireland, Scotland and Wales)

One in Four UK

One in Four is an organisation run for and by people who have experience of sexual abuse. One in Four provides a unique service to individuals, both directly and indirectly: directly, through individual therapy and helpline support; indirectly, through campaigning, policy making, in-house research, training, and consultancy work with statutory and non-statutory agencies.

Address: One in Four UK, 219 Bromley Road, Catford, SE6 2PG

Tel: 020 8697 2112 (24-hr answerphone)

Fax: 020 8697 8022

Email: admin@oneinfour.org.uk

Web: www.oneinfour.org.uk

OA: Overeaters Anonymous

12-step group for people with all forms of eating distress.

Address: OAGB Ltd, 483 Green Lanes, London, N13 4BS

Tel: 07000 784 985

Web: www.oa.org (follow links to UK and local meetings)

The Patients' Association

The Patients Association is a national charity providing patients with an opportunity to raise concerns and share experiences of healthcare with the aim towards improvement of services and patients rights.

Tel (Helpline, UK only): 0845 608 4455

Email: helpline@patients-association.com

Web: www.patients-association.com

The PDSA Animal Welfare

Address: PDSA, Sunderland Administration Centre, 18 Fawcett Street, Sunderland, SR1 1RH

Tel: 0800 731 2502

Web: www.pdsa.org.uk

Rape Crisis England and Wales

Rape Crisis (England and Wales) provides co-ordination for the national network of Rape Crisis Centres across England and Wales. Rape Crisis Centres provide a range of specialist services for women and girls that have been raped or experienced another form of sexual violence – whether as adults or as children. On the website you will find information about rape and sexual violence and details of your nearest Rape Crisis Centre. There is also information for family, friends, students and professionals.

Web: www.rapecrisis.org.uk

Scottish Women's Aid
Address: Women's Aid Federation of Scotland, 2nd Floor, 132 Rose Street, Edinburgh EH2 3JD
Tel: 0131 226 6606
Tel (Free helpline): 0800 027 1234 (available 24 hours)
Fax: 0131 226 2996
Email: contact@scottishwomensaid.org.uk
Web: www.scottishwomensaid.org.uk

Shakti Women's Aid
An Edinburgh-based organisation for Black and Ethnic Minority women, children and young people experiencing domestic abuse. Other languages available on website.
Tel: 0131 475 2399
Web: www.shaktiedinburgh.co.uk

Victim Support
Victim support provides confidential emotional and practical support (such as court witness service) for victims and witnesses of crime.
Supportline address (for letters only): Victim Support, Hannibal House, Elephant and Castle Shopping Centre, London, SE1 6TB
Tel (Helpline): 0845 30 30 900
Email: supportline@victimsupport.org.uk
Web: www.victimsupport.org.uk

Women's Aid Federation of England
Women's Aid is a national charity working to end domestic violence against women and children. There are lots of links to local services and also free resources to download.
Address: Women's Aid Federation of England, PO Box, 391Bristol, BS99 7WS
Tel: 0117 944 4411
Tel (free helpline): 0808 2000 247 (open 24 hours)
Email: helpline@womensaid.org.uk
Web: www.womensaid.org.uk

Women's Aid Federation of Northern Ireland
Address: Women's Aid Federation of Northern Ireland, 129 University Street, Belfast, BT7 1HP
Tel: 028 9024 9041
Tel (Helpline): 0800 917 1414
Email (General enquiries): info@womensaidni.org
Web: www.niwaf.org

OTHER RESOURCES:
THE REPUBLIC OF IRELAND

AA: Alcoholics Anonymous
12-step group for people who experience problems with alcohol. Local group listed at the front of telephone directory.

> National contact address: AA, Unit 2, Block C, Santry Business Park, Swords Road, Dublin 9
> Tel: 01 842 0700
> Fax: 01 842 0703
> Email: gso@alcoholocsanonymous.ie
> Web: www.alcoholicsanonymous.ie

Al-Anon
12-step recovery group which offers understanding and support for families and friends of problem drinkers in an anonymous environment, whether the alcoholic is still drinking or not.

> Address: AA Information Centre, Room 5, 5 Caple Street, Dublin 1
> Tel (Helpline): 01 873 2699 (Monday–Friday 10:30–14:30)
> Email : info@al-anon-ireland.org
> Web: www.al-anon-ireland.org

Information for Co. Cork:
> Address: Al-Anon, PO Box 55, Togher, Cork
> Tel: 0210 431 1899

Alateen
Alateen is part of the Al-Anon fellowship and is for young people, aged 12–17 inclusive, who are affected by a problem drinker. Alateen members share their ideas and experience in order to gain a better understanding of alcoholism and to lessen its impact on their lives. Contact through Al-Anon above.

> Al-Anon opening hours 10:30–14:30, Monday–Friday
> Address: Alateen, Room 5, 5 Caple Street, Dublin 1
> Tel: (01) 8732699
> Email : info@al-anon-ireland.org

Information for Co. Cork:
> Address: Alateen, PO Box 55, Togher, Cork
> Tel: 0210 431 1899

Aware
A national voluntary organisation providing support, awareness and information around depression, including local support groups and telephone support.

> Address: Aware, 72 Lower Lesson Street, dublin 2
> Tel: 01 661 7211
> Tel (Helpline): (Lo-call) 1890 303 302
> Email: info@aware.ie
> Website: www.aware.ie

BeLonG To
Youth project for lesbian, gay, bisexual and trans youth.
>Address: BeLonG To, Parliament House, 13 Parliament Street, Dublin 2
>Tel: 01 670 6223
>Fax: 01 670 6219
>Email: info@belongto.org
>Web: www.belongto.org

Also available via BeLonG To: the IndividualiTy (Trans youth group), and Ladybirds (young women's LBT group).

BodyWhys: The Eating Disorder Association of Ireland
Support meetings, online, telephone and one-to-one support for those living with all forms of eating distress.
>Address: BodyWhys, PO Box 105, Blackrock, Co Dublin
>Tel: 01 283 4963
>Tel (Helpline): (Lo-call) 1890 200 444
>Fax: 01 205 6959
>Email: info@bodywhys.ie
>Email Support: alex@bodywhys.ie
>Web: www.bodywhys.ie

ChildLine
Run by the Irish Society for the Prevention of Cruelty to Children, provides free and confidential support for children and young people by telephone, text and online.
>Tel: 1800 66 66 66 (24 hours)
>Web: www.childline.ie

CODA: Codependents Anonymous
12-step group for people who wish to develop healthy relationships with themselves and others.
>Email: outreach@coda.org
>Web: www.coda.org (go to 'world meetings' to find local groups)

Irish meeting information also available from The Rutland Centre
>Tel: 01 494 6358

Crisis Pregnancy Agency
The Crisis Pregnancy Agency is a government funded planning and co-ordinating body established to formulate and implement a strategy to address the issue of crisis pregnancy in Ireland. It has publications, resources and links to services such as Positive Options (see below).
>www.crisispregnancy.ie

Debtors Anonymous
See UK listing, p. 228.

DisABILITY.ie
User-led information and support for people with disabilities.
> Office hours 09:00–17:00, Monday–Friday
> Tel: 01 505 9435
> Email: info@disability.ie
> Web: www.disability.ie

See also:
Disability Federation Ireland: Web: www.disability-federation.ie
Enable Ireland: Web: www.enableireland.ie

Dublin Rape Crisis Centre
Free support services for females and males who have experienced rape and/or sexual abuse recently or in the past.
> Address: Dublin Rape Crisis Centre, 70 Lower Leeson Street, Dublin 2
> Tel (Freephone): 1800 77 88 88
> Tel: (01) 661 4911
> Fax: (01) 661 0873
> Email: rcc@indigo.ie
> Web: www.drcc.ie

Irish Association for Counselling and Psychotherapy
Provides list of fully accredited, qualified and registered therapists in Ireland. It is a good idea to discuss self-injury practice with potential therapist as practice varies widely.
> Address: IACP, 21 Dublin Road, Bray, Co. Wicklow
> Tel: 01 272 3427
> Fax: 01 286 9933
> Web: www.irish-counselling.ie

The Irish Blue Cross (Ireland) Animal Welfare
> Address: The Irish Blue Cross Animal Welfare, 15A Goldenbridge Industrial Estate,
>   Tyrconnell Road, Inchicore, Dublin 8
> Tel: 01 416 3030
> Fax: 01 416 3035
> Email: info@bluecross.ie
> Web: www.bluecross.ie

Irish Family Planning Association
The IFPA is a charitable organisation in existence since 1969. The IFPA is committed to an Ireland where there is full access to high quality information, education and health services regarding sex, sexuality, conception, contraception, safe abortion and sexually transmitted infections. They provide sexual and reproductive health information, crisis pregnancy counselling, clinical services, education and training.
> Address: IFPA Head Office, 60 Amiens Street, Dublin 1
> Tel: 01 806 9444
> Tel (National Pregnancy Helpline): 1850 49 50 51
> Fax: 01 806 9445
> Email: post@ifpa.ie
> Web: www.ifpa.ie

Irish Patients' Association
The Irish Patients' Association is a national charity providing patients with an opportunity to raise concerns and share experiences of healthcare with the aim towards improvement of services and patients rights.

Address: Unit 1, First Floor, 24 Church Road, Ballybrack, Co Dublin
Tel: 01 272 2555
Tel (Out of hours emergency): 087 659 4183
Fax: 01 272 2506
Email: info@irishpatients.ie
Web: www.irishpatients.ie

The European Patients' Charter for Ireland is available online from the Irish Patients' Association: www.irishpatients.ie

L.inC: Lesbians in Cork
Lesbians in Cork is a network and community resource centre based in Cork city. L.inC was established in 1999 and is for women who identify as lesbian or bisexual, including transgender people (or those in transition) who identify as lesbian or bisexual.

Address: L.inC, 11a White Street, Cork
Tel: 021 480 8600
Email: info@linc.ie
Web: www.linc.ie

See also Cork Lesbian Line, a free helpline for women of all ages dealing with issues of sexual orientation:

Tel 021 431 8318 (Thursday 20:00–22:00)
Email: lesbianlinecork@gmail.com

LOOK (Loving Our Out Kids – formerly Parents' Support)
Support service for parents of LGBT people.

Tel: 087 253 7699
Email: info@lovingouroutkids.org
Web: www.lovingouroutkids.org

Belonging, produced by the Swedish Federation for LGBT Rights. www.rfsl.se

MABS: Money Advice and Budgeting Service
MABS is a national, free, confidential and independent service for people in debt or in danger of getting into debt. It is funded and supported by the citizens' information board.

Tel (Helpline): 1890 283 438 (09:00–20:00, Monday–Friday)
Callers from Northern Ireland or outside Ireland can contact the helpline on:
00 353 1 8129350 (09:00–17:00, Monday–Friday)
Email: helpline@mabs.ie
Web: www.mabs.ie

NA: Narcotics Anonymous Ireland
12-step recovery group for those for whom drug use is a problem.
> Address: NA, PO Box 1368, Cardiff Lane, Dublin
> Regional Office: 4/5 Eustace Street, Dublin 2
> Tel: 01 672 8000
> Email: info@na-ireland.org
> Web: www.na-ireland.org

NASC: The Irish Immigrant Support Centre
Provides support and referral on a whole range of issues from reproductive health and procedures for asylum seekers to community groups and a speakers panel.
> Open: 09:00–17:30, Monday–Friday, closed for lunch 13:00–14:00
> Address: NASC, Enterprise House, 35 Mary Street, Cork
> Tel: 021 431 7411
> Fax: 021 431 7002
> Email: info@nascireland.org
> Website: www.nascireland.org

Niteline
Niteline is a confidential, anonymous, non-directive and non-judgemental listening service run by students for students (see also Niteline, UK listing, p. 230).
> Open: Thursday–Sunday 21:00–02:30; Monday 21:00–01:30
> Tel: 1800 793 793
> Web: www.ucd.ie/niteline

One in Four
Support for females and males who have experienced sexual abuse and their loved ones.
> Address: One in Four, 2 Holles St, Dublin 2
> Tel: 01 662 4070
> Fax: 01 611 4650
> Email: info@oneinfour.org
> Web: www.oneinfour.org

Open *Heart* House, Dublin
Open *Heart* House was established in 1997 and is a HIV-positive member-led organisation with a mission to empower and enhance the lives of people living with HIV and AIDS. It is the only voluntary agency of its kind in Ireland.
> Address: Open Heart House, 2 St Mary's Place, Dublin 7
> Tel: 01 830 5000
> Fax: 01 860 1285
> Email: info@openhearthouse.ie
> Web: www.openhearthouse.ie

OA: Overeaters Anonymous
12-step group for people with all forms of eating distress. For information on meetings:
> Tel: 01 278 8106
> Web: www.oa.org (follow links to Ireland and local meetings)

Outhouse
Lesbian, gay, bisexual and trans community resource centre (not accessible to people with physical disabilities).
>Address: Outhouse, 105 Capel St, Dublin 1
>Tel: 01 873 4999
>Email: info@outhouse.ie

Positive Options
Positive Options provides a free information service listing organisations which offer counselling and information in relation to dealing with a crisis/unwanted/unplanned pregnancy. Positive Options also provides information about the law and abortion in Ireland and support to partners.
>Web: www.positiveoptions.ie
>Free text list to 50444

Ruhama: Supporting Women Affected by Prostitution
Ruhama is a Dublin-based NGO which works with women involved in prostitution and other forms of commercial sexual exploitation, including women who are victims of sex trafficking.
>Address: Senior House, All Hallows College, Drumcondra, Dublin 9
>Tel: 01 836 0292
>Fax: 01 836 0268
>Email: admin@ruhama.ie
>Web: www.ruhama.ie

Student Union of Ireland LGBTQ Support
>Web: www.usi.ie

TENI: Transgender Equality Network Ireland
TENI is a non-profit organisation supporting the transgender community in Ireland in all its variety. TENI raise awareness about gender diversity through support, education and advocacy.
>Addresses Dublin: TENI, 2nd Floor, Ballast House, Aston Quay, Dublin 2
>Tel (Office): 01 633 4687
>Tel (Support): 085 147 7166 (19:00–22:00, text anytime)
>Address Cork: TENI c/o The Other Place, South Main Street, Cork
>Tel (Support): 085 108 3935 (or contact the Cork Gay Project on 021 4278470)
>Email: info@teni.ie
>Web: www.teni.ie

Victim Support
Confidential support service for individuals, their families and others who have been affected by crime.
>Tel: 1850 211 407
>Text: 085 133 7711
>Email: info@crimevictimshelpline.ie
>Web: www.crimevictimshelpline.ie

Women's Aid

Support and services for women in or leaving abusive relationships.

Address: Everton House, 47 Old Cabra Road, Dublin 7

Tel (National free helpline): 1800 341 900

Tel: 01 868 4721

Fax: 01 868 4722

Email: helpline@womensaid.ie

Web: www.womensaid.ie

BIBLIOGRAPHY

Alexandra, N & Clare, L (2004) You still feel different: The experience and meaning of women's self-injury in the context of lesbian and bisexual identity. *Journal of Applied and Community Social Psychology, 14*, 70–84.

Angrossino, MV (1998) *Opportunity House: Ethnographic studies of mental retardation.* Walnut Creek, CA: AltaMira Press.

Arnold, L & Magill, A (1998) *What's the Harm?* Abergavenny: The Basement Project (see Appendix 3: Resources).

Arnold, L & Magill, A (1998) *Making Sense of Self-Harm.* Abergavenny: The Basement Project (see Appendix 3: Resources).

Arnold, L & Magill, A (1998) *The Self-Harm Help Book.* Abergavenny: The Basement Project (see Appendix 3: Resources).

Arnold, L & Magill, A (1998) *Lifting the Lid.* Abergavenny: The Basement Project (see Appendix 3: Resources).

Arnold, L & Magill, A (1998) *Hurting Inside.* Abergavenny: The Basement Project (see Appendix 3: Resources).

Arnold, L & Magill, A (1998) *New Strength in Numbers.* Abergavenny: The Basement Project (see Appendix 3: Resources).

Arnold, L &Magill, A (1998) *Self-Harm: A resource pack.* Abergavenny: The Basement Project (see Appendix 3: Resources).

Arnold, L & Magill, A (2007) *Getting it Right* (2nd ed). Abergavenny: The Basement Project (see Appendix 3: Resources).

Babiker, G & Arnold, L (1997) *The Language of Injury.* Leicester: BPS Publications.

Banks, A & Banks, SP (1998) *Fiction and Social Research: By ice or fire.* Walnut Creek, CA and London: AltaMira Press.

Blackman, L (2007) Psychiatric culture and bodies of resistance. *Body and Society, 13*(2), 1–23.

Bornstein, K (1995) *Gender Outlaw: On men, women and the rest of us.* New York: Vintage Books.

Bracken, P & Thomas, P (2002) Time to move beyond the mind body split. *British Medical Journal, 325*, 1433–4.

Bracken, P & Thomas, P (2005) *Postpsychiatry: Mental health in a postmodern world.* Oxford: Oxford University Press.

Brain, R (1977) *Kolonialagent: A novel with an appendix.* London: Faber.

Breggin, P (1971) *The Crazy from the Sane.* New York: Lyle Stewart Inc.

239

Breggin, P (1991) *Toxic Psychiatry.* New York: St. Martin's Press.

Bristol Crisis Service for Women (1996) *Women and Self-Injury: A survey of 76 women.* Bristol: The Mental Health Foundation.

Bristol Crisis Service for Women (2004) *For Friends and Family.* Bristol: BCSW (see Appendix Three: Resources).

Bristol Crisis Service for Women (2004) *The Pain Inside.* Bristol: BCSW (see Appendix Three: Resources).

Bristol Crisis Service for Women (2006) *Good Practice Guidelines.* Bristol: BCSW (see Appendix Three: Resources).

Bristol Crisis Service for Women (2006) *Self-Help for Self-Injury.* Bristol: BCSW (see Appendix Three: Resources).

Bristol Crisis Service for Women (2006) *Self-Injury Support and Self-Help Groups.* Bristol: BCSW (see Appendix Three: Resources).

Bristol Crisis Service for Women (2006) *Women from Black and Minority Ethnic Groups and Self-Injury.* Bristol: BCSW (see Appendix Three: Resources).

Bristol Crisis Service for Women (2007) *The Rainbow Journal.* Bristol: BCSW (see Appendix Three: Resources).

Bristol Crisis Service for Women (2007) *Understanding Self-Injury.* Bristol: BCSW (see Appendix Three: Resources).

Bristol Crisis Service for Women (2009) *Hidden Pain: Self-Injury and people with learning disabilities.* Bristol: BCSW (see Appendix Three: Resources).

Brontë, E (1847/1992) *Wuthering Heights.* Hertfordshire: Wordsworth Classics (with introduction and notes by JS Whitley).

Clarke, L & Whittaker, M (1998) Self-mutilation: Culture, contexts and nursing. *Journal of Clinical Nursing, 7,* 129–37.

Denzin, NK (2003) *Performance Ethnography: Critical pedagogy and the politics of culture.* Thousand Oaks, CA: Sage.

Department of Health (2006) *A Vision for Change: Report of the Expert Group on Metal Health Policy.* Dublin: Stationary Office.

Ellis, C (2004) *The Ethnographic I.* London: Rowman & Littleford.

Ellis, C & Bochner, AP (1992) Telling and performing personal stories: The constraints of choice in abortion. In C Ellis & M Flaherty (eds) *Investigating Subjectivity: Research on lived experience* (pp. 79–101). London: Sage.

Ellis, C & Bochner, AP (2000) Autoethnography, personal narrative, reflexivity. In NK Denzin & YS Lincoln (eds) *Handbook of Qualitative Research* (2nd ed, pp. 733–65). London: Sage.

Favazza, AR (1996) *Bodies Under Siege: Self-mutilation and body modification in culture and psychiatry* (2nd ed). Baltimore, MD: Johns Hopkins University Press.

Foucault, M (1989) *The Birth of the Clinic: An archaeology of medical perception.* London: Routledge.

Foucault, M (2001) *Madness and Civilisation: A history of insanity in the Age of Reason.* London: Routledge.

Fox, KV (1996) Silent voices: A subversive reading of child sexual abuse. In C Ellis & AP Bochner (eds) *Composing Ethnography: Alternative forms of qualitative writing* (pp. 330–56). Walnut Creek, CA: AltaMira Press.

Garland Thomson, R (1997) *Extraordinary Bodies: Figuring physical disability in American culture and literature.* New York: Columbia University Press.

Gollust, SE, Eisenberg, D & Golberstein, E (2008) Prevalence and correlates of self-injury among university students. *Journal of American College Health, 56*(5), 491–8.

Gray, R (2002a) *Standing Ovation: Performing social science research about cancer.* Walnut Creek, CA: AltaMira Press.

Gray, R (2002b) Making a mess and spreading it around: Articulation of an approach to research based theatre. In AP Bochner & C Ellis (eds) *Ethnographically Speaking: Autoethnography, literature and aesthetics* (pp. 57–75) Walnut Creek, CA: AltaMira Press.

Gray, R (2004) No longer a man: Using ethnographic fiction to represent life history research. *Auto/Biography, 12*(1), 44–61.

Hewitt, K (1997) *Mutilating the Body: Identity in blood and ink.* Bowling Green, OH: Popular Press.

Holland, M (ed) (2000) *The Oscar Wilde Anthology.* London: HarperCollins.

Inckle, K (2007) *Writing on the Body? Thinking through gendered embodiment and marked flesh.* Newcastle-upon-Tyne: Cambridge Scholars Publishing.

Inckle, K (2008) Policing the body: A conversation from the edge of normative femininity. In A Sparkes (ed) *The Auto/Biography Yearbook 2007* (pp. 75–94) Sussex: Clio Publishing.

Inckle, K (2010) Telling tales? Using ethnographic fiction to speak Embodied 'Truth' *Qualitative Research, 10*(1), 27–47.

Jones, V, Davies, R & Jenkins, R (2004) Self-harm by people with learning disabilities: Something to be expected or investigated? *Disability and Society, 19*(5), 487–500.

Kenrick, J (2007) *Red Tears.* London: Faber & Faber.

Laing, RD & Esterson, A (1970) *Sanity, Madness and the Family.* Middlesex: Pelican.

Liebling, H et al. (1997) Why do women harm themselves? Surviving special hospitals. *Feminism and Psychology, 7,* 427–37.

LifeSIGNS (now FirstSigns) (2004) *The LifeSIGNS Self-Injury Awareness Booklet: Information for people who self-injure/self-harm, their friends, family, teachers and healthcare professionals.* FirstSigns Self-Injury Guidance and Network Support: www.firstsigns.org.uk

Lorde, A (1982) *Zami: A new spelling of my name.* Freedon, CA: Crossing Press.

McCarthy, M (1996) Sexual experiences and sexual abuse of women with learning disabilities. In M Hester, L Kelly & J Radford (eds) *Women, Violence and Male Power* (pp. 119–29). Milton Keynes: Open University Press.

McNiff, S (2004) *Art Heals: How creativity cures the soul.* Boston and London: Shambala.

Mental Health Commission (2007) *Knowledge Review: Code of practice on admission, transfer and discharge to and from an approved centre.* Dublin: Mental Health Commission.

Mental Health Commission (2008) *Quality Framework: Mental health services in Ireland.* Dublin: Mental Health Commission.

Mental Health Foundation (2006) *Truth Hurts: Report of the National Inquiry into Self-Harm among Young People.* London: Mental Health Foundation.

Miller, A (1990) *For Your Own Good: The roots of violence in childrearing.* London: Virago.

Miller, A (1995) *Pictures of a Childhood.* London: Virago.

Mind (Croydon) (1997) *Visible Memories* [DVD]. Available from The Basement Project and Mind (see Appendix Three: Resources).

Morris, J (1991) *Pride Against Prejudice: Transforming attitudes to disability.* London: Women's Press.

Moyer, M (2008) Working with self-injurious adolescents using the safe kit. *Journal of Creativity in Mental Health, 3*(1), 60–8.

National Institute in Health and Clinical Excellence (2004) *Self-Harm: The short-term physical and psychological management and secondary prevention of self-harm in primary and secondary care.* London: NICE.

Newham Asian Women's Project (1998) *Growing Up Young, Asian and Female in Britain: A report on self-harm and suicide.* London: Newham Asian Women's Project and Newham Innercity MultiFund.

O'Brien, K (1941/1982) *The Land of Spices.* Dublin: Arlen House (with preface by Lorna Reynolds).

Orbach, S (1999) *The Impossibility of Sex: Stories of the intimate relationship between therapist and patient.* London: Penguin.

Pelias, RJ (2004) *A Methodology of the Heart: Evoking academic and daily life.* Walnut Creek, CA, Lanham, MD, New York and Oxford: AltaMira Press.

Pembroke, LR (1996) *Self-Harm: Perspectives from personal experience* (2nd ed). Originally published by Survivors Speak Out and forthcoming as a free download from www.kreativeinterventions.com

Pembroke, LR (2007a) Harm-minimisation: Limiting the damage of self-injury. In H Spandler & S Warner (eds) *Beyond Fear and Control: Working with young people who self-harm* (pp. 163–72). Ross-on-Wye: PCCS Books.

Pembroke, LR (2007b) *Dedication to the Seven; Catatonia* [DVD]. London: Mind Publications.

Reinharz, S (1992) *Feminist Methods in Social Research.* Oxford and New York: Oxford University Press.

Richardson, L (1992) The consequences of poetic representation: Writing other, rewriting the self. In C Ellis & MG Flaherty (eds) *Investigating Subjectivity: Research on lived experience* (pp. 125–37). London: Sage.

Ronai, CR (1992) A night in the life of an erotic dancer/researcher. In C Ellis & MG Flaherty (eds) *Investigating Subjectivity: Research on lived experience* (pp. 102–24). London: Sage.

Ronai, CR (1996) My mother is mentally retarded. In C Ellis & AP Bochner (eds) *Composing Ethnography: Alternative forms of qualitative writing* (pp. 109–31). Walnut Creek, CA: AltaMira Press.

Rothblatt, M (1996) *The Apartheid of Sex: A manifesto on the freedom of gender.* Pandora: London.

The Royal College of Surgeons (2007) *Children in Hospital: Rights and responsibilities of children and parents.* Dublin: Royal College of Surgeons.

Sacks, OW (1991) *A Leg to Stand On.* London: Picador.

Sandahl, C (2003) Queering the crip or cripping the queer? Intersections of queer and crip identities in solo autobiographical performance. *GLQ: Journal of Lesbian and Gay Studies, 9*(1–2), 25–56.

Sedgwick, P (1982) *Psycho Politics.* London: Pluto Press.

Servan-Schreiber, D (2005) *Healing without Freud or Prozac: Natural approaches to curing stress, anxiety and depression.* London: Rodale.

Shakespeare, T et al. (1996) *The Sexual Politics of Disability: Untold desires.* London and New York: Cassell Press.

Shaw, C & Hogg, C (2004) Shouting at the spaceman: A conversation about self-harm. In D Duffy & T Ryan (eds) *New Approaches to Preventing Suicide: A manual for practitioners* (pp. 167–77). London: Jessica Kingsley.

Shaw, C & Shaw, T (2007) A dialogue of hope and survival. In H Spandler & S Warner (eds) *Beyond Fear and Control: Working with young people who self-harm* (pp. 25–36). Ross-on-Wye: PCCS Books.

Shaw, C & Shaw, T (2009) *harm-ed.* Dublin presentation. Unpublished paper for New Ways of Understanding Self-Injury: Ireland's National Self-Injury Awareness Day, Trinity College Dublin, March.

Shingler, A (2007) *Only Smarties Have the Answer* [DVD]. London: Mind Publications.

Smith, B (2002) The (in)visible wound: Body stories and concentric circles of witness. *Auto/Biography, 10*(1), 121–31.

Smith, G, Cox, D & Saradjian, J (1998) *Women and Self-Harm.* London: Women's Press.

Spandler, H (1996) *Who's Hurting Who? Young people, self-harm, and suicide.* Manchester: 42nd Street.

Spandler, H & Warner, S (eds) (2007) *Beyond Fear and Control: Working with young people who self-harm.* Ross-on-Wye: PCCS Books.

Sparkes, AC (2002) Fictional representations: On difference, choice and risk. *Sociology of Sport Journal, 19*, 1–24.

Sparkes, AC (2003) Bodies, identities, selves: Autoethnographic fragments and reflections. In J Denison & P Markula (eds) *Moving Writing: Crafting writing in sports research* (pp. 51–76). New York: Peter Lang.

Sparkes, AC (2007) Embodiment, academics, and the audit culture: A story seeking consideration. *Qualitative Research, 7*(4), 521–50.

Strong, M (2000) *A Bright Red Scream: Self-mutilation and the language of pain.* London: Virago.

Sutton, J (1999) *Healing the Hurt Within: Understand and relieve the suffering behind self-destructive behaviour.* Plymouth: Pathways.

Szasz, T (2007) *The Medicalization of Everyday Life.* New York: Syracuse University Press.

Thomas, P & Bracken, P (2001) Postpsychiatry: A new direction for mental health. *British Medical Journal, 322*, 724–7.

Thomas, P & Bracken, P (2004) Critical psychiatry in practice. *Advances in Psychiatric Practice, 10*, 361–70.

Tillman-Healy, L (1996) A secret life in the culture of thinness: Reflections on body, food, and bulimia. In C Ellis & AP Bochner (eds) *Composing Ethnography: Alternative forms of qualitative writing* (pp. 76–108) Walnut Creek, CA: AltaMira Press.

Turp, M (2003) *Hidden Self-Harm: Narratives from psychotherapy*. London: Jessica Kingsley.

Ussher, J (1991) *Women's Madness: Misogyny or mental illness?* London: Harvester Wheatsheaf.

Yalom, ID (1991) *Love's Executioner and Other Tales of Psychotherapy*. Harmondsworth: Penguin.

Beyond Fear and Control

Working with young people who self-harm

(a 42nd **street reader**)

Helen Spandler &
Sam Warner (eds)

This radical book is about supporting young people who use self-harm as a way of coping with distress. It aims to move practice beyond fear and control of such young people towards more empowering ways of working. It demonstrates why we need to give up the idea of stopping young people harming themselves, and why we need to start listening, supporting and empowering them to take control of ther own lives.

Beyond Fear and Control brings together practitioners, activists and service users from a wide range of service contexts who have developed new and innovative ways of helping young people who self-harm. These include group work, work in prisons, counselling, housing support, legal rights, direct payments and activism. It covers underlying, causative issues such as abuse, neglect, oppression, discrimination and trauma-based dissociation.

Helen Spandler is a research fellow in the Department of Social Work, University of Central Lancashire.
Sam Warner is a consultant clinical psychologist and research fellow in the Department of Psychology and Speech Pathology, Manchester Metropolitan University.

ISBN 978 1 898 05987 5
Paperback, pp. 192
£18.00 (£16.00 online)

www.pccs-books.co.uk

LIVING WITH VOICES
50 STORIES OF RECOVERY

PROF MARIUS ROMME

DR SANDRA ESCHER

JACQUI DILLON

DR DIRK CORSTENS

PROF MERVYN MORRIS

ISBN 978 1 906254 22 3
pp 346 2009 £20.00 (£18.00 online)

This is the third book in a series that includes *Accepting Voices* (Romme and Escher 1993) and *Making Sense of Voices* (Romme and Escher, 2000). It contains nine chapters outlining the 'recovery model' versus the 'disease model' of hearing voices, and these are consolidated by 50 stories of personal recovery.

Living with Voices proves the value of 'accepting' and 'making sense of' voices, arguing that voices are not a sign of madness, but a reaction to serious problems in life. It demonstrates that it is entirely possible to overcome problems with hearing voices and how harmful it is to associate hearing voices with schizophrenia.

> *This is essential reading for mental health workers of all professions, which challenges conventional thinking, empowers mental health service users, and looks forward to a more humane approach to psychiatric care.*
>
> Richard Bentall, Professor of Clinical Psychology, Bangor University; author of *Madness Explained* and *Doctoring the Mind*.

> *The groundbreaking development in modern mental health is recognition of the crucial importance of the first-hand experience and accounts of service users themselves. This book is a breakthrough because for the first time we hear about and can make sense of 'hearing voices' through the direct voice of fifty service users themselves. This is a must-read book for all concerned with mental health issues from senior psychiatrists to current service users.*
>
> Peter Beresford, Professor of Social Policy and Director of the Centre for Citizen Participation, Brunel University

www.pccs-books.co.uk